Intercultural Experience and Education

Brian Morgan DLLL, York u.
S540 Ross, (416) 544-8795

Languages for Intercultural Communication and Education
Editors: Michael Byram, *University of Durham, UK* and Alison Phipps, *University of Glasgow, UK*

The overall aim of this series is to publish books which will ultimately inform learning and teaching, but whose primary focus is on the analysis of intercultural relationships, whether in textual form or in people's experience. There will also be books which deal directly with pedagogy, with the relationships between language learning and cultural learning, between processes inside the classroom and beyond. They will all have in common a concern with the relationship between language and culture, and the development of intercultural communicative competence.

Other Books in the Series
Developing Intercultural Competence in Practice
  Michael Byram, Adam Nichols and David Stevens (eds)

Other Books of Interest
Foreign Language and Culture Learning from a Dialogic Perspective
  Carol Morgan and Albane Cain
The Good Language Learner
  N. Naiman, M. Fröhlich, H.H. Stern and A. Todesco
Language, Culture and Communication in Contemporary Europe
  Charlotte Hoffman (ed.)
Language Learners as Ethnographers
  Celia Roberts, Michael Byram, Ana Barro, Shirley Jordan and Brian Street
Language Teachers, Politics and Cultures
  Michael Byram and Karen Risager
Motivating Language Learners
  Gary N. Chambers
New Perspectives on Teaching and Learning Modern Languages
  Simon Green (ed.)
Teaching and Assessing Intercultural Communicative Competence
  Michael Byram

Please contact us for the latest book information:
Multilingual Matters, Frankfurt Lodge, Clevedon Hall,
Victoria Road, Clevedon, BS21 7HH, England
http://www.multilingual-matters.com

LANGUAGES FOR INTERCULTURAL COMMUNICATION AND EDUCATION 2
Series Editors: Michael Byram and Alison Phipps

Intercultural Experience and Education

Edited by

Geof Alred, Michael Byram and Mike Fleming

MULTILINGUAL MATTERS LTD
Clevedon • Buffalo • Toronto • Sydney

Library of Congress Cataloging in Publication Data
Intercultural Experience and Education/Edited by Geof Alred, Michael Byram and Mike Fleming
Languages for Intercultural Communication and Education: 2.
Papers presented at two symposia held at the University of Durham.
Includes bibliographical references and index.
1. Multicultural education–Congresses. 2. International education–Congresses.
I. Alred, Geof. II. Byram, Michael. III. Fleming, Michael (Michael P.). IV. Series.
LC1099.I563 2002
370.117–cd21   2002026327

British Library Cataloguing in Publication Data
A catalogue entry for this book is available from the British Library.

ISBN 1-85359-607-8 (hbk)
ISBN 1-85359-606-X (pbk)

Multilingual Matters Ltd
UK: Frankfurt Lodge, Clevedon Hall, Victoria Road, Clevedon BS21 7HH.
USA: UTP, 2250 Military Road, Tonawanda, NY 14150, USA.
Canada: UTP, 5201 Dufferin Street, North York, Ontario M3H 5T8, Canada.
Australia: Footprint Books, PO Box 418, Church Point, NSW 2103, Australia.

Typeset by Archetype-IT Ltd (http://www.archetype-it.com).
Printed and bound in Great Britain by the Cromwell Press Ltd.

Contents

Foreword

A colleague of mine at Durham University (if I dare assume such a relationship with a distinguished academic, I a mere unacademic appointee) kindly proposed that I should write the Foreword for a book to which he and certain other sparkling minds have contributed. The headings of the different items have something in common: '*Intercultural Experience and Education*' is the overall title, and it takes on various aspects of the advantages of an intercultural background over a blinkered mono-cultural one. My first modest reaction was that I was hardly qualified to air my views on such matters, until I realised, from the very theme of this book how very lucky I have been.

As one who, in Yugoslav terms, is ethnically filthy, and inordinately proud of the fact, it follows that I have never succeeded in pretending to be predominantly British despite the happy accident of birth which caused my mother to deliver me in London. In fact, I am full of admiration for politicians like Michael Portillio and Michael Howard who were so successful in disguising their respectively Spanish and Romanian origins that they became outstanding Conservative members of Parliament in an epoch of dogged mono-culturalism.

I was in trouble from the very beginning. The subject of so-called musical appreciation for one term at my preparatory school was the composer Tchaikovsky. During the end of term exams a cunning question was 'Name one Russian composer'. You can no doubt guess the correct answer. Unfortunately I refused to take the hint, and put down Nikolai Rimsky-Korsakov. After the responsible authorities had consulted an encyclopedia, I was not encouraged, but upbraided before the whole school by a vindictive lady teacher, who accused me of 'showing-off'. This is, to my mind, typical of a British prejudice, the mistrust and dislike of knowledge, and therefore of anything which smells even mildly of intellectualism. There is even, among learned judges, a cult of ignorance. Sometimes they interrupt a murder trial to ask a question to which they should know the answer, and probably do. It is just advisable at moments to subtly underline their fallibility, while stressing that the majesty of ermine and wig reiterates their final authority over the more wretched of human destinies whatever the circumstances.

My mother was of French origin, although half-Russian. Another quite different concept of living came with those genes. A respect for the human intellect which many British would feel instinctively to be unwise. Also a glorification of the relatively short republican tradition as a natural and desirable form of government. And they still regard the British Monarchy with nostalgia and envy – so long as it remains British, and does not taint their rampant tradition of republicanism. Lady Thatcher, the one leading politician one could never accuse of multicultural thinking, and who in fact has made mono-culturalism the basis of her political thinking, reminded the French, on her arrival in Paris as a guest to celebrate the 200th Anniversary of the French Revolution, that they had committed an unpardonable sin in beheading their monarch. She had conveniently forgotten in her determination to occupy the moral high ground that in 1649, a century and a half earlier, the British had done precisely that to Charles I.

It is the moment for a little balance of power. In modern times, the Germans have been burdened with the accusation of militarism. This is perhaps because they were given their first opportunity to enjoy this evil very late in history. For centuries they constituted the Holy Roman Empire, an agglomeration of states none of which was powerful enough to see much future in military adventure. This temptation was first introduced to the German psyche when Napoleon began marching and continued marching all over Europe, using Hessians against Prussians, Saxons against Bavarians and so on. This habit of employing mercenaries to swell his ranks has inevitably tested German unity and as a direct consequence of the Napoleonic wars, Prussia emerged as the pre-eminent Germanic power, and militarism was well on the way after Bismarck's 'Anschluss', an act of union in which individual states centralised their energies without losing their identities completely, and which the nation's complicated voting procedures reflects all too faithfully to this day. For a while, German militarism became the outstanding disturbance to Europe's peace of mind. I personally believe that British militarism was just as noticeable as the German variety, with the cardinal difference that, whereas German militarism invariably led to war, the British variety only led to parades. At times the British were deeply resentful towards the Germans because war broke out during a parade.

Naturally the world moves on apace, and many of the stereotypes of yesterday vanish like leaves in autumn. The ringing words of Cecil Rhodes, uttered a century and more ago – 'Remember that you are an Englishman, and have therefore won first prize in the lottery of life' – sound pleasantly absurd today. Nevertheless, on more abstract ground, the upholders of the colonial mind believe sincerely that the British have planted the Union Jack squarely in humour, and that nobody can take that away from them. 'Our ability to laugh at ourselves' is a phrase of seeming demureness but which is as unashamedly arrogant as every other self-assessment of its kind.

Many thoughtful Britons refuse to believe that the Germans have any humour whatsoever. In fact, as someone who has played before German, British and French audiences, I would say the German audience is more overtly intellectual than the British, although its ability to produce decibels of merriment leaves nothing to be desired. It is also more tolerant towards serious moments, not manifesting undue unrest at a sudden change of climate or direction in the text. The French, who have long ago planted their flag into logic just as the British have theirs in humour, often require points explained to them with an evident loss of subtlety and irony.

We have only touched on three cultures very briefly and inadequately. The ensuing book will go much further, and in depth.

Perhaps I may leave you with the following afterthought. In order to attain the truth, the French subtract, the Germans add, and the British change the subject.

Peter Ustinov
Chancellor of the University of Durham

Series Editors' Preface

Intercultural Experience and Education expands the field of 'interculturality' beyond the usual fields of foreign language education and cross cultural training. It focuses on the experience of being intercultural, fully aware that experience and being are not the same, but that both are importantly about developing relations with members of other social and cultural groups. A wide range of domains are represented in this volume, including ethnography, psychotherapy and drama as well as education. This book takes the intercultural project into the heart of education, both within and outwith the classroom. As such it lays the foundation for fresh approaches to being intercultural and for analysing intercultural experience.

This book is one of a series which aims to analyse and respond to the changing contexts within which education is developing in the contemporary world. It has become a commonplace to describe the world as a village, to call for better cross-cultural communication and greater social harmony and tolerance. The authors of the UNESCO report *Learning: The Treasure Within* called for more emphasis on 'learning to live together', as well as on 'learning to know', the traditional purpose of education. Learning to live together involves the ability to understand each other, to communicate, to interact with others. Language and intercultural education has a significant role to play, and a key purpose of this series is to encourage the study of languages and cultures in ways which can ultimately enrich practice. On the one hand, there is a need for studies which inform the ways in which teaching can be structured and methods developed. On the other, studies of individuals' responses to experience of other cultures can all help to redefine the nature of language and intercultural teaching and learning and its educational and social purposes.

This series thus includes books which describe and analyse successful practice within and beyond the walls of the conventional classroom, and it also includes books which develop new theories, critique existing models and explore new combinations of disciplines. There are many different and innovative ways of contributing to the field of Languages, Intercultural Communication and Education. Consequently, both monographs and edited volumes of conceptual theorising and/or empirical studies are within our scope. It is essential that education and the variegated academic fields of modern languages and cultures respond to and provoke change in an imaginative way, and Multilingual Matters has provided us and our contributors with an opportunity to explore linguistic and cultural experience and education from many different angles.

Alison Phipps and Michael Byram

Contributors' Biographical Notes

Dr Geof Alred is a BPS Chartered Psychologist, counsellor trainer, counsellor in private practice, and former university student counsellor. His research interest include metaphorical understanding, language in therapy, mentoring, and intercultural experience, in particular the experience and long term significance of student residence abroad.

Lothar Bredella, born 1936, studied English, German, philosophy and sociology at Erlangen and Frankfurt/Main (Germany) and Bristol (England). Since 1975 full professor in Giessen. President of the German Association for American Studies (1984–87) and of the German Association for Foreign Language Research (1991–93). From 1994 to 2000 speaker of the postgraduate programme 'Didaktik des Fremdverstehens' (Pedagogy of Intercultural Understanding). Author of several books and more than 100 articles. Editor of more than a dozen anthologies.

Professor Mike Byram is a foreign linguist in the sense that he has both studied and learnt three languages and cultures/literatures – all imperfectly. He has taught languages in secondary school and has been involved in initial teacher education for many years. His research has focused on the education of linguistic minorities and the cultural dimension of language teaching. He is Special Adviser to the Council of Europe Modern Languages Division.

Dr Leah Davcheva works for the British Council in Bulgaria and manages projects in the fields of cultural studies and intercultural education and training. She co-ordinates an intercultural studies post-graduate distance learning course for language teachers. Her interests include the intercultural dimension of the foreign language classroom, evaluating learning materials from an intercultural perspective, and practices of cultural representation.

Dr Michael Fleming is Senior Lecturer in Education and Director of Initial Teacher Training at the University of Durham where he has worked since 1989. Previously he taught in secondary schools in the North East of

England. He has written several books and a number of chapters and papers on the teaching of English and drama.

Dr Elizabeth Murphy-Lejeune is a Lecturer in the French Department, Saint Patrick's College, Dublin. Her main research interests are the sociology of the stranger, international migration and mobility, intercultural studies, and the European dimension in education. She has just published a book on the European student stay abroad entitled *Student Mobility and Narrative in Europe: The New Strangers* (Routledge, 2002).

Celia Roberts is Senior Research Fellow in the Department of Education and Professional Studies, King's College London. Her research interests are in intercultural communication, institutional discourse, language socialisation and micro-ethnography. Her publications include: *Language and Discrimination* (1992, with Jupp and Davies); *Achieving Understanding* (1996, with Bremer *et al.*); *Talk, Work and Institutional Order* (1999, with Sarangi) and *Language Learners as Ethnographers* (2001, with Byram *et al.*).

Phyllis Ryan is a professor at the Universidad Nacional Autonoma de Mexico in the Departamento de Lingüística Aplicada of the Centro de Enseñanza de Lenguas Extranjeras. She teaches in the masters' degree programme and is directing doctoral theses. Her research focuses on intercultural perceptions of foreign language teachers and students in multilingual settings in Mexico and internationally. She is co-editor of the collection, *Language: Issues of Inequality*.

Dr Amita Sen Gupta is a BPS Chartered Psychologist and formerly a Senior Lecturer in Psychology. She has also worked as a counsellor and has been involved in cross-cultural counselling training. Her special interests include teaching psychology from an intercultural perspective and cultural aspects of self and identity. Her research has focused on different aspects of intercultural/international education and identity.

David Stevens lectures in English in Education at the School of Education of Durham University, having taught English in various secondary schools for fifteen years. He is interested in researching and teaching about the creative aspects of native language education, especially in a broadly intercultural context.

Dr Susanne Weber is a researcher and lecturer at the Institute for Economics and Business Education and Management Training, Georg-August-University Göttingen (Germany). Her major research interest actually is intercultural learning and development.

Geneviève Zarate has been working in the field of French as a foreign language for 25 years, first of all abroad, and then extended this work to the methodology of language teaching in its cultural and linguistic diversity. She investigates the ways in which representations of other countries function by analysing them in a framework of cultural distance and proximity, mediation and geographic mobility. She is currently Professor at the National Institute of Oriental Languages and Civilisations in Paris (l'Institut National des Langues et Civilisations Orientales de Paris), where she is responsible for the co-ordination of the teaching methodologies of the 90 languages from all continents that are taught at the Institute. She also supervises doctoral theses at the Université de Paris III.

Chapter 1

Introduction

GEOF ALRED, MIKE BYRAM and MIKE FLEMING

Choosing a title for this book caused us more than usual difficulty. We were sure that we wanted to refer to 'intercultural experience' and to 'education' but it was the link word which proved difficult. Intercultural experience 'in' and 'as' education would together reflect the contents and purpose of the book but neither would do alone. A complex title with two link words would, however, be opaque to readers until they grasped our intention, so we settled for the more neutral 'and'. Our intention is nonetheless clear, even if complex and ambitious. We and our contributors want to do two things:

- extend the range of use of the concept of 'interculturality' beyond its usual use in discussions of multicultural education, foreign language education and cross-cultural training; and
- explore the ways in which extending the concept in this way can develop and re-align ways of thinking and acting in education, including those domains mentioned earlier where it is already familiar.

By extending the concept of 'interculturality' outside its usual frame of reference we are inviting educators to examine the practical and theoretical conseqences of seeing their work in new ways. However it is also our aim that those who already see themselves working within the area of 'interculturalism' will also be prompted to extend and deepen their understanding of what they do. Understanding is largely about making connections; extending the concept of 'interculturality' is intended to make rich connections both within and outside the field as traditionally defined. Given the origins and staring point of our work, it is perhaps inevitable that a majority of contributions come from within 'education', but our intention is to avoid casting experience as peripheral to education. We believe that by making connections between what are often conceived as separate

1

domains, there will be an opportunity to look afresh at the educational significance and potential of intercultural experience.

The term 'intercultural' has been used by various groups of educators and trainers. In the USA and in Europe, it has been used by those who prepare people for short or longer term residence in another country when, for professional and work-related reasons, they find themselves obliged to leave the familiarity of their own cultural environment (Dahlen, 1997).

In Germany, it has been used in the phrase '*interkulturelle Erziehung*' to refer to the need for the education system to respond to the multiplicity of ethnic groups in contemporary German society. A similar phrase and usage can be found in France. In Germany, too, the phrase '*interkulturelle Didaktik*' refers to the ways in which foreign language teaching should respond to new aims of preparing learners for interaction with people of different cultural identities (Müller-Jacquier, 2000). We ourselves have used the term 'intercultural speaker' to define the language learner who also acquires knowledge and skills of cultural mediation or interpretation, and not just a linguistic competence modelled on a native speaker (see Kramsch, 1998).

In this book, we want to extend the use of the word 'intercultural' and the concept of 'interculturality' beyond these established usages to other domains of experience which can be characterised as by being between cultures. We wish to do so because we think such domains exist and can be illuminated by the concept, and because we think the concept is useful for educationalists beyond the circle of those concerned with the 'foreign' and 'the strange' in the most immediate and obvious sense. Our first step needs therefore to be an analysis of what we mean by the concept for as well as extending its range we need also to delimit it, for there is a sense in which virtually any human encounter can be described as intercultural but if the concept is extended too far it loses its value. To describe all human interaction as an exercise in interculturalism may be true but only at the expense of being vacuous and thereby unlikely to provide any fresh insights into educational practice.

Being Intercultural

We begin therefore by setting our limits. This is important because the word 'culture' itself now appears in so many contexts. Indeed 'culture' almost replaces 'context' in much discourse in education and social sciences

That human beings are cultural beings, shaped by their specific environment through processes of socialisation (Berger and Luckmann, 1966) is evident. That there is no natural 'essence' which can be revealed under the surface of what is acquired in socialisation is also evident. Insofar as formal education systems play a significant role in socialisation and contribute to the creation of a sense of national identity in many cases, it is important that educationists be aware of the development of cultural identities in their pupils and students. Nonetheless this perspective is too wide for our purposes; our focus is on a more specific kind of experience than that of primary and secondary socialisation.

It is also evident that human beings cannot be understood or educated simply as individuals. By nature, we are social and it is in the interaction with others that we develop. This too must be part of the educationist's awareness but it is also a wider perspective than ours. Our focus is on social interactions, and human beings as social actors but our concept of interculturalism is limited in a particular way.

Our focus is more on the ways in which human beings inevitably form groups (in addition to those based on nationality or ethnicity) which give them a sense of security and which in turn lead individuals to favour insider members of their groups over outsider members of other groups (Tajfel, 1981). People born and socialised into specific groups tend to assume that the conventions and values by which they live within their groups are inevitable and 'natural'. It is when they have some kind of experience which leads them to question these given conventions and values – but not necessarily to reject them – that they begin to become 'intercultural' in our sense.

This questioning of the 'natural' and recognition of the arbitrary nature of the given, crucial to the concept of interculturality, may take place in many ways but is most often a consequence of stepping outside the closed boundaries of one's groups and experiencing the conventions and values by which people in other groups live. In the most common uses of the concept of interculturality, in the education disciplines concerned with multi-ethnic societies or foreign language teaching or cross-cultural training, the focus has been gaining experience of a different national or ethnic group. We have, however, consciously talked of the individual's experience of their own social groups in the plural because we want to emphasise that social identities are not only related to national and ethnic groups. The formation of in-groups and the consequent identification of out-groups takes place at many levels and offers different forms of security, but also different opportunities for experiencing otherness.

The extension of the concept of interculturality to the experience of other groups their conventions, their beliefs, values and behaviours – in short, their cultures – is our interest in this book.

It is helpful to distinguish between 'intercultural experience' and 'being intercultural'. The former is simply a statement of fact, of an encounter between particular groups; the latter, however implies a more qualitative judgement about the nature of such an encounter. Experience of otherness in a range of ways creates a potential for questioning the taken-for-granted in one's own self and environment. Being intercultural is, however, more than this. It is the capacity to reflect on the relationships among groups and the experience of those relationships. It is both the awareness of experiencing otherness and the ability to analyse the experience and act upon the insights into self and other which the analysis brings. Experience alone is therefore not enough.

Experience of other national cultures and critical reflection on one's own, even though the latter does not always follow from the former, is clearly not a new phenomenon. It is, however, one which is becoming more familiar and visible to more people, as a consequence of contemporary social change. The mobility of populations and individuals consequent on globalisation of national economies and on the internationalisation of communications and travel is a phenomenon much commented on both in mass media and academic discourses. It is represented in this book in a number of chapters, for example Phyllis Ryan's account of a woman who has lived in several countries and languages, contrasted with a language learner who has not yet been outside her country.

Yet being intercultural, being interested in, curious about and empathetic with people of other groups is not synonymous with being 'international', being a constant traveller, being constantly in search of somewhere else. Nor is it synonymous with abandoning one's own groups and rejecting one's social identities. On the contrary, it leads to a heightened awareness of these, and of the interaction between 'own' and 'other', an interaction which, whilst maintaining distinctions, creates a sense of communality, of community. The locus of interaction is not in the centripetal reinforcement of the identity of one group and its members by contrast with others, but rather in the centrifugal action of each which creates a new centre of interaction on the borders and frontiers which join rather than divide them.

This centre is experienced not only in relation to others, but also in relation to oneself. It is said that travel broadens the mind. That is often so, as several chapters in this book demonstrate, but our contention is that travel, taken as shorthand for intercultural experience, also has the potential to deepen the mind. An inevitable consequence of intercultural experience is that it presents a challenge to customary modes of perception, thought and feeling. Hence, when intercultural experience leads to creative, rather than defensive, learning a concomitant is serious self-reflection and examination, bringing with it consequences for self-understanding and self-knowledge. A blunt, but powerful, example would be someone discovering his or her latent racism through contact with people towards whom, as a collective group, they have held derogatory and hostile views, and gaining some measure of insight about why they were racist. Another example would be a student realising that after all they do have the resources to survive and thrive as a temporary resident in a foreign country. In both cases, a potential in the learner has been brought out into the open provoked by new experience. In crossing frontiers externally, the learner has crossed and possibly dissolved frontiers within. When such change takes hold and becomes incorporated into the person's sense of themselves, a step towards being an intercultural person has been taken, paving the way for further steps, and a deeper, more complex, sense of belonging to groups, communities, societies and nationalities. Psychologically, a person's centre shifts, greater competence and comfort in being in-between socially, culturally and internationally is matched by a more profound, tolerant and integrated sense of self. Frontiers become less barriers and prohibitions and more gateways and invitations.

Interculturality as/in Education

Experience, we said, is not a sufficient, even though perhaps a necessary, condition for interculturality. There must also be reflection, analysis and action. The fact that these do not inevitably flow from experience suggests a particular role for education and educators. Such a role has been claimed for foreign language education where the potential encounter with social groups – ethnic and/or national – who speak other languages is evident (Byram & Zarate, 1997; Byram, 1997; Kramsch, 1993; Bredella, 1992; Zarate, 1986). Since we believe that intercultural experience is not only in encounters with speakers of other languages, and not only in mobility from one country to another, we believe that other domains of education also have a role to play – and we wish to extend the range of the concept and theory to practice and theorising in these domains.

Indeed, we seek to include all domains where serious learning can take place. Our range is not exhaustive, but we include examples that constitute a mix that is unusual, itself an intercultural endeavour. For example, one frontier crossed is to include a perspective based upon psychotherapy. Whilst dealing with human distress is not central to educational practice, there is no doubt that in therapy serious learning takes place. Smail (1980), for instance, has argued for a learning perspective in describing the changes that therapy can bring about, and much therapy is about helping people to question basic assumptions about themselves and others, and to adopt new ways of looking at themselves and their world. Smail identifies the kinds of learning that take place in therapy conducted in a western cultural context, in terms of such things as human agency, autonomy, responsibility, meaning, good faith, self in relationship. More specifically, people who seek therapy often have the experience of encountering a way of relating with another person that is profoundly different from their usual transactions with others. Discussions of cross-cultural therapy, increasingly relevant for precisely the same reasons as the general educational case made here, address the same thorny and urgent issues as confront any teacher of a modern language or student studying abroad (Lago and Thompson, 1996; Hays, 2001; Pedersen *et al.*, 2002).

Our vision of the extension into these other domains is ambitious. We think it only worthwhile if it leads to transformation of other domains of education and therapy. We are not interested in 'adding-on' an intercultural dimension such that counsellors in training are merely given an extra issue to consider if they are to counsel someone from a different ethnic national, linguistic group. Neither are we simply interested, for example, in adding to the teaching of English a dimension which is called 'literature from other cultures, written in English'.

The transformation we wish to initiate is that, through reflection, analysis and action, experience of any kind of otherness can be seen as intercultural experience. It should be part of the purposes of education and therapy to promote a sense of interculturality, an intercultural competence, which is fundamental to education, perhaps always has been so, but is all the more significant in the contemporary world.

Our vision thus stated might appear to be the product of theory, with ensuing chapters conceived as illustrations of theory. In fact, the vision arose from the chapters or, more accurately, from two symposia at the University of Durham where versions of the chapters were presented.[1]

The symposia were themselves occasions of intercultural experience and reflection. They brought together people of different national, language, academic disciplinary groups and cultures. On the first occasion the format was traditional; presentation and discussion of papers. On the second, the presence of new people, 'outsiders' with whom we wished to interact, led to a format of workshop and seminar. The composition of the groups on both occasions was dictated by opportunity and chance, not planned to be representative or comprehensive in terms of disciplines, nationalities or any other social groups. This too was a reflection of all intercultural experience. There is no such thing as the 'complete' or 'finished' intercultural experience.

Our vision is not complete or finished either. We do not claim either here or in the chapters which follow, to have presented a comprehensive and finished theory or practice of the transformation in education and therapy adumbrated earlier. We are aware, too, that the chance composition of our group means that our chapters do not exhaust the potential explorations of interculturality in the domains and disciplines from which we originate but we stress that the variety of our experiences illustrates the potential for transformation.

In the same vein, we have not attempted to group the chapters into sections since any particular grouping would over-emphasise one characteristic of a chapter to the detriment of others. One possible grouping was to divide the chapters as follows:

(1) those which deal with the domains usually associated with interculturality (Weber, Bredella, Davcheva, Zarate);
(2) chapters which have a close link to these domains through a focus on experience which fits everyday concepts of 'foreign culture' (Murphy-Lejeune, Roberts, Byram);
(3) chapters which have a link which is less immediately obvious, but stems from a shared concern with language, communication and relationship (Ryan, Byram, Alred); and
(4) chapters which start from a different point and from a different domain/discipline and demonstrate that experience of otherness is not only present when it is marked by a foreign language (Sen Gupta, Fleming, Stevens).

A second grouping could distinguish those chapters which deal with pedagogy (Bredella, Sen Gupta, Stevens, Roberts) from those which analyse experience.

As no one grouping is more significant than others we have decided to present the chapters in alphabetical order by author. What all of the chapters have in common is an intention to deepen and extend the concept of interculturality and what 'being intercultural' means, and to explore their relevance to wider educational debate.

Geof Alred's chapter argues that intercultural experience can be found both in the obvious interculturality of residence in another country and in the work of the counsellor therapist. He illustrates this both from the accounts given by university students of languages living in another country with the declared purpose of improving their language skills, and from the accounts given by therapists of their practice and principles in their work with clients. The 'Year Abroad', as it is called, for the linguists is a major experience of change through living between two cultures; and Alred describes how he too found himself between cultures, between discourses and between languages as he trained as a therapist. The intercultural experience requires therefore, a re-consideration of assumptions and identities which is far more significant than the acquisition of language as a formal system, to which most research attention has been paid in language education. Hence it is clear that therapy theory can inform our way of thinking about intercultural experience in education, and *vice versa* that therapy, when seen in a post-psychological mode as social process, learn from ways of thinking about intercultural experience.

Lothar Bredella's chapter argues for a flexible model of intercultural understanding which makes sense of the claim that it is possible to understand a foreign culture (contrary to the assumptions of psychological and cultural determinists). The limitations of Lockean and structuralist conceptions of language are identified, the former because it assumes that individual speakers have the freedom to decide what words mean, the latter because it pays insufficient attention to the agency of speaker and listener. In contrast a pragmatic concept of language is able to describe the complexity of understanding and to reconcile the private and public nature of language. Intercultural understanding is seen as the negotiation between two contexts and perspectives which accepts the preservation as well as the change in the learners' identity. It requires a flexibility of mind which allows us to cross borders and accept differences, so that we neither subsume another culture into our familiar categories or over romanticise it. Intercultural understanding is not necessarily a betrayal of one's own culture as assumed by identity politics. A flexible model of intercultural understanding allows us to mediate between relativism and ethnocentrism.

Michael Byram's chapter examines the concept and experience of being *bicultural* with a view to defining more precisely what might be involved in being *intercultural*. Research and other illustrative material shows that having two cultural/ethnic identities and holding two sets of values and beliefs is both complex and difficult and, in some cases, can be very painful. It is particularly difficult for those who acquire another culture as an adult as opposed to those who are bicultural through primary socialisation. This has implications for understanding what being intercultural entails. It is not a matter of experiencing a change in cultural/ethnic/national identity but rather a change in attitude towards other cultures. The role of education in developing intercultural competence involves change not just in behaviour but also at cognitive and affective levels. It also involves a level of conscious awareness which is not necessarily part of being bicultural. In order to become intercultural it is necessary for individuals to become aware of the relativity of their own culture through experience of other cultures.

Leah Davcheva's chapter reports on an intercultural project involving Bulgarian student teachers who planned and taught lesson in English schools. Using data drawn from observations, informal discussions and written journals kept by the participants, the chapter analyses and evaluates the student teachers' development in terms of their intercultural awareness, attitude to teaching and learning and classroom behaviour, and professional relationships. Details are provided of the background to the project as well as the process of participant selection and training. The growing commitment in the Bulgarian school system to the cultural dimension of language in foreign classrooms and the need for study programmes and training methods to go beyond merely imparting background information about the dominant target culture provided an impetus for the work. The analysis of the participants' growth in terms of intercultural awareness traces their developing pedagogical theory as well as the degree to which they were prompted to reflect on their own culture. The project provides a possible model for training student teachers of foreign languages to teach interculturally.

Mike Fleming explores teaching and learning in and through drama as a valuable form of intercultural education. He summarises a number of ways in which drama can promote cultural and intercultural awareness. The educational potential of the more oblique of these is made explicit through reference to the Wittengensteinian concept of 'forms of life'. Language, as part of a form of life, is embedded in significant human behaviour and is only intelligible as such. The meaning of language, of what people say and write, is deeply bound up with the specific contexts of their activity and interaction. A goal of intercultural education is to enable learners to apprehend the cultural dimension of forms of life. To this end, the use of fictitious contexts in drama can simplify the complexity of everyday life, including its language, creating the space and conditions for learners, as both participant and observer, to experience and reflect upon intercultural encounters and themes of diverse kinds. Drama has relevance to intercultural education precisely when it is itself conceived as intercultural experience.

Elizabeth Murphy-Lejeune describes the experience of living abroad as a student, and the learning that can result, based upon interviews with returning students. She emphasises the holistic nature of this learning, and how demanding of the individual it can be. Several broad areas of learning are identified: general and local knowledge of the host society, and language proficiency; becoming independent and self-confident; social competence; and personal and interpersonal attitudes. The chapter highlights the importance of a student's willingness to enter into the life of the host society, as a temporary resident, with energy and enthusiasm. Such an approach can offset the inevitable challenge of encountering unfamiliarity and strangeness, and lead to a successful adaptation. Central to adaptation are certain personal qualities, such as tolerance and flexibility, and a self-conscious stance of being between cultures, and being comfortable and effective as an 'intercultural person'. When successful, living abroad is experienced as 'an untried and refreshing meeting place', which engenders serious reflection about oneself, and where living is experienced as a liberating and maturing process.

Celia Roberts discusses how the practice of ethnography can contribute to learning during residence abroad. Using the example of an Introduction to Ethnography course undertaken by modern language students in higher education, Roberts illustrates how the notion of *learning ethnographically* is educationally valuable in two ways: first in terms of learning about others' worlds, such as the societies and communities where modern language students temporarily reside as part of their studies; and second, in terms of learning about oneself and gaining reflexive knowledge of social and cultural practices. Ethnography and a post-modern consciousness of culture as 'travelling' situates the student learner as being 'in between' cultures, and encourages her/him to understand that cultural knowledge and self-knowledge are socially constructed; to de-centre her/his own cultural identity; to recognise the affective dimension in intercultural experience, and the holistic nature of intercultural learning; to use the ethnographic process to develop a reflexive intercultural understanding so that reflexivity becomes an habitual attitude when encountering newness and otherness; and to appreciate issues of power and politics in social and cultural practices. Roberts gives a brief description of the Introduction to Ethnography course, and uses student quotes to support her case for learning ethnographically from intercultural experience.

Phyllis Ryan's chapter is concerned with the question of whether and to what extent a person can become intercultural in the classroom. She develops this by letting two women whom she considers to be intercultural people speak in their own ways about their experience. They are contrasting cases. One has lived in various countries and learned their languages at different stages of her life; the other has never left her country but is involved in language learning and acquiring several languages. They talk about their experience of interculturality and give their views on the relationship between language learning and becoming intercultural. Marty, who has lived and worked in several countries, feels that this experience is essential. Guadelupe, who has never been outside Mexico, suggests that language learning can lay the foundation for becoming intercultural but that it need not necessarily do so; it depends on the language – English learned as a *lingua franca* in Mexico is not conducive to interculturality – and it depends on learners' initial attitudes, although these may change as a consequence of exposure to appropriate language teaching. Ryan concludes that these two cases suggest a need for further research on the potential of language teaching as a location for becoming intercultural.

Amita Sen Gupta draws on her own teaching experience, to present a discussion of an example of intercultural education created within the context of a 'Psychology and Culture' course taught in an international school. Students study psychological topics in a way that foregrounds the intercultural dimension of both the curriculum and classroom activities. The pedagogy encourages and requires students to examine their own cultural identity, through engagement with others in a multi-cultural classroom and through self-reflection. The challenges, difficulties and demands of this for students and staff are illustrated by quoting from essays written during the course. The teaching approach fosters the intercultural quality of students' learning in a number of ways: a dynamic and interactive learning environment; copious use of discussion groups; and the requirement that students keep a journal of their learning. By these means, the richness of intercultural encounters and learning from them is maximised. The outcomes are considerable and profound, in terms of self-knowledge as a cultural being and a critical perspective towards education as a cultural system. Students learn to learn from the unpredictable and discover something new about themselves. Sen Gupta concludes that these achievements would not be possible if the intercultural nature of the educational experience were not intentionally and constantly kept in the foreground.

David Stevens' chapter examines what an intercultural classroom might look like in terms of native language teaching, in this case English. The importance of English as an arts-based subject is stressed in the context of teaching which attends to the significance of student-centred self-discovery. It is important to feel easy about one's own cultural identity if another culture is to be understood. Fostering openness to experience is an essential ingredient of the intercultural classroom. The reading of literature is seen as a personally liberating force, a rediscovery of innocence, of a sense of wonder and of strangeness. Good art and especially poetry 'notices things'. Native language teaching ought to stress intercultural concerns in order to counter a narrowly conceived ethnocentric native-language education seen narrowly as the simple imparting of cultural heritage. Examples of poetry teaching (particular the work of Craig Raine and William Blake) are used to show how pupils can be helped to see everyday experience in new ways and to foster a non-literal understanding of the world. To teach interculturally is to awaken children's and pupils' eyes to the possibilities of wonder.

Susanne Weber's chapter describes an approach to developing intercultural competence which is rooted in the world of business and commerce but which is of a more general import. She argues for the integration of the 'mindful identity negotiation' approach, referring to the need for analysis of successful intercultural interaction which is holistic and not just focused on communication processes. However, mere analysis is not enough and learners need to be active and involved in social interaction and group negotiation if they are to engage fully with the various dimensions of intercultural interaction. She then describes an experiment with young people from a vocational school and some of the techniques which help them to simulate intercultural interaction and then also reflect upon it.. This chapter thus demonstrates what can be done in the classroom when a well-founded theoretical framework is applied in imaginative ways.

Geneviève Zarate's chapter argues for the recognition in an 'international marketplace' of a specific vision of intercultural competences. The recognition should be in the concrete form of cross-frontier acceptance of the assessment of intercultural competences. The specific vision she offers is of an intercultural person whose competences are a product of a biography involving experience of otherness and the capacity to adapt and develop identities which are created in experience. She presents a number of illustrative biographies from a research project which analysed Franco-Australian relationships during the period of nuclear testing in the Pacific. The assessment of the intercultural person should not be, as traditionally, on the basis of comparison with a native speaker, but rather in its own terms as a recognition of the significance of being able to operate in a 'third space' between cultures. One consequence of this is to uncouple linguistic and cultural competences so that each can be recognised in its own right; a second is to give more weight to the transfer of competences from one language or culture learning situation to another – and to validate the transfer in assessment. The chapter thus presents a vision of how intercultural people develop and how the assessment of their competences could stimulate change in educational thinking.

Coda

The book has had a long period of gestation! It began in September 1999 at the first symposium and this introduction is being written in September 2001, at a point when it is impossible to ignore the events of 11 September in the USA. Whilst these and other destructive episodes in contemporary world history threaten our understanding, it is clear that catastrophies of this kind arise when boundaries are seen as places of division and conflict instead of as opportunities for encounter and growth. The events of 11 September have strengthened our conviction that interculturalism should be at the heart of education.

Durham, 29 September 2001

Note

1.   In a separate but related project, our group also edited a collection of articles describing current classroom practices. Byram *et al.* (2001).

References

Berger, P. and Luckmann, T. (1966) *The Social Construction of Reality*. Harmondsworth: Penguin.

Dɪᴀᴅᴀʟʟᴀ, L. (1992) Tᴏ ᴡᴀᴅᴏ ᴀ ᴩᴏᴅᴀᴏᴏᴏʏ ᴏf ɪɴᴛᴏʀᴄᴜʟᴛᴜʀᴀʟ ᴜɴᴅᴇʀsᴛᴀɴᴅɪɴɢ *Amerikastudien* 37, 559–94.

Byram, M. (1997) *Teaching and Assessing Intercultural Communicative Competence*. Clevedon: Multilingual Matters.

Byram, M., Nichols, A. and Stevens, D. (eds) (2001) *Developing Intercultural Competence in Practice*. Clevedon: Multilingual Matters.

Byram, M. and Zarate, G. (1997) Defining and assessing intercultural competence: Some principles and proposals for the European context. *Language Teaching* 29, 14–18.

Dahlen, T. (1997) *Among the Interculturalists – An Emergent Profession and its Packaging of Knowledge*. Stockholm: Stockholm Studies in Social Anthropology

Hays, P.A. (2001) *Addressing Cultural Complexities in Oractice: A Framework for Clinicians and Counselors*. Washington, DC: American Psychological Association.

Kramsch, C. (1993) *Context and Culture in Language Teaching*. Oxford: Oxford University Press.

Kramsch, C. (1998) The privilege of the intercultural speaker. In M. Byram and M. Fleming (eds) *Language Learning in Intercultural Perspective. Approaches Through Drama and Ethnography*. Cambridge: Cambridge University Press.

Lago, C. and Thompson, J. (1996) *Race, Culture and Counselling*. Buckingham: Open University Press.

Müller-Jacquier, B. (2000) Interkulturelle Didaktik. In M. Byram (ed.) *Routledge Encyclopedia of Language Teaching and Learning*. London: Routledge.

Pedersen, P.B., Draguns, J. G, Lonner, W.J. and Trimble, J.E. (2002) *Counseling Across Cultures* (5th edn). Thousand Oaks, CA: Sage.

Smail, D. (1980) Learning in psychotherapy. In P. Salmon (ed.) *Coming to Know*. London: Routledge and Kegan Paul.

Tajfel, H. (1981) *Human Groups and Social Categories. Studies in Social Psychology*. Cambridge: Cambridge University Press.

Zarate, G. (1986) *Enseigner une culture étrangère*. Paris: Hachette.

Chapter 2

Becoming a 'Better Stranger': A Therapeutic Perspective on Intercultural Experience and/as Education

GEOF ALRED

Introduction

This chapter presents a *prima facie* case for a dialogue between a thera-peutic perspective and the study of intercultural experience. It is an attempt to show that therapeutic theory and practice carry lessons for un-derstanding intercultural experience and for developing appropriate educational responses to it. It also acknowledges, as others have (Bimrose, 1996; Krause, 1998; McLeod, 1999), that therapy can profit from adopting an intercultural perspective, and must if therapy is to be inclusive in plural-ist multicultural societies.

In an educational context (whether formal or informal) an experience of interculturality can be both liberating and threatening, whatever the age of those involved, and a 'pedagogy of intercultural experience' is needed in order to enable individuals to benefit rather than suffer. Intercultural expe-rience has the potential to be highly significant. Whether it is or not, in any particular case, is another matter, but entering a situation in which the fa-miliar is drastically reduced and customary ways of responding to circumstances are seriously challenged has the potential to change an indi-vidual in important ways. A student living abroad and working as a teaching assistant wrote home about personal change he was experiencing:

> My life most certainly has changed radically from the first to the second term. However this was not an immediate process. From Christmas up until the half-term break in the middle of February things were much the same as the first term, that is to say it was tolerable as long as I didn't

14

think too much about what I was missing in England. However it was after this half-term break that suddenly, virtually overnight, my outlook changed. I felt a sense of well being previously inexperienced. To meet again the people I knew here was a revelation. Before I considered them to be people with whom I spent my time whilst in France. Now I realise that they are people with whom I enjoy myself and feel comfortable. This is generally true. France used to be a way of life in which I found myself but now it is my way of life.[2]

This represents a profound shift in relationship with the adopted society and in self-perception. Another student describes herself shortly after a similar sojourn abroad:

I mean each day that goes past at the moment I seem to be changing, made of change. It's just different people that I'm meeting, but definitely sort of being in France started the ball rolling . . . It's given me an awful lot more self-confidence and awareness that I can actually do something . . . which before, you know, I was just . . . going through school and University and doing what was expected of me. But now, you know, I've actually done something. I mean, just the example of going to London, I took the school trip to London, okay there were three other teachers there but I really felt as though if I hadn't been there an awful lot of them wouldn't have enjoyed it as much as they did.

I'm very much more bubbly and lively than I used to be. I'm not the sort of person who gets very high or very low, but I do, I mean, I don't tend at the moment, I'm quite happy because I'm, not getting depressed at all, but I do tend to be getting very, very lively. It's something I never used to do before. I used to be quite a placid person who tended to listen an awful lot. I think, you know, I've got more confidence now, self-confidence. I just talk more, I've got more to say.

This student is describing important personal change, attributable to the experience of living abroad. Therapy is also about important change, and there are a number of points of contact between therapy and intercultural experience that suggest exploration of the parallel between them may contribute to a 'pedagogy of intercultural experience'. Whatever the initial motivation of a person seeking therapy, it can, and usually does, contribute towards greater self-understanding, growth and development, and movement towards more resourceful and effective living (Smail, 1980). The chapter will mention briefly empathy, caution and curiosity, language in therapy, and therapy training, and conclude with some general observations about a pedagogy of intercultural experience.

Intercultural situations are diverse and in general, theoretically inclined discussions, there is a danger of unwittingly homogenising the heterogeneous. However, I believe a common denominator of experience in varied intercultural situations is a meeting between individuals who are different in important respects and who present one another with the experience of 'otherness'. There are cases where the otherness is obvious, such as in the case of living abroad, and there are cases where otherness is seen in an encounter that previously was regarded as an encounter with the familiar. Both types of case, and mixtures of them, are common in therapy, and a central activity in therapy is mediation between therapist and client, the person seeking help, as the degree of otherness/sameness shifts and changes in the therapeutic process.

Much theorising about interculturality draws upon psychological theory. It would, I believe, be an exaggeration to say that psychology is a foundational subject in this area, but it does provide a common point of reference for understanding. An obvious example is the phenomenon of 'culture shock', and explanations of it (Furnham & Bochner, 1986). Similarly, therapy traditionally draws heavily on psychology. Here it is claimed that psychology is foundational, although now an alternative view is emerging (Pederson, 1991) and an argument for a post-psychological approach (McLeod, 1999). I do not want, however, to draw on general psychological theories, but instead am looking for points of contact between therapy and intercultural experience, in the belief that there is a distinct dialogue between the two to be joined.

As part of my introduction, I would like to sketch those experiences in my background that have led to the current interest. It began through involvement in research with Mike Byram (Alred, 1998; Byram & Alred, 1992) into cultural learning arising from a period of residence abroad. The context was an investigation of the experience of students undertaking a year abroad as teaching assistants, as part of a modern language degree – what is commonly referred to as the Year Abroad.

The purpose of the study was to gain an understanding of the experience of the Year Abroad from the student's perspective. Students working as assistants in schools (30 British students spending a year in France and 17 French students in British schools) were studied. Data were collected mainly through semi-structured interviews. A major focus was the development of students' knowledge of the culture and society in which they were living and the interaction of that knowledge with the circumstances of their residence. These two aspects were linked by the students' capacity to adapt to living abroad and the consequences for personal development (Alred, 1998).

The overall findings were positive – students were challenged, generally valued their sojourn and reported extensive cultural learning. Few, if any, escaped difficult experiences, and most experienced some loneliness. Certain situational factors, such as accommodation, financial circumstances and support within the school, played a significant role in the degree of success students enjoyed, and in how stressful living abroad proved to be. Many students reported marked changes in self-perception, personal development and maturity. By the end of the year, an initial emphasis on language *per se* had given way to attention to language in context, to the use of language in social exchange and being part of a social world. Several students described the Year Abroad as a major episode in their lives. Experiences amongst the group of interviewees were varied, ranging from a seemingly inconsequential period of 'time out' from regular studies to changes that could best be described as a profound transformation in self-understanding and outlook on life. A small minority felt less confident after a year living and working abroad.

Reading between the lines of the data, I felt that much was left unsaid by interviewees, and that their involvement in our research was no substitute for a proper opportunity to digest their experience and to appreciate its significance for them. It was apparent that within their degree course as a whole, the Year Abroad was poorly integrated. Its educational value, in the broadest sense, went unrecognised. My suspicion was, and remains, that we, as researchers, did not get a full picture of how hard the Year Abroad could be and of the emotional demands it made. Perhaps, also, we did not get a full picture of how good it could be.

A link between this research and therapy came about in two ways. First, there seemed to be a parallel with therapy training, in that becoming a therapist can be seen as an intercultural experience, of engaging with the values, beliefs and discourses of the world of therapy. There is an emphasis on personal development and self-knowledge, as a concomitant of and prerequisite for being effective as a therapist. My own training over a period of two years involved one day a week as a trainee, and four days a week as a university lecturer engaged in teacher education. Over time, I came to experience this pattern in my working life as intercultural. I inhabited alternately two worlds, one very familiar and one full of newness, strangeness and otherness. The tension between the two was energising, and I became conscious of mediating between worlds separated by beliefs, values and practices. Learning was both directed outwards, in that I came to see afresh the familiar world through the perspective of the training course culture, and personal, in that I became more aware of myself as an inhabitant of two worlds. I seemed to be living on the boundary, physically and psychically, between them. Being a mediator was a powerful stimulus to learn, about myself, about others and about the business of therapy. One manifestation was a heightened sensitivity to language. Strictly speaking, I was moving between discourses, but I prefer to say I was speaking different languages, and importantly, was learning a new language as part of becoming a therapist. The term 'discourse' wasn't strong enough to convey the richness of both the experience and the learning that ensued.

Second, I encountered modern language students who came for therapy at a university counselling service and whose troubles involved their Year Abroad. Here I came to appreciate at first hand the enormity of this undertaking for some students, and there is both systematic and anecdotal evidence that troubled students do introduce the experience of the Year Abroad, and other periods away from regular study, into conversations with therapists (Khoo *et al.*, 1994; Brice, personal communication). There certainly is evidence of the deleterious effects of homesickness amongst students making the transition to university (Fisher, 1989; Fisher & Hood, 1987). Recently, the Association for Student Counselling devoted a conference to this general area. The conference title was 'Culture and Psyche in Transition: A European Perspective on Student Psychological Health' (ASC, 1996).

Preparation for the Year Abroad

Early research into the Year Abroad tended to focus on change in linguistic proficiency. A recent review by Coleman (1995) highlights a significant feature of this research: almost all studies of linguistic gains during the Year Abroad reveal high individual variation, mirroring variation in the overall quality of the sojourn. Coleman speculates that an important factor in explaining varied outcomes is the extent of informal learning that results when a student engages actively in the host society (our data would support this speculation). This, in turn, depends on other factors, including a student's readiness and ability to be open and flexible in new situations, the circumstances of the sojourn and the encouragement and preparation to engage provided by the sending institution. Hence, Coleman (1997) has emphasised the importance of preparation that addresses the broader context of the Year Abroad. He identifies four desirable components: recognition of the role of personality in responding to experiences whilst abroad; self-awareness; intercultural competence; and appropriate learning strategies. In current research, Hall and Toll (1999) have also recognised the complexity and breadth of learning during residence abroad:

> [A]ny learning at the preparation stage needs to draw upon the student's prior experience and current knowledge, feelings and attitudes in order to influence what takes place during, and possibly after, the

residence stage. Awareness raising activities/tasks should offer students insights into the processes involved in adapting to change and, ultimately, being 'intercultural people'. (Hall & Toll, 1999: 9)

There exist examples of educational practice which address through preparation the broader context of the Year Abroad experience highlighted by our research. For example, the 'language learner as ethnographer' (Roberts *et al.*, 2001) is a holistic approach to learning whilst living abroad in which students carry out a 'downsized ethnographic inquiry' (Jurasek, 1996: 225). The student becomes better able to talk relativistically and contextually about 'otherness', and so becomes better able to engage with 'otherness', to truly culturally mediate. It is an emotionally demanding achievement.

Another approach outwardly quite different from ethnographic inquiry but sharing similar aims is one which develops students' personal resources for living abroad (Cormeraie, 1995). Students are helped to appreciate the dimensions of their own cultural identity in order that they can understand how other belief systems and attitudes are encoded in other societies. The rationale is that the development of complex thinking about cultural difference through greater self-knowledge and awareness increases the self-confidence to be open to the challenges of living abroad.

The two approaches are as the faces of the same coin, and taken together point to a complex relationship between, on the one hand, an ability to adapt to and function well abroad and, on the other, self-knowledge and personal qualities. These twin aspects are a central determinant of the outcomes of the Year Abroad and reinforce the conclusion from our own research that learning through living abroad as a modern language student involves changing as a person. The parameters of such change can be expressed in the notion of 'intercultural competence' (Byram, 1997; Jensen, 1995) which comprises 'the ability to behave appropriately in intercultural situations, the affective and cognitive capacity to establish and maintain intercultural relationships and the ability to stabilise one's self identity while mediating between cultures.' (Jensen, 1995: 41).

Empathy, Caution and Curiosity

Essential to the ability to mediate between cultures is sensitivity to the feelings of other people and the ability to empathise with their experience (Byram, 1995; Watkins, 1999). Amongst therapists, there is widespread recognition that empathy is a powerful source of therapeutic effect. For example:

Much of the art of therapy depends on being able to place oneself within the experience of the other and to feel, in some measure, what it is like to be him. (Lomas, 1993)

The focus on empathy is predicated upon the belief that there is a bridge to be crossed between two people, the therapist and the client. Understanding and sharing are not immediate or easy to achieve. There is a degree of 'otherness' between the two people. The client, in her/his experience, is initially unknown to the therapist and subsequently becomes less unknown. The experience of becoming known is therapeutic for the client, it leads to whatever is confusing, painful or distressing in her/his self and her/his circumstances becoming less so. Lomas works within a psychoanalytic tradition where interpretation, rather than empathy, is a central goal. However, he recognises its importance, and that interpretation, however justified by being seen eventually to be accurate, can be an impediment. The assumptions, beliefs and values encapsulated in a theory from which interpretation derives must be transcended if empathic understanding is to be achieved. Theory, as a determinant and reflection of a cultural mindset, can become baggage that impedes travelling to meet the client, especially the strangeness and otherness that they present.

Forming an empathic bridge between two people's experience is complex and paradoxical. It involves the therapist in staying in touch with her/himself whilst entering the client's world – it is a subtle double act. If it is not, it becomes either sympathy or an intellectual understanding, both of which are incomplete. In humanistic approaches to therapy, and person-centred therapy in particular, empathy is one of a number of conditions the therapist aims to achieve. Another is congruence or being genuine. A third is acceptance of the client, refraining from judgement that might prevent truly and empathically 'meeting' and understanding the client. It requires recognition of one's biases and prejudices and a willingness to set them to one side. The ability to offer these conditions can be developed. All require self-awareness and self-knowledge on the part of the counsellor. Developing as a therapist is again a double act – getting to know others goes hand in hand with getting to know oneself.

Empathy is not all or nothing. There are degrees of empathy, (there are, indeed, scales of empathy used in research and training [Truax & Carkuff, 1967]). Therapists recognise that a high degree of empathy will not be achieved nor, indeed, will be necessary all of the time. However, when it does occur, it is likely to be highly effective, primarily in fostering the client's learning and ability to change but also for the therapist in coming to understand the worldview and the world of the client. An important part of this learning may be that the culture of the client becomes more transparent and known, less strange and foreign, and recognition that s/he has resources for being part of a social world. In addition, and over time, the therapist may become more empathic in general and better able to tolerate and work with the strangeness that clients bring.

However, empathy varies not only in degree but in its expression. There are cultural differences in how empathy is communicated. Like all human qualities, claiming, or wanting to believe, that it is universal does not mean a 'pedagogy of empathy' can be generalised across cultures. For example.

> In contrast to the American emphasis on verbal articulateness and expression, Asians often convey their empathic awareness nonverbally. In Korea, it is called 'heart-to-heart' communication. Within close intimacy relationships, it is considered impolite, if not insulting, to verbalise one's thanks or other marks of appreciation. To actually say it in words to the other implies that you are not so intimate, and more like outsiders or strangers to each other. This is often very difficult for Americans to understand. Even more foreign to North American modes of communication is that Asian women in particular have dozens of different kinds of silences by which they communicate to each other, especially in the family. This takes considerable empathic attunement on the part of the other, as psychoanalysts know from the different kinds of silences in session. (Roland, 1996: 108)

An implication here for education is that 'empathy training' in one culture, any one approach to therapy, is no guarantor of that aspect of intercultural competence. If wider lessons are to be learned from the therapeutic perspective, they are likely to come from therapy where cultural difference is marked, acknowledged and worked with.

In fact, cross-cultural therapy goes beyond empathy. Empathy is not enough. Krause (1998), for example, has described the therapist's task as ethnographic, and advocates an approach that seems very close to what an intercultural person might do when encountering the 'otherness' of someone from a foreign culture:

> In practice this means that the therapist must be cautious. She may decide on a period in the beginning of therapy, in which understanding and how to understand is the main issue, a sort of ethnographic mode. This means going slowly, enquiring and eliciting descriptions of relevant aspects of clients' lives. It means noting analogic communication and doxic information and finding a way of being respectfully curious with clients about this. It means asking about action, both action observed in the therapy room and action described. It also means reading and making herself familiar with the salient themes from the client's social and cultural backgrounds and checking these out with clients themselves. It means checking out whether understanding is shared. And it means being curious about misunderstandings and about times when negotiation of a public

space between client and therapist has broken down. Such a period at the beginning of therapy can help the therapist develop a way of asking ethnographic questions, that is to say questions about specific circumstances, about local context and about detail. (Kraus, 1998: 174).

Krause here is talking to therapists but her dialogue is two-way, between ethnographers and therapists, hers is an 'intercultural dialogue'. She believes that the standpoint of therapy can encourage ethnography to 'take proper account of inner worlds' (p. 3), of both parties in an intercultural encounter. Therapist and intercultural person alike are empathic, cautious and respectfully curious when approaching the 'other'.

Language, Identity and Therapy

Intercultural experience often involves learning/speaking a second language, and can present challenges and indeed threats to a person's sense of themselves. As has been observed:

[I]n order to be a wit in a foreign language you have to go through the stage of being a half-wit – there is no other way. If the problem is not addressed explicitly, learners may just be aware of it as a constant resistance against opening their mouths. (Harder, 1980: 269)

And, 'When we give up our mother tongue for another language we are truly disabled and bereft' (van Deurzen, 1996: 57). The relationship between language and identity is another point of contact between interculturality and therapy, and the accompanying belief that talking, in a certain way, can bring about significant personal change and sense of belonging and being part of a social world.

In the field of language study, Evans (1988), for example, has argued that 'To learn a new language is to create a new identity *irrespective of the foreign culture or foreign experience*' (p. 79, italics in original). Language is the principal means by which the process of identity formation takes place. His argument is based upon a detailed study of the professional lives of modern linguists, drawing upon psychological and psychosocial theories to explore the identities of people who become modern linguists. He makes brief mention of examples from therapy where clients (or, patients, as they are termed, as the examples are drawn from psychoanalytic cases) who are bilingual use this resource to manage themselves emotionally and their relationships with others. For example:

I think another reason why I was so attracted to a foreign language was that there was quite a lot of anxiety or unease in my associations with my mother tongue. This was associated with my family life. My mother, with whom I learned to speak the language, was unsatisfied and unfulfilled and quite an angry person and a lot of those undertones were picked up by me in the use of language. English, my mother tongue, was slightly contaminated by the emotional input from my family. So there were lots of phrases and lots of expressions that used to make me anxious. When I discovered another language, French, I could learn these idioms, I could learn these expressions and the use of them was in some way delightful, new and not emotionally laden. I could put my own emotional content into those phrases, those expressions, they could be fun, they could be light, whereas an awful lot of the idiomatic use of English to me was laden with my mother's experience and I needed to get away from that. It had to be something I could make my own that didn't belong to my mother. But that was at an unconscious level. (Quoted in Evans, 1988: 78–9)

Here a second language is liberating, allowing the shedding of emotional baggage and the forging of a more independent identity. That the person concerned later recognises that the motivation to learn French was unconscious indicates complex and profound learning about herself as a bilingual person. Before gaining this insight, and here I can only speculate in this case, the person may have embraced French as an escape and defence against anxiety associated with her early years. So a second language can be used to limit growth as well as promote it. Evans gives a further example of this contradictory aspect of being bilingual, in which speaking a foreign language was an alternative to silence:

Although the women discussed here used a second language as a language of repression, it saved them from having to resort to long periods of silence . . . children who for neurotic reasons are unable to talk are nearly always able to sing the words of songs: *a second language might be compared to the singing of silent children: both free the words of the emotional charge which burdens and inhibits the use of the native tongue.* (Italics added by Evans, 1988: 81)

These psychological, intrapersonal aspects came to the fore because the context was a therapeutic one. Other such examples can be found in a small but growing literature in this area (Burck, 1997; Stanley, 2000). However, there are well-known examples from elsewhere. One such is Eva Hoffman's account of learning English when, as a Polish girl of 13 she moved to live in Canada and struggled with whether to write her diary in English or Polish. She describes learning about herself as she learned a second language:

Refracted through the double distance of English and writing, this self – my English self – becomes oddly objective, more than anything, it perceives. It exists more easily in the abstract sphere of thoughts and observations than in the world. For a while, this impersonal self, this cultural negative capability, becomes the truest thing about me. When I write, I have a real existence that is proper to the activity of writing – an existence that takes place midway between me and the sphere of artifice, art, pure language. This language is beginning to invent another me. However I discover something odd. It seems that when I write (or, for that matter, think) in English, I am unable to use the word 'I'. I do not go so far as the schizophrenic 'she', but I am driven, as by a compulsion, to the double, the Siamese-twin 'you'. (Hoffman, 1989: 121)

The relationship between language and identity could not be expressed more starkly. The educational implication of this close relationship is an imperative to attend to language and to become a sensitive user of language, especially in situations where language becomes problematic or in some way, less reliable, less in the service of our needs and concerns. The sensitivity is not confined to the structures, rhythms and nuances of language but includes recognition that a different language can lead to a different way of expressing oneself, and indeed experiencing oneself. Van Deurzen (1998: 58) recognises her own shifting self in different linguistic communities:

I learnt that I had to let myself get much more passionate, if I ever wanted to speak French well, and then of course I had to learn to get much more phlegmatic and rational when trying to get my English right: each time bringing out different aspects of my character, leaving the Dutch pragmatism somewhat behind.

In therapy training, a common approach is to develop skilful language behaviour, such as active listening – skills practice is the stock-in-trade of much therapy training. An alternative approach regards therapy 'as a craft that calls upon an understanding of drama, creative writing and rhetoric' (McLeod, 1997). Here, attention is given to style, the ways in which we speak, and the poetic quality of our language. 'Conversational therapy' (Hobson, 1985) is based on a certain kind of conversation premised on the belief that therapist and client are 'alone together' working towards common ground between two phenomenal worlds.

Education for Intercultural Experience, Training for Therapy

Other points of contact between interculturality and therapy could be mentioned. The implication is that if there are lessons to be learned about the former from the latter, then, in some sense, an intercultural person is like a therapist. The definition of intercultural competence recognises this through the emphasis on openness and the ability to function in conditions of uncertainty and encounter with otherness. In broad terms, the lessons might be about the profundity of what is prized in being able to function optimally in intercultural situations. Therapy is good at teaching that certain human qualities, such as empathy, acceptance, respectful curiosity and openness, are hard won. More specifically, therapy teaches that these qualities have inner and outer aspects: being open to others, especially others who represent otherness, is dependent upon being open to oneself. And being open to oneself means being open to the 'otherness' in oneself – to that which is outside consciousness. To be intercultural is to be a 'stranger to ourselves' (Kristeva, 1991), as well as to others. An opening toward the other's experience and reality presents an opportunity to see and question as assumptions one's own attitudes and the taken-for-granted in one's reality. Hence, a pedagogy of intercultural experience must combine opportunities and provocations and support to look inside as well as outside. This is necessary when anticipating (Comeraie, 1995) and when reflecting upon intercultural experience.

Lessons may also be drawn in the other direction, in that there is an emerging view of therapy as a social process. The emphasis here is on social identity and a sense of belonging. McLeod (1999), for example, draws on social constructionist philosophy to sketch a post-psychological approach, in which:

> The role of the counsellor is to act as a bridge back into participation in the social world. At the moment of seeking counselling, the person is in some respect outside of everyday life. There is some part of their experience, their story, which cannot be shared with others. The task of the counsellor is to help the person to rejoin the human conversation. The social anthropologist Victor Turner, who has studied the role of shamans and healers in other cultures . . . , describes such people as liminal figures, on the edge of society. Counsellors, too, are liminal figures, who exist on the edge of social groups or institutions for the purpose of helping individuals re-enter the social world. (p. 218; bold in original)

To become such a therapist requires a training that might be described as intercultural, although McLeod uses the term 'multicultural'. To quote:

> Counsellor education and training is grounded in multiculturalism; it is only from a comparative perspective that the cultural construction of one's own identity can become apparent. It is necessary for counsellors to be able to locate their approach within its social and historical context . . . . Training needs to include development of the capacity to appreciate the intricacies of language use through the study of topics such as narrative, discourse and conversation. (p. 221)

To become a therapist requires self-knowledge and an understanding of one's own identity, an appreciation and acceptance that this is a construction, a sensitivity to language in its various uses, in order to occupy temporarily, and with confidence and competence, a liminal position between a person who is currently outside somewhere they would like to belong.

This chapter is an invitation to dialogue between domains that ordinarily do not meet. Before concluding, I quote a call for dialogue that seems to speak with equal force to both domains, to language educators and to therapists and their trainers:

> Let me be more specific about the kind of dialogical capacities I am referring to: the allowing of the other and the self to freely arise and to be given the space for expression; to allow the other to exist autonomously from myself; patiently to wait for relations to occur in this open horizon; to move toward difference not with denial or rejection but with tolerance, curiosity, and a clear sense that it is in the encounter with otherness and multiplicity that deeper meanings can emerge . . . [Such dialogue] presupposes a capacity to take a third-person perspective on the self, so that one can reflect on how one's actions and attitudes have affected the other and the situation. As these capacities develop, the self moves from being an unreflective center that finds the other to be either like oneself or as needed to be to serve the self's ends, to a self who is able to step to the side, who is aware of the co-creating nature of the interaction with the other, who knows that the other's experience departs from the self's – often in radical ways. In this chasm, where such departures differentiate self and other, there is a choice available to penetrate it through attempts at dialogue and understanding. This penetration is never only an opening toward the other's experience and reality. It signals a willingness to see and question as assumptions one's most cherished attitudes: the core of our own beliefs, approaches, and commitments. To be able deeply to entertain the difference that the other poses we must, as well, be able to disidentify from our passionately held beliefs, and be able to see what ideologies they are based on and to be able to interrogate the function and effects of these beliefs. (Watkins, 1999: 255–6)

Conclusion: The Therapist and the Intercultural Person

One important difference between a therapist and an intercultural person, someone who is able to function optimally and effectively in intercultural situations, someone who is at home when 'not at home', so to speak, is sociological. Most therapists are, in some way, associated with the professionalisation of therapy and support its status as a legitimate social practice. Any therapist worth their salt has credentials. And, despite the proliferation of therapeutic services in western societies in recent decades, it remains a minority activity. Being intercultural, in contrast, is altogether more diffuse, fluid and common. A central argument of this book is that intercultural experience is not confined to overtly cross cultural or multi-cultural situations, but rather occurs whenever worldviews come into contact and engage, and is a potential whenever two people meet.

However, it is interesting to note that in many cases a formative influence in becoming a therapist is moving from one culture to another, usually as a result of emigration, sometimes involuntary emigration (Henry, 1977). From a survey of 4000 therapists practising in three American cities in the 1970s, Henry found, not surprisingly, wide variation in ethnicity and religious affiliation, but also a high proportion of therapists having overt and substantial intercultural experience. They had moved from one society, usually European, to American society. Hence many therapists 'have been exposed to more than one set of cultural influences' (p. 49). They have had direct experience of the 'newness', 'strangeness' and 'otherness' of a foreign culture, and have occupied the position of the 'outsider' on the margin of a culture they seek to join. Life experience has, perhaps, prepared them to occupy the liminal position that enables them to do their work (Williams, 1999).

Intercultural experience, in its broadest sense, is unavoidable. We all have experiences of, and can learn from, being astonished, enthralled, bedazzled, confused, contradicted, unaccepted, alienated, misunderstood, welcomed, accepted, understood. Such experiences can be contrived but more usually they occur in the flow and flux of life. The observation of the contribution of informal learning during student residence abroad (Coleman, 1995) is important, and is amply illustrated in the stories told by students in the research referred to earlier. The quality and value of living and working abroad were invariably the result of a complex of factors and influences. A successful outcome was often fortuitous, and herein lies an educational challenge: how to give direction and purpose to the learning that occurs when living interculturally, so that it contributes to intercultural competence, and not intercultural incompetence. Van Deurzen (1998: 81), herself a therapist and person of considerable intercultural experience aptly expresses the educational payoff of intercultural experience:

> [W]e can become better strangers to each other and thus better known to each other and ourselves.

Becoming a 'better stranger' was expressed by one student in our research as: '[W]hen I came back, I would say I was European rather than

English'. And progress towards intercultural competence is described in her verdict on her sojourn:

> I would describe it as a very, very positive year abroad, that certainly helped me to become more aware of myself and more confident in myself. I can't say that I've learned an awful lot about teaching because it was very much related to French teaching and there are different ideas in England, British schools. I think, yes, the main thing I've learned about is about myself more than anything else. And it's improved my language no end, I can actually speak French now, which is what it was supposed to do.

For educators in this field, the challenge begins with truly listening to what learners say.

Note
1. Quotes from students during or after their Year Abroad and the research described here are from ESRC project 'Residence Abroad and the Cultural Perceptions of Foreign Students in HE' (1996).

References

Alred, G. (1998) *Being Abroad – Becoming a Linguist: A Discussion of the Psychosocial Effects of the Year Abroad. (CRILE Working Papers: Research Issues in the Year Abroad.)* Lancaster: Centre for Research in Language Education, Lancaster University.

Association for Student Counselling (1996) *Culture and Psyche in Transition: A European Perspective on Student Psychologial Health.* Rugby: British Association for Counselling in association with the Forum Européen de l'Orientation Académique, FEDORA.

Bimrose, J. (1996) Multiculturalism. In R. Bayne, I. Horton, and J. Bimrose (eds) *New Directions in Counselling.* London: Routledge.

Burck, (1997) Language and narrative: Learning from bilingualism. In R.K. Papadopoulos and J. Byng-Hall (eds) *Multiple Voices: Narrative in Systemic Family Psychotherapy* (pp. 64–85). London: Duckworth.

Byram, M. (1995) Acquiring intercultural competence. A review of learning theories. In L. Sercu (ed.) *Intercultural Competence: A New Challenge for Language Teachers and Trainers in Europe Vol. 1: The Secondary School.* Aalborg: Aalborg University Press.

Byram, M. (1997) 'Us and Them' and foreign language learning. Inaugural Lecture, University of Durham.

Byram, M, and Alred, G. (1992) *Residence Abroad and the Cultural Perceptions of Foreign Language Students in Higher Education.* Report to the Economic and Social Research Council, Research Grant No. R000231196.

Coleman, J. (1995) The current state of knowledge concerning student residence abroad. In G. Parker and A. Rouxeville (eds) *'The Year Abroad': Preparation, Monitoring, Evaluation, Current Research and Development.* London: AFSL/CiLT.

Coleman, J. (1997) Residence abroad within language study. *Language Teaching* 30, 1–20.

Cormeraie, S. (1995) Cross-cultural training: Perceptions and personal growth. In G. Parker and A. Rouxeville (eds) *'The Year Abroad': Preparation, Monitoring, Evaluation, Current Research and Development*. London: AFSL/CiLT.

Evans, C. (1988) *Language People*. Milton Keynes: Open University Press.

Fisher, S. (1989) *Homesickness, Cognition and Health*. Hove, Sussex: Lawrence Erlbaum.

Fisher, S. and Hood, B. (1987) The stress of transition to university: A longitudinal study of vulnerability to psychological disturbance and homesickness. *British Journal of Psychology* 78, 425–41.

Furnham, A. and Bochner, S. (1986), *Culture Shock: Psychological Reactions in Unfamiliar Environments*. London: Methuen.

Hall, S. and Toll, S. (1999) Raising intercultural awareness in preparation for periods of residence abroad. www.lancs.ac.uk/users/interculture/reports.htm#sp1

Harder, P. (1980) Discourse as self expression: On the reduced personality of the second language learner. *Applied Linguistics* 1, 262–270.

Henry, W.E. (1977) Personal and social identities of psychotherapists. In A.S. Gurman and A.M. Razin (eds) *Effective Psychotherapy: A Handbook of Research*. Oxford: Pergamon Press.

Hobson, R. (1985) *Forms of Feeling: The Heart of Psychotherapy*. London: Routledge.

Hoffman, E. (1989) *Lost in Translation*. London: Vintage.

Jensen, A.A. (1995) Defining intercultural competence: A discussion of its essential components and prerequisites. In A.A. Jensen, K. Jaeger and A. Lorentsen (eds) *Intercultural Competence: A New Challenge for Language Teachers and Trainers in Europe. Vol II: The Adult Learner*. Aalborg: Aalborg University Press.

Jurasek, R. (1996) Using ethnography to bridge the gap between study abroad and the on-campus language and culture curriculum. In C.J. Kramsch (ed.) *Redefining the Boundaries of Language Study*. Boston, MA: Heinle and Heinle.

Krause, I. (1998) *Therapy Across Culture*. London: Sage.

Khoo, P.L.S., Abu-Rasain, M.H. and Hornby, G. (1994) Counselling foreign students: A review of strategies. *Counselling Psychology Quarterly* 7(2), 117–31.

Kristeva, J. (1991) *Strangers to Ourselves*. New York: Columbia University Press.

Lomas, P. (1993) *Cultivating Intuition: An Introduction to Psychotherapy*. Northvale, NJ: Jason Aronson.

McLeod, J. (1997) *Narrative and Psychotherapy*. London: Sage.

McLeod, J. (1999) Counselling as a social process. *Counselling: The Journal of the British Association for Counselling* 10(3), 217–22.

Pederson, P.B. (1991) Introduction to Part 1: A conceptual framework. *Journal of Counseling and Development* 70 (1), 6–12.

Roberts, C., Byram, M., Barro, A., Jordan, S. and Street, B. (2001) *Language Learners as Ethnographers*. Clevedon: Multilingual Matters.

Roland, A. (1996) *Cultural Pluralism and Psychoanalysis: The Asian and North American Experience*. New York: Routledge.

Smail, D. (1980) Learning in psychotherapy. In P. Salmon (ed.) *Coming to Know*. London: Routledge and Kegan Paul.

Stanley, M. (2000) Different tongues: The experience of counsellors/psychotherapists in Britain who practise in English, where English is not their mother tongue. Unpublished MA thesis, University of Keele.

Truax, C.B. and Carkuff, R.R. (1967) *Toward Effective Counseling and Psychotherapy*. Chicago: Aldine.

van Deurzen, E. (1998) *Paradox and Passion: An Existential Approach to Therapy and Counselling*. Chichester: Wiley.

Watkins, M. (1999) Pathways between the multiplicities of the psyche and culture. In J. Rowan and M. Cooper (eds) *The Plural Self: Multiplicity in Everyday Life*. London: Sage.

Williams, S. (1999) The therapist as outsider: The truth of the stranger. *British Journal of Psychotherapy* 16(1), 3–15.

Chapter 3

For a Flexible Model of Intercultural Understanding

LOTHAR BREDELLA

In an illuminating essay, Theo Harden explores the limits of intercultural understanding. The essay ends with the following words:

> He/she [the learner] has to be able to draw the line exactly where 'understanding' becomes a threat to his/her identity. Instead of creating the illusion that it is possible to 'understand' a foreign culture it is therefore probably wiser to prepare the learner for the difficult position of the respected outsider, who, no matter how much he/she might try, will never fully 'understand' and will never be fully 'understood'. (Harden, 2000: 120f)

I will take these reflections on intercultural understanding as a starting point for some critical questions: Should intercultural understanding necessarily come to an end when it becomes a threat to one's collective identity? Is the preservation of one's collective identity the highest goal? What about students who want to change and enrich their collective identities by learning a foreign language and understanding others? Why is understanding others an illusion? In the first sentence Harden regards it as possible and desirable, at least to a certain extent. What is the role of a 'respected outsider' who will never 'fully' understand and will never be 'fully understood'? Does this imply that an insider will 'fully' understand and be fully understood? These questions indicate that we have to clarify what we mean by intercultural understanding and establish what its goals should be.

In the first three sections of the first part I will show how our concept of intercultural understanding depends on our concept of language. Then I will deal with psychological as well as cultural determinism, which both regard intercultural understanding as impossible. The final section of the first part, I will describe what is constitutive of intercultural understand-

31

ing. In the second part of my contribution I will take up the question of whether intercultural understanding should be subordinated to the preservation of one's collective identity.

Towards a Pedagogy of Intercultural Understanding

The Lockean concept of language

According to a widespread common-sense concept of language we use words and sentences to convey meanings to others and assume that these words and sentences have the same meaning for speakers and listeners. This belief can easily be shaken by critical reflection: Why should speakers and listeners share the same meanings, if we consider the fact that they have different biographies, live under different conditions and are free to attribute meanings to the words in connection with their respective experiences? Considering this question, we will almost certainly come to the conclusion that it is unlikely that speakers and listeners will associate the same meanings with the words spoken and heard. In his *Essay Concerning Human Understanding* John Locke develops a concept of language which confirms the sceptical conclusion about understanding I have just mentioned. Locke points out that individual speakers have the freedom to decide what their words and sentences mean, so that it is unlikely that the words have the same meanings for speakers and listeners:

> And every Man has so inviolable a Liberty, to make Words to stand for what *Ideas* he pleases, that no one hath the Power to make others have the same *Ideas* in their Minds, that he has, when they use the same Words, that he does. (Locke cited in Taylor, 1992: 32)

Locke stresses the agency of the speaker and the voluntary nature of the act of signification. His concept of language is well expressed by Talbot Taylor when he writes:

> it is not possible for me to signify, by the words I use, any but my own ideas. Signifying is an act performed by the speaking agent, an act in which she utters some sounds as 'marks' of her own ideas. (Taylor, 1992: 33)

Locke points out that, if we are careful with the use of words, we might be able to avoid misunderstandings, but there is no guarantee that we understand what the other means. If we agree with Locke's concept of language, we might say with Harden that understanding others is an illusion. Yet, before we draw such a conclusion, let us look at a different concept of language.

The Saussurean concept of language

Whereas Locke stresses the agency of the speaker and the voluntary nature of signification, Ferdinand Saussure stresses that the act of signification is not private but public. Not the individual speaker but language as a system, *langue*, determines what for example the words 'jealousy' and 'silliness' mean. Their meaning is beyond the reach of the individual speaker. The agency of the speaker that plays such an important role in Locke's concept of language disappears in Saussure's. Taylor describes Saussure's concept of language as being closed:

> Rather, the sign is determined solely by its structural place in the linguistic system. It is not nature, or God, or reason, or tradition, or the voluntary choice of an individual or of society as a whole that determines which concept is associated with which acoustic image (that is, that determines what the sign, as a 'unified duality' is). It is language as a whole which determines the sign. (Taylor, 1992: 85)

According to Saussure, we understand each other not by grasping the other's ideas through words but rather by sharing the same linguistic sign. From the view of structuralist linguistics we might say that Locke's concept of language is simply wrong, as he did not realise that meaning is not private but public (cf. Taylor, 1992: 119).

The question, however, is whether the structuralist model of language does justice to our experience of language and understanding. Do the listener's agency and personal and sociohistorical experiences play no role in understanding what is said?

The pragmatic model

According to pragmatics, the structuralist model of language is right in stressing the public nature of language which constrains and guides us, but it is one-sided. In order to understand an individual utterance it is not enough to know the language as a system; one also needs to know something about the speaker's and listener's prior knowledge and their expectations about the special situation in which they communicate. Language is not a closed system independent of culture but inherently connected with it. Structural linguistics stresses the impersonal aspect of language at the expense of the interpersonal one.

Roger D. Sell, who is well aware of the achievements of structural linguistics, points out that it de-historised, de-personalised and de-humanised language use: 'In Western linguistics, the exclusion of interpersonality was sometimes so complete that language was almost thought of as a kind of smoothly efficient machine' (Sell, 2000: 42). A pragmatic concept of language attempts to integrate what structuralist linguistics excludes and

re-establishes the relative agency of speaker and listener. In order to understand an utterance, as already indicated, we must take into account the
speaker's and the listener's background knowledge and their interpretive
and reasoning abilities:

> Both speaker and hearer make use of background knowledge, the situ-
> ational context, and memory of past communicational experiences in
> attempting to accomplish their respective reasoning tasks; but they
> perform these *acts* of reasoning as *individuals*. (Taylor, 1992: 128)

Pragmatics replaces the Lockean idea of communication as the carrying
of ideas through words from speakers to listeners with the idea that speakers make listeners perform certain acts of interpretation and reasoning so
that speakers and listeners see things in a similar light:

> What remains distinctive of the pragmatic theories is the assumption
> that, in order to reach the goal of a 'rough' mutual understanding (that
> is, to come onto the 'same train of thought'), speaker and hearer *must*
> perform complex acts of reasoning. (Taylor, 1992: 128)

Words are clues that allow speakers and listeners 'to agree on 'the essential lines' of what is meant' (Taylor 1992: 129). Such a view underlines the
concept of understanding as interaction. Traditionally, we assume that a
text conveys meaning to the reader in such a way that those who are linguistically competent can extract the meaning from it. However, if we
assume that a text offers us clues and gives us directions, then readers
create its meaning under its guidance. The pragmatic concept of language
is able to describe the complexity of understanding and to reconcile the
private and public nature of language. Yet, as we shall see in the next
section, the insight into the readers' and listeners' active role in understanding makes critics doubt that understanding others is at all possible.
On a higher level we return to the Lockean scepticism in a radicalized form.

Psychological determinism

From the insight into readers' active role, psychological determinists
conclude that the readers' dispositions and interests determine what a text
means to them. Whereas in the traditional view of reading, author and text
are more important than the reader, in the new one the reader is so dominant that author and text can be neglected as irrelevant. David Bleich (1975:
3) formulates the basic assumption of the psychological or subjective
model of reading when he writes: 'To say that perceptual processes are different in each person is to say that reading is a wholly subjective process
and that the nature of what is perceived is determined by the rules of the
personality of the perceiver'. In a similar way Norman Holland points out

that it is not the writer but the reader who is in control of the process of signification:

> In reading, I bring to a text schemata from previous literary experiences, from my historical or critical knowledge, my sense of human nature, my values, my preferences in language, my politics, my metabolism – I bring all these things to bear on the text, and the text feeds back to me what I bring to it either positively or not at all. It rewards my hypotheses or, so to speak, ignores them. That is all the text does, for it is always I who am in control. It is I who ask questions of the text and I who hear and interpret its answers. (Holland, 1985: 7)

Holland seems to give a convincing description of the reading process, but we might ask the critical question of how readers could acquire their historical and critical knowledge of the text if they always ignore what does not confirm their expectations. Psychological determinists are right in criticizsing the concept of a passive and docile reader, but they are wrong when they ignore the author's intention and reduce the text to a meaningless arrangement of black dots on a white sheet of paper from which we are unable to see the world in a new light. This concept of reading leads to a narcissistic world view from which there will be a rude awakening. Narcissus who was so enraptured by his own image in the water that he wanted to embrace it, drowned.

Cultural determinism

Stanley Fish is a severe critic of Bleich's psychological determinism. It is not the reader's personality but the strategies of the interpretive community which decide what a text means. Both, however, agree that a text is powerless in conveying meanings to readers. They only disagree about the answer to the question of how we impose our meanings on the text. Like Locke, Bleich stresses that individuals project their desires and values into the text, whereas Fish, like Saussure, stresses the public nature of signification which is beyond the individual's control:

> the strategies in question are not his [the recipient's] in the sense that would make him an independent agent. Rather, they proceed not from him but from his interpretive community of which he is a member; they are, in effect, community property, and insofar, as they at once enable and limit the operations of his consciousness, he is too. (Fish, 1980: 15)

Like structuralism, cultural determinism minimalises the significance of the individual reader. What we understand is not determined by the reader's individual psychological dispositions but by the strategies of his / her interpretive community. Therefore members of one and the same community understand each other but regard as incomprehensible what is said in another community:

> Members of the same community will necessarily agree because they will see (and by seeing, make) everything in relation to that community's assumed purposes and goals; and conversely, members of different communities will disagree because from each of their respective positions the other 'simply' cannot see what is obviously and inescapably there. This, then, is the explanation for the stability of interpretation among different readers. (Fish, 1980: 15)

For pedagogical and political reasons Fish supports the belief that we are necessarily egocentric and ethnocentric because such an attitude liberates us from the obligation to listen to others. For Fish, the goal of reading consists not in understanding others but in enhancing our sense of importance by imposing our meaning on the text (Fish, 1980: 368). He praises cultural determinism because it 'relieves me of the obligation to be right (a standard that simply drops out) and demands only that I be interesting (a standard that can be met without any reference at all to an illusionary objectivity)' (Fish, 1976: 195f.). Fish rejects the attempt to understand others as 'illusionary objectivity' and stresses that we have no obligation to listen to others. The others' views are either inaccessible or 'false, or mistaken, or partial, or immature, or absurd' (Fish, 1980: 361). Such an attitude justifies egocentrism and ethnocentrism. Now, before I outline a different concept of understanding, let me consider the post-colonial critique of intercultural understanding.

The post-colonial critique of understanding

In his famous book *Orientalism* Edward Said asserts that we cannot understand others. What we are really after when we pretend to understand them is our domination over them. The real motive in understanding is the will to power. Therefore Said (1978: 3) can sum up his evaluation of Orientalism in the following words: 'In short, Orientalism [is] a Western style for dominating, restructuring, and having authority over the Orient'. In a similar way, James Clifford (1986:7) argues that ethnologists who want to understand foreign cultures must realise that they are constructing nothing but 'powerful "lies" of exclusion and rhetoric'. According to this cultural determinism, we cannot help but impose our categories on the foreign culture. We might believe that we understand others in an objective way, but in reality we are prisoners of our own culture. This implies that western poets and philosophers as individuals might want to say positive things about the Orient, but what they actually say about it proves to be negative. When we speak about a foreign culture, we are not individuals but representatives of our culture, who cannot help but serve the interests of our own culture:

> For if it is true that no production of knowledge in the human sciences can ever ignore or disclaim its author's involvement as a human subject in his own circumstances, then it must also be true that for a European or American studying the Orient there can be no disclaiming the main circumstances of his actuality: that he comes up against the Orient as a European or American first, as an individual second. (Said, 1978: 11)

According to Said we are unable to create a critical distance to our own culture: 'Even the most imaginative writers of an age, men like Flaubert, Nerval, Scott, were constrained in what they could either experience or say about the Orient' (Said, 1978: 43). Yet such cultural determinism raises a series of critical questions: How is it possible that Said is able to distance himself from his own culture? When Said's critics pointed out that, according to his own premises, his book could not claim to be a true account of *Orientalism* but only an expression of the interests of Oriental cultures, he asserted that Orientalism is not 'a defense either of the Arabs and Islam' but an objective description of Orientalism (Said, 1985: 92f.). Cultural determinists are caught in a performative contradiction. They can only make true statements about cultural determinism if they assume that they are not products of cultural determinism. Said (1987: 326) himself says at the end of his book: 'I would not have undertaken a book of this sort if I did not also believe that there is scholarship that is not as corrupt, or at least as blind to human reality, as the kind I have been mainly depicting'.

If cultural determinism could stand unchallenged, cultural imperialism would be inevitable. It can, however, be challenged because 'human beings can have sufficient independence and flexibility of mind to criticize their own grouping' (Sell, 2000: 95). Said's assertion that western orientalists, poets, and philosophers must necessarily say negative things about the Orient is not true. Therefore we need a different concept which questions the epistemological assumptions of psychological and cultural determinism.

Constitutive elements of a theory of intercultural understanding

The objections of psychological and cultural determinists to intercultural understanding must be taken seriously. There is a tendency in our thinking to subsume what is strange and foreign under our familiar categories. Martha Nussbaum (1998:118) calls this tendency *descriptive chauvinism*: 'It consists in recreating the other in the image of oneself, reading the strange as exactly like what is familiar'. And there is also *descriptive romanticism*, which is 'the expression of a romantic longing for exotic experiences that our own familiar lives seem to deny us' (p. 123). We praise the foreign culture because we find our own culture boring or inhumane. Whereas *descriptive chauvinism* subordinates the familiar under one's own category, *descriptive romanticism* highlights the differences between cultures and stresses the mystery and strangeness of the foreign culture. Yet in both cases our expectations determine what the foreign culture is like. Intercultural understanding, however, means that we must overcome the dominance of our expectations, categories and interests and recognise those of the other culture.

The decisive question of whether or not intercultural understanding is possible depends on the answer to the question of whether we have the flexibility of mind which allows us to cross borders and accept differences. Pragmatics has made us aware of the fact that even in our own culture there are differences which must be overcome if we want to understand others. In each case, listeners and speakers are differently situated; they have different biographies and often have different social positions. Sell formulates a basic insight into the nature of understanding when he writes: 'Between any two communicants, there will always be differences of recall or awareness or attitude, however slight, which make communication at once desirable, worthwhile, and sometimes problematic' (Sell, 2000:120).

We often believe that intracultural understanding is unproblematic because we share the same beliefs and values, whereas intercultural understanding is impossible because we are determined by our own categories and interests. Yet, if psychological and cultural determinists were right, even intracultural understanding would be impossible:

> For communication between differently positioned people to stand any chance of satisfying both parties, the human imagination must be sufficiently autonomous to empathize with modes of being and doing that are different from the ones valorized within its most immediate milieu. (Sell, 2000: 4).

In criticizing determinism, Sell points out that our empathy and imagination allow us to perceive and understand what differs from our categories and interests. We can evoke the others' beliefs and attitudes in our mind and compare them with our own. Without such an ability, communication would be impossible:

> The self-projective ability is what underlies the power of interpersonal communication in the first place, and it is an ability of which people really can avail themselves, giving and taking across every conceivable cultural divide. Naturally entering into a process of self-discovery through self-alienation, they may even become different people as they go along. (Sell, 2000: 101)

Intercultural understanding means that we can reconstruct the context of the foreign, take the others' perspective and see things through their eyes. This implies that we are able to distance ourselves from our own categories, values and interests. This, of course, does not imply that our own cultural context and our own perspective do not play a role in understanding others. They necessarily come into play when we criticise what we understand. Understanding is a process of negotiation between the context in which something is said and done and the context in which it is perceived. It is also a process of negotiation between the inner perspective – we see things through the others' eyes – and the outer perspective – we see things through our own eyes. But such a process of negotiation can only begin if we possess the flexibility of mind to reconstruct the context of production and assume the inner perspective.

Having described intercultural understanding so far, we can discuss what Harden might have meant when he said that understanding is an illusion and that we can never fully understand others and will never be fully understood by them. Harden is right in stressing that understanding is an unlimited process. There can never be understanding in an absolute sense. But this does not mean that understanding is an illusion. The alternative – either understanding is possible in an absolute sense or it is an illusion – is problematic and does not help to clarify what goes on in understanding. It is never an either-or.

Often it is assumed that understanding means that we become identical with what we understand. And since this is impossible, the belief in understanding is rejected as an illusion. Yet we can understand a slave or a slaveholder without becoming one. In a similar way, we can understand a member of a foreign culture without becoming one. There is an existential unbridgeable gap between the others and us. We can put ourselves in their position, but this does not mean that we become identical with them. We *know* that we are putting ourselves in the other's position. Understanding would cease if it were no longer able to distinguish between the context of production and that of reception.

Critics of understanding often argue that we cannot understand what we have not experienced. When reading Toni Morrison's novel *Beloved* in one of my classes, some students pointed out that we cannot understand the novel because our ancestors were not slaves. This argument can have the critical function of making us aware of what slavery does to people so that even our emphatic and imaginative understanding which the novel encourages may find its limits. But we can only experience these limits if we read the novel. A general refusal to read the novel would prevent us from gaining such critical insights. When Agnes Heller discusses the question of whether we can understand what we have not experienced, she comes to the conclusion:

> We need never have been in Othello's shoes in order to experience his jealousy; in fact, we need never have been jealous at all. We need not have been madly in love, to be moved to tears by the death of Tristan and Isolde, we need never have felt desire for vengeance in order to feel through Electra's rancor. Of course, this does not mean that we are jealous along with Othello, in love along with Tristan, or desire vengeance along with Electra, but rather that we are to empathize with these feelings, because we understand the situations that have elicited them and the feelings themselves. (Heller, 1979: 122f.)

Understanding Othello means that we put ourselves in his position and realise why he acts as he does, given his character and the social situation in which he acts. We will feel compassion and fear with him because we can imagine that we could be in a similar position. Yet such a belief is only possible if we are not completely identical with him and thus can see what he is unable to see.

We take an interest in others whose situation may differ radically from our own because our self-respect is at stake when we understand and evaluate their actions, thoughts and feelings.

At the end of the first part I would like to sum up what I regard as the constitutive elements of intercultural understanding. The reconstruction of the context of production and of the inner perspective is a prerequisite for intercultural understanding but, as we have seen, the context of reception and our outer perspective also come into play when we evaluate what others think, feel and do and consider their relevance for us. Intercultural understanding is the negotiation between the two contexts and perspectives. The result may sometimes be a 'third position' which transcends the two contexts and the two perspectives.

We must be aware of the fact that the goals of understanding can differ. In some situations we will put the emphasis on the reconstruction of the context of production and the inner perspective. In other situations we will put the emphasis on the context of reception and the outer perspective when we want to find out whether we approve or disapprove of what we understand. And in yet another situation it will be necessary to develop a 'third position' which transcends the others' views and our own so that we can act together. A model of intercultural understanding should describe what is constitutive of intercultural understanding and be flexible enough to acknowledge the different goals of intercultural understanding. In the second part of my contribution I will argue that a flexible model of intercultural understanding will have to accept the preservation of as well as the change in the learner's identity.

Intercultural Understanding and Identity Politics

I began my contribution with a quote from Harden: 'He/she [the learner] has to be able to draw the line exactly where 'understanding' becomes a threat to his/her identity'. It is understandable that people in a period of post-colonialism and globalisation are concerned about the restoration or preservation of their cultural and ethnic identities, but we should also consider that through colonisation and globalisation people have acquired multicultural identities and that the restoration and preservation of a narrowly defined collective identity might be experienced as a form of tyranny.

The justification and critique of identity politics

Identity politics has its origin in the experience of people who are regarded as inferior because they belong to a certain group. In order to overcome this feeling of inferiority they have to re-evaluate their collective identity. If black is regarded as ugly, Blacks will have to re-write such an evaluation and stress that black is beautiful. Thus they can turn what is a cause of shame into a cause of pride and self-esteem. In a famous essay Charles Taylor points out that 'a person or group of people can suffer real damage, real distortion, if the people or society around them mirror back to them a confining or demeaning or contemptible picture of themselves' (Taylor, 1994: 25). According to Alain Finkielkraut, identity politics makes it possible for the colonised to reject the demeaning images imposed by colonialism and to re-establish their original culture:

> The theme of cultural identity permitted the colonized to stop being mimics, allowing them to replace their degrading parody of the invader with the affirmation of their cultural difference, to turn into a subject of pride what they had been taught to be ashamed of. (Finkielkraut, 1995: 67f.)

Considered from this perspective, identity politics is beyond criticism. People have the right and obligation to fight against discrimination. Yet, as Stuart Hall points out, identity politics is 'the constitution of some defensive collective identity against the practices of racist society' (Hall, 1991: 52). People who in the 1950s and 1960s came to England from former colonies considered themselves to be British subjects but were not accepted as such. Thus they had to return to their native culture to find a place from which they could speak and interpret the world. Many immigrants, though, have more than one identity and they want to see their different identities recognised. In general, one can say that identity politics becomes problematic if it ignores the complex situation and prescribes how people should behave in order to be accepted members of their group.

In the autobiographical story 'Child of the Dream', Clarisse Nesbit describes how she is rejected by Blacks because she does not live up to their definition of a Black person. She is called 'white girl' or 'wannabe' because she goes to college and does not speak slang (Nesbit 2000: 161). If one behaves differently, identity politics can be as cruel as forced assimilation: 'Why did they hate me for being a little different? Sounding educated and being interested in things other than what they were interested in didn't make me any less black, did it?' (Nesbit, 2000: 161). Kwame Anthony Appiah criticises identity politics for prescribing too narrowly what it means to be a loyal member of a group: 'It is at this point that someone who takes autonomy seriously will want to ask whether we have not replaced one kind of tyranny with another' (Appiah, 1996: 99). For Finkielkraut identity politics is problematic in principle because it regards the collective identity as the highest value and demands from individuals that they subordinate themselves to the group norms:

> At the very moment the Other got his culture back, he lost his freedom: his personal name disappeared into the name of the community; he became an example, nothing more than an interchangeable representative of a particular class of beings. (Finkielkraut, 1995: 75)

In a similar way Steven C. Rockefeller (1994:88) is critical of identity politics: 'To elevate ethnic identity, which is secondary, to a position equal in significance to, or above, a person's universal identity is to weaken the foundations of liberalism and to open the door to intolerance'. Like Rockefeller, Michael Ignatieff (1993: 248) sees the dangers of a multiculturalism which regards one's own collective identity as the final frame of reference: 'Being only yourself is what ethnic nationalism will not allow. When people come, by terror and exaltation, to think of themselves as patriots first, individuals second, they have embarked on a path of ethical abdication'.

Identity politics can easily lead to the exclusion of others. Thus Gertrud Nunner-Winkler (1998: 280) regards 'the right to difference' with suspicion. She points out that after the Holocaust it is no longer possible to argue for racial purity, but that it is politically correct to argue for cultural purity and the 'right to difference,' although both can fulfil the same function, a fear of mixing: 'Underlying the manifest demand for a "right to difference" is the same old racist structure: namely, a deep-seated phobia of interbreeding' (Nunner-Winkler, 1998: 280). In a similar way, Finkielkraut says that it does not make much difference whether we reduce individuals to their race or to their culture:

> We believe we have since discredited the concept of race, but have we really made any progress? Like the racists before them, contemporary fanatics of cultural identity confine individuals to their group of origin. Like them, they carry differences to the absolute extreme, and in the name of multiplicity of specific causalities destroy any possibility of a natural or cultural community among peoples. (Finkielkraut, 1995: 79)

Whereas intercultural understanding allows us to learn from the foreign culture and to reflect critically on one's own culture, identity politics demands that we distance ourselves from other cultures and must be loyal to our own culture:

> Thus education no longer seeks to provide students with the tools to choose among the many beliefs, opinions, and customs that make up their heritage, but to plunge them instead into this ocean of traditions, *head first*. (Finkielkraut, 1995: 82)

A plea for assimilation

In his autobiography, Eric Liu criticises the belief that he should think, feel and behave like a Chinese because he is of Chinese origin. He finds this essentialist concept of culture expressed in the following proverb: 'You can take a Chinese out of China, but you can't take the China out of a Chinese' (Liu, 1998: 10). This implies that wherever the children of Chinese parents are born and raised, they are Chinese and must be loyal to their Chinese culture. Yet for Liu one is not a Chinese because one's ancestors are Chinese but because one decides to act Chinese:

> And whether it [Chinese culture] is transmitted to the Overseas Chinese depends, ultimately, on consent rather than descent. Chineseness isn't a mystical, more authentic way of being; it's just a decision to act Chinese' (p. 10).

Liu, who regards himself as an American, is aware of the fact that he is accused of having betrayed his Chineseness:

> The assimilist is a traitor to his kind, to his class, to his own family. He cannot gain the world without losing his soul. To be sure, something is lost in any migration, whether from place to place or from class to class. But something is gained as well. And the result is always more complicated than the monochrome language of 'whiteness' and 'authenticity' would suggest. (p. 36)

In *East of Eden* John Steinbeck describes Lee, a Chinese-American who was born in the United States in the middle of the 19th century and attended the University of California. He speaks English fluently, but the dominant culture regards Chinese-Americans as inassimilable and forces him to speak pidgin English because a Chinese-American who speaks English fluently is considered to be untrustworthy and regarded as an impostor. Identity politics stresses how people have suffered under enforced assimilation but ignores the suffering which results from the refusal to allow assimilation (cf. Bredella, 1999). Liu (1998: 77) highlights the paradox that at the end of the 20th century, assimilation is possible for Asian-Americans, but identity politics forbids it: 'Walls that once existed to keep a minority group out [are] now . . . maintained to keep them *in*'.

For Liu, a culture that allows assimilation will be changed by accepting the people who have been excluded. Therefore assimilation brings about change, whereas identity politics preserves the status quo, the powerlessness of the minorities: 'The vocabulary of 'assimilation' has remained fixed all this time: fixed in whiteness, which is still our metonym for power; and fixed in shame, which is what the colored are expected to feel for embracing the power' (p. 35).

Liu is afraid of the possibility that the minorities who claim that their identity is not shaped by the *nation* but by their *descent* will be rejected in critical situations by 'those who belong to the nation' (p. 123). An essentialist concept of culture which implies that you cannot take China out of a Chinese will justify racist statements like the following which was published in the *Los Angeles Times* at the outbreak of the war between the United States and Japan: 'A viper is nonetheless a viper wherever the egg is hatched – so a Japanese-American, born of Japanese parents, grows up to be a Japanese not an American' (p. 119).

Intercultural understanding as an enrichment of one's identity

In the novel *Almost a Woman* Esmeralda Santiago explores the paranoia of the proponents of identity politics. Negi, the protagonist of the novel, who came from Puerto Rico to the United States as a child, becomes a dancer in the new Japanese-inspired production for Children's Theater in New York and plays the role of the member of Indian royalty. Her Puerto Rican friend Jaime is concerned about her interest in Indian dance: 'There's something wrong with this . . . We should be out there fighting for the rights of our people. . . . We need to champion our art and theater. Let the Hindus worry about their own' (Santiago, 1998: 286). Yet Negi does not accept this line of argument. Her interest in Indian dance does not mean that she is against Puerto Rican culture and for Indian culture: 'My devotion to Indian dance, I argued, wasn't part of a conspiracy to promote their civilization over Puerto Rico's'. Like Appiah and Rockefeller, Negi stresses the need for the development of her own personal identity which will profit from her interest in Indian dance. Yet for Jaime her devotion to Indian dance is part of a conspiracy and a betrayal of her Puerto Rican culture. 'If we lose Puerto Ricans to other cultures, we lose Puerto Rican culture'. Negi, however, contradicts him: 'Why should I be less Puerto Rican if I danced Bharata Natyam? Were ballet dancers on the island less Puerto Rican because their art originated in France? What about pianists who performed Beethoven? Or people who read Nietzsche?' (p. 286f.). The emphasis on the preservation of differences is limiting if it forbids members of one culture to enjoy the achievements of another one.

Identity politics should help to preserve the diversity of cultures, but, as Martha Nussbaum points out, the logic of identity politics implies that we are only interested in our own:

> Why would one love or attend to a Hispanic fellow citizen, on this view, if one is oneself most fundamentally an Irish-American? Why should one care about India, if one defines oneself as above all an American? Only a human identity that transcends these divisions shows us why we should look at one another with respect across them. (Nussbaum, 1998: 67)

Identity politics in a multicultural society often assumes 'that everything will be just fine, as long as none of them [the various cultures] gets a disproportionate share of classroom hours or funding' (Sell, 2000: 267) and as long as one culture does not influence the other. In this context empathetic understanding of others is regarded with suspicion because it might weaken one's own identity.

In the novel *A Change of Skies* Yasmine Gooneratne explores how immigrants from Sri Lanka relate to their new Australian culture. In a highly satirical scene, the protagonists, Bharat and Navaranjini Mangala-Davansinha, host a religious ceremony at their house. Mr Kyako, the leader of the Asian community in Sydney, arrives before the guests to make sure that everything is in order. He assures Bharat that he is very satisfied with what he sees but is upset by some Keyt paintings. Since they show nude women, Bharat believes that Mr Kyako objects to these paintings for moral and religious reasons. But he learns that Mr Kyako does so for cultural reasons. Bharat has to remove them because they were not produced by a Sinhalese artist but by one of 'Dutch extraction' and because they show Indian influences:

> Mr Keyt may be a good artist (even though I may not personally care for his work), but he does not represent those traditions . . . Mr Keyt

does not represent our good Sinhala traditions because he cannot, Bharat. How can he? He is, I am told, of Dutch extraction. A Burgher. And, I am informed,' Mr. Kyako added with serious displeasure, 'that his painting reveals Indian influences'. (Gooneratne, 1991: 91)

The exclusive concern for one's own culture is a form of ethnocentrism that does not allow us to respect others. For Mrs Kyako the Australians are 'brutes': 'My husband warned me from the start: "Be careful, Padmini," he said. "Always be on your guard! These people are not like us. They know only violence"' (p. 81). And later she adds: 'As my husband is always saying to me, "Padmini, Padmini, what can you expect of barbarians and ex-convicts?"' (p. 82). For Mr and Mrs Kyako, Asians must preserve their Asian identity in Australia but Bharat points out that immigrants cannot help but ask themselves what kind of cultural identity they will develop:

There is a question I still ask myself after many years in an alien country: when is it exactly that the immigrant throws overboard every other idea, every other possible destination, and decides that here, and in no other place he will make his home? (p. 151)

This disquieting experience has a liberating effect: 'Until we choose where we shall settle, and decide (in our own time) to make ourselves known, displaced people such as ourselves enjoy a liberty that others may well envy' (p. 281).

The restoration and preservation of one's collective identity might be liberating in certain cases but in others it might be oppressive. Therefore we need a flexible model of intercultural understanding which allows learners to preserve or to change their identity. One's primary affiliations must not necessarily be 'with one's local group, whether religious or ethnic or based on sexuality or gender' (Nussbaum, 1998: 109f.). We do not lose our soul if we transcend our cultural and ethnic identity.

Conclusion

I have argued for a flexible model of intercultural understanding from three different perspectives, as follows.

First, whether we regard intra- and intercultural understanding as possible or impossible depends on our concept of language. Those who argue that it is impossible stress that the meanings of words are private, so that we will not be able to guess what the other really means. This concept of language is well expressed by John Locke: 'Every Man has so inviolable a Liberty, to make words stand for what Ideas he pleases'. Yet this concept of language has been severely criticised. Its critics stress that meanings are not personal but public. Therefore we can learn foreign languages. Yet the acquisition of a language as a system alone does not enable us to understand others. According to Saussure we must distinguish between language as a system, *langue*, and an utterance, *parole*. In order to understand an utterance, not only linguistic but also social and cultural knowledge is required. In order to understand the other's utterance we must reconstruct the context of the utterance. Therefore we need a flexible model which allows us to 'make use of background knowledge, the situational context, and memory of past communicational experiences' (Taylor, 1992: 128, quoted earlier), in order to understand what the other means with his or her utterance.

Second, for a variety of critics, intercultural understanding is impossible because we cannot help but see others through our own categories and interests, which determine what we perceive. Therefore the claim to understand others is an illusion. In reality, it is an act of violence by which we subsume what is foreign and different under our own categories and interests. Thus, for its critics understanding means that we reduce what is foreign to what we already know. Yet this description of understanding ignores that our minds are flexible enough to learn something new and reconstruct different frames of reference. Just as we are able to learn foreign languages we are able to understand foreign cultures. Ethnologists and anthropologists have reconstructed different value systems and different ways of thinking and feeling. The real problem begins when we evaluate what we have understood. Are there transcultural values or must each culture be evaluated by its own values? If we accept the latter possibility, we cannot criticise a racist culture. To be able to criticise it, we must refer to values which differ from those of the racists. If, however, we evaluate others by our own values, we are ethnocentric. Therefore we need a flexible model of intercultural understanding which allows us to mediate between relativism and ethnocentrism and to develop a third position which transcends the values of the foreign culture and those of our own.

Finally, understanding another culture has an effect on our cultural identity. Will it weaken it or will it strengthen it? Should we allow ourselves to be influenced by the foreign culture or should we reject it because it will estrange us from our own culture? In the last 30 years, identity politics has demanded that people resist the influence of foreign cultures and preserve their cultural, ethnic and social identity. I have briefly outlined the reasons for identity politics but I have also referred to those who point out that identity politics prevents people from social mobility and from enriching their identities by accepting influences from different cultures. We need a flexible model of intercultural understanding which makes learners aware of these different implications of intercultural understanding and helps them to make their own decisions.

Critics of intercultural understanding often confront us with the alternative: either absolute understanding is possible or there is no understanding at all. Thus the critics crave for certainty, a certainty which we, finite human beings, cannot gain. And in our everyday encounters with people from foreign cultures it would be inhumane to declare that understanding is impossible because it would imply that we cannot listen to others and see the world through their eyes and that egocentrism and ethnocentrism have to be accepted as 'natural' phenomena of our human condition and can no longer be criticised. Intra- and intercultural understanding is a process in which misunderstandings often occur but in which understanding is also possible. Therefore we need a flexible model which takes these different situations into account.

References

Appiah, Kwame Anthony (1996) Race, culture, identity: Misunderstood connections.' In Kwame Anthony Appiah and Amy Gutman (eds) *Color Conscious: The Political Morality of Race* (pp. 30–105). Princeton, NJ: Princeton University Press.

Bleich, David (1975) *Readings and Feelings: An Introduction to Subjective Criticism*. Urbana, IL: National Council of Teachers of English.

Bredella, Lothar (1999) Nightmares of misrecognition in multicultural texts. In Carin Freywald and Michael Porsche (eds) *The American Dream. Festschrift für Peter Freese* (pp. 79–96). Essen: Die Blaue Eule.

Clifford, James (1986) Introduction: Partial truths. In James Clifford and George E. Marcus (eds) *Writing Culture. The Poetics and Politics of Ethnography* (pp. 1–26). Berkeley, CA: University of California Press.

Finkielkraut, Alain (1995) *The Defeat of the Mind*. New York: Columbia University Press.

Fish, Stanley (1976) Interpreting 'Interpreting' the Variorum. *Critical Response* 3, (Fall) 191–96.

Fish, Stanley (1980) *Is There a Text in This Class? The Authority of Interpretive Communities*. Cambridge, MA: Harvard University Press.

Gooneratne, Yasmine (1991) *A Change of Skies*. Sydney: Picador.

Hall, Stuart (1991) Old and new identities, old and new ethnicities. In Anthony D. King (ed.) *Culture, Globalization and the World-System* (pp. 41–68). New York: Macmillan.

Harden, Theo (2000) The limits of understanding. In Theo Harden and Arnd Witte (eds) *The Notion of Intercultural Understanding in the Context of German as a Foreign Language*. Oxford: Lang.

Heller, Agnes (1979) *A Theory of Feelings*. Assen: Van Gorcum.

Holland, Norman (1985) Reading readers reading. In Charles R. Cooper (ed.) *Researching Responses to Literature and the Teaching of Literature. Points of Departure* (pp. 3–21). Norwood, NJ: Ablex.

Ignatieff, Michael (1993) *Blood and Belonging. Journeys into the New Nationalism*. London: BBC Books.

Liu, Eric (1998) *The Accidental Asian*. New York: Vintage.

Morrison, Toni (1988) *Beloved*. New York: Plume.

Nesbit, Clarisse (2000) Child of the dream. In Laurel Holliday (ed.) *Dreaming in Color, Living in Black and White. Our Own Stories of Growing up Black in America* (pp. 156–64). New York: Pocket Books.

Nunner-Winkler, Gertrud (1998) Normal elements of ethnocentrism. In Dieter Haselbach (ed.) *Multiculturalism in a World of Leaking Boundaries* (pp. 279 308). Münster: LIT.

Nussbaum, Martha C. (1998) *Cultivating Humanity: A Classical Defense of Reform in Liberal Education*. Cambridge, MA: Harvard University Press.

Rockefeller, Stephen C. (1994) Comment. In Charles Taylor *et al.* (eds) *Multiculturalism. Examining the Politics of Recognition* (Introduced by Amy Gutman) (pp. 87–98). Princeton, NJ: Princeton University Press.

Said, Edward W. (1978) *Orientalism*. New York: Vintage 1987.

Said, Edward W. (1985) Orientalism reconsidered. *Cultural Critique* 1 (Fall) 89–107.

Santiago, Esmeralda (1998) *Almost a Woman*. New York: Vintage.

Sell, Roger D. (2000) *Literature as Communication*. Amsterdam/Philadelphia, PA: John Benjamins.

Steinbeck, John (1963) *East of Eden*. London: Heinemann.

Taylor, Charles (1994) The politics of recognition. In Charles Taylor *et al.* (eds) *Multiculturalism: Examining the Politics of Recognition* (Introduced by Amy Gutmann) (pp. 25–73). Princeton: Princeton University Press.

Taylor, Talbot J. (1992) *Mutual Understanding: Scepticism and the Theorizing of Language and Interpretation*. London: Routledge.

Chapter 4

On Being 'Bicultural' and 'Intercultural'

MICHAEL BYRAM

The purpose of this chapter is to see whether an examination of the concept and experience of being 'bicultural' can help to define more precisely what might be involved in being 'intercultural'. This, in turn, might lead to more precise recommendations for pedagogy in language teaching and in any other teaching which hopes to contribute to education as intercultural experience. For, although this argument will be made with foreign/second language learning in mind, all that will be said here applies to experience of different social groups within a society, with ostensibly the same language and the same culture but in fact with their own language and culture varieties.

So the first stage of the argument is descriptive, i.e. attempting to define what being 'bicultural' means, whereas the second part is prescriptive, i.e. suggesting what needs to be done to ensure language education and/or other dimensions of education provides intercultural experience and develops intercultural competence. The main question I am interested in elucidating is whether becoming intercultural involves a change in one's relationship to the culture(s) into which one has been socialised, i.e. some change in cultural identity, as well as some change in attitudes towards other cultures and one's own. In this context, the definition of 'culture' I shall use is the 'shared beliefs values and behaviours' of a social group, where 'social group' can refer to any collectivity of people from those in a social institution such as a university, a golf club, a family, to those organised in large-scale groups such as a nation or even a 'civilisation' such as 'European'. The beliefs in question are the 'shared meanings' (Taylor, 1971) which justify and underpin their behaviours and the 'social representations' (Farr & Moscovici, 1984) they hold in common. There are, too, shared 'values' which include the values attached to their beliefs and behaviours, and the attitudes they have towards their shared social representations.

Being Bicultural

Social identity theory (Tajfel, 1981) suggests that individuals interact on two levels: in interpersonal and intergroup behaviour. When circumstances are such that group characteristics are prominent – the presence of another language is one indicator of group difference and therefore accentuates the presence of group characteristics – individuals categorise themselves and others in terms of their belonging to groups, i.e. they act at the second level. The empirical work in social identity theory shows how individuals can be influenced by groups and their individuality, their personal identity, dominated by their group identity; how individuals respond to other individuals in terms of such categorisation; how this leads to comparison and competition which is, in turn, a basis for self-esteem – when a person's group is successful in competition with others, the person's self-esteem is increased. Group membership can be created artificially, as experiments have shown (Tajfel, 1981; Sherif & Sherif, 1969) but it is usually a result of the process of socialisation.

Through the processes of primary and secondary socialisation (Berger & Luckmann, 1966), individuals become members of many social groups. Becoming a member of a social group involves incorporating its culture (cf. Bourdieu's 1977 concept of 'habitus') but also being accepted by others in the group and defining oneself as a member of the group (Tajfel, 1981). Being a member of a group is thus a consequence of self-ascription, but it is also reinforced by other-ascription, by being categorised by others as a member of a group (Barth, 1969). Most of the groups to which an individual belongs complement each other. One can be a member of a golf club and a football club, of a school and a family, although there may be some degree of conflict in the cultures involved (some families do not accept all the beliefs, values and behaviours that a school expects of the children of the family). Others are mutually exclusive: one cannot be a member of both Newcastle and Sunderland football supporters' clubs, I think, or at least not openly so; there will be situations in which one needs to keep silent about membership of one whilst claiming membership of the other.

Where people from two social groups interact and are in competition, they force each other to act in terms of their identification with one or the other group – very evident when the groups are nation-states at war or when football teams and their supporting groups meet. When one group is dominant, it can force individuals into the category of the minority group and this can have detrimental effect on the self-esteem of the individuals, if they perceive the minority group as low status. As we shall see later, this is problematic for people who would like to belong to more than one group but are forced to choose by people who perceive the groups as mutually exclusive, and therefore the identities associated with them as mutually exclusive.

There are mutually exclusive identities with reference to membership of national/ethnic groups. With Edwards (1985), I distinguish between ethnic groups which focus on membership by descendance and shared culture, and national groups which are ethnic groups with political ambitions. This is different again from the notion of a state, although nations often wish to realise their political ambitions in the form of a homogeneous nation-state, most recently in Yugoslavia, but also in the 19th century in Wales, and still today in Ireland. However, the drive towards political representation and nation-state independence is not a necessary development, as Oommen (1999: 2–3) argues:

> a nation is essentially a cultural entity and it is not natural for a nation to establish its own state, as is widely believed. Such theories and experiences are European and do not fit the reality of South Asia.

Membership of ethnic national groups has to be either mutually exclusive or, if an individual wishes to be in two (or more) groups, they have to manage this carefully, since most members of an ethnic group are monoethnic and tolerate poorly the presence of 'hybrids'.

My illustrations are taken from South Tyrol, Italy, where young people who are bilingual, born of one parent from the German minority and one from the Italian majority, have difficulty because the expectation is that one is either German or Italian, with both parents from the same ethnic group.

The first quotation shows the power of other-ascription: other children will not allow one to be both German and Italian, and it is the language which is seen as the symbol of ethnicity, as is often but not always the case:

> Was it difficult to become bilingual?
> I would say that I haven't had any particular problems in the languages, but with the (other) children. Because I was in the German school, they looked on me as if I was an Italian, and in the Italian school they considered me to be German.

So the tactic for the person with adequate linguistic competence is to identify with the ethnicity of the people with whom one is interacting at a given moment:

> Because I was always quite good in both languages. If I was in German groups, I spoke German, and they didn't notice that I was an Italian, and have an Italian mother, and if I was among Italians, they always thought that I'm Italian. So I never had difficulties. (Egger, 1985: 178)

The question which now arises, however, is how the individual experiences this process of ascription by self and other, what the effect is upon identity. Unfortunately there is only a little systematic and theoretically well-founded research which tells us what is involved in being bicultural, analogous for example to Second Language Acquisition research which describes the process of acquisition or to discourse analysis which analyses the language processes of interaction between people of different languages and cultures (and therefore of different social identities, although this is not an issue addressed directly) (Scollon & Scollon, 1995). Norton (2000) has studied women immigrants in Canada, and Miller (1999) has analysed the changing identities of young immigrants in Australia. Both focus on issues of power in the community, of developing new social identities, and the significance of language learning in this context, but do not pursue the psychological impact of being obliged to learn another language and the effect on the individual's existing social identities.

Another literature which has attempted to theorise bicultural identity arises from counselling and psychotherapy (Valdez, 2000; Poston, 1990; Herring, 1995). This literature attempts to explain how particularly young people have to deal with choice between usually two cultural identities which they could accept but which are seen as mutually exclusive by the cultural groups in question. The conflict is experienced particularly by young people with biracial (Afro-American and Euro-American) identities but also by Hispanic-Americans with parents from Hispanic and Euro-American ethnic groups. This literature focuses inevitably on the problems experienced and on how therapists can help their clients to overcome the problems but the existence of such problems is perhaps more widespread than is often realised, as the following extract from an interview with Italian immigrants to Belgium shows. Despite having lived for more than twenty years, the sense of anomie is strong and the power of other-ascription very evident:

- Do you feel Belgian or still Italian?
- Well let's say it's difficult. We have taken on all the customs here, but it's difficult to say we're Belgian because of that, just as it's difficult to say that we're not Belgians, either. Since all our children are here, . . . so we're neither one nor the other . . . Here we're foreigners, and at home we're foreigners too . . . All the people of our age, a whole generation, left Italy . . . so when we go back to Italy, we're treated like foreigners, since the new generation doesn't know us . . . Personally, I'm alright wherever I am earning a living . . . I don't have anything against the Belgians or against the Italians . . .

In the final analysis, we feel just as foreign over there. We go there, and we are foreign too, so when we go back, they say 'Ah the immigrants are here'. We're foreigners here and there, really. We have nowhere really. Well we're used to the Belgian rhythm, I think. We don't even pay attention any more to the word 'foreigner', but from time to time, it gets to us, you know. (Byram & Leman, 1990: 90)

There is, however, a distinction to be made between biculturals who become bicultural through primary socialisation and those who move to another culture as adults. Studies of the former include the acquisition of deaf bicultural identity (Holcomb, 1997) and the biculturalism of 'Kikokushijo', children of Japanese expatriates, which concluded from four case-studies of teenage kikokushijo that

> [A]lthough the four individuals were of diverse personalities and attitudes, their stories all reflect a bicultural self that made it difficult to fit comfortably and naturally in any one society. (Kanno, 2000: 378)

This was attributed both to the host societies and to some individuals' lack of will to participate in those societies, and there is a tendency for the literature to identify problem cases, but one study shows how, though there may be stages of 'denial or confusion', it is possible for a bicultural to arrive at a stage of 'integration' (Garrett, 1996). The narrative of the life of a member of the Eastern Band of Cherokee Indians, is analysed in terms of a five-stage model of bicultural identity, leading ultimately to 'integration', defined as follows:

> a secure, integrated identity with the ability to function effectively in both cultures. In addition, they understand the meanings behind various cultural values, beliefs, expectations, and practices of which they are a part. (Garrett, 1996: 18)

The description which the interviewee offers in his own words suggests very explicitly that a person can hold within themselves two cultural, ethnic identities and, because he gained acceptance by both groups – as a highly regarded medical doctor – it seems that being two people is not difficult for him:

> I think who I am, is that I truly am two people, matter of fact. Doc Amoneeta Sequoyah used to call me 'Gagoyoti' in other words 'two people'. In Cherokee, that's a way of saying, well you're this and you're that. For me a lot of my conflicts in earlier years were because I wasn't sure who I was. Was I Indian, was I white, you know, what was a mixture of person, where did I belong? I knew deep down inside, I didn't belong with that class of people who felt they were better than others. And I knew that the people I came from, the Cherokees, there was something very special. (p. 18)

Despite the successful outcome, this person, too, had experienced conflict and a sense of not knowing where he belonged. Again this is bound up with how other people, especially the dominant majority group attribute an identity to the individual whether the individual wishes it or not.

A particular striking instance of this is caught by Eva Hoffmann in her account of becoming a resident of Canada, and ultimately a Canadian:

> We make our way to a bench at the back of the room; nothing much has happened, except a small, seismic mental shift. The twist in our names takes them a tiny distance from us – but it's a gap into which the infinite hobgoblin of abstraction enters. Our Polish names didn't refer to us; they were as surely us as our eyes and hands. These new appellations, which we ourselves can't yet pronounce, are not us. They are identification tags, disembodied signs pointing to objects that happen to be my sister and myself. We walk to our seats, into a roomful of unknown faces, with names that make us strangers to ourselves. (Hoffman, 1989: 105)

Hoffman's experience as described in the rest of her book suggests that she never felt quite at ease with North American values, beliefs and behaviours despite the majority of her life being spent there. The power of primary socialisation in one cultural environment is such that 'late' acquisition of another cultural identity is not the same as bicultural primary socialisation.

Similarly, the account by Christina Bratt Paulston of her own bicultural experience is that of someone whose primary socialisation was into a monocultural Swedish environment and who then moved, like the Italians in Belgium, like Hoffmann to Canada, to another country, the USA.

Paulston draws on a particular model of culture which identifies three dimensions: cognition, affection and action. Under cognition, she suggests that a characteristic of being bicultural is to be 'able to interpret what the same phenomenon means from the viewpoint of two cultures' – also a characteristic, I shall argue, of the interculturally competent person. It is, however, when she talks about the affective dimension that there is an implicit link with the notion of socialisation:

> Under the Affection domain, Kleinjans posits the following levels: perception, appreciation, reevaluation, reorientation, identification. Perception and appreciation simply refer to the coming to know and to like aspects of another culture, like food and music as well as aesthetic and moral values.. . . Reevaluation is the process of changing one's values. 'It might mean a shift in priorities, the giving up of certain values for new ones, or an enlargement of one's value system.' Reorientation means changing the direction of one's life, 'spurred by values he has

adopted from the second culture.' Identification is becoming one with the people of the other culture; 'A person changes citizenship'. (Paulston, 1992: 124)

This is very reminiscent of Berger and Luckman's (1966: 176ff) discussion of re-socialisation, which, in the extreme case, is described as 'alternation' where, as in religious conversion, an individual abandons one set of beliefs and values for another. They argue, however, that there are degrees of transformation of beliefs and values lying between the extreme of alternation and the normal process of secondary socialisation. As long as there are no abrupt discontinuities in the individual's subjective biography and new beliefs and values are not incompatible with existing ones, then re-socialisation of the extreme kind does not take place.

Paulston is a professional linguist who has no trouble with being bilingual but finds it difficult to be bicultural. However, it is not her bi/multilingualism which is the most important issue. Degrees of competence in two or more languages are only relevant, as we saw earlier, in as far as they allow people to hide one of their identities; it is not the degree of competence itself which makes one more or less bicultural. Since the monolingual members of one group cannot usually evaluate the competence of someone speaking the language of the other group, it is simply the fact that they do so which is important. If they decide that the person's competence in their own language is not that of a native speaker, then they ascribe that person to membership of another group. (Children in Japan assume that anyone who is obviously not Japanese and speaks English must be American.[3] (personal communication by Yoko Arashi).)

Paulston, however, suggests that there are such levels of incompatibility for the person who experiences conflicting cultural values:

> At these levels I don't believe it is possible to be bicultural. When I took out US citizenship, I had to give up my Swedish citizenship; I could not have both. And so it is with conflicting cultural values; in the same way as one just can't believe in the overriding importance of consensus and conciliation of group interests at the same time as one believes in confrontation and the overriding rights of the individual in solving problems.

So she suggests that there are different levels of beliefs and values, some of which are unalterable, for which there is no alternation, and others of which can be chosen to suit the circumstance, i.e. there is a kind of deliberate alternation:

> So what happens, I think, is that the individual picks and chooses. Some aspects of culture are beyond modification. Many Americans

comment on my frankness, but Swedes never do. Now I wouldn't want to claim that Swedes lie less than Americans, but I do think there is more emphasis on the value of always telling the truth (or saying nothing) in the socialisation process of Swedish children. I know some people dislike me for it, and still I don't change because I simply cannot. But many aspects of culture are within the bounds of modification; one can learn to be half an hour late and not consider it moral slackness; one can learn to eat with one's fingers and still feel like an adult. But such modifications mainly concern surface behaviour, behaviour one can switch back and forth.

She also points out that when an individual has conflicting values imposed on them, the result may be some form of psychopathology. The experience of the young people in South Tyrol is fortunately not so extreme but there are certainly indications of liking with constant pressure, being drawn in two directions.

Sometimes it happens that the individual is not allowed to pick and choose between his two cultures but will have conflicting values imposed on him. The result is often some form of psychopathology. Seward (1958) in her fascinating collection of case studies documents the stress of such individuals, like the Japanese Nisei boy torn between his desire to espouse modern egalitarian values and the imposition of his father's strictly traditional Japanese values. His response to such conflict was mental breakdown, the inability (refusal?) to function with any cultural rules. (Paulston, 1992: 126)

If we follow Paulston, then, at levels of behaviour where there are no conflicts present, it is possible to be bicultural in some respects, but where there are conflicting values at other 'deeper' levels, it is not. She refers to biculturalism rather than multiculturalism because at any given moment, in the various experiences of different countries she describes, the issue is the relationship between her one set of values and those of the society around her, be it American, Moroccan or Swedish. However an individual may experience different societies at different points in their biography and therefore accumulate more than two sets of behaviours and 'perceptions and appreciations' to use her and Kleinjans' terminology. Nonetheless she remains convinced that at the levels of reorientation and identification, the individual cannot accommodate conflicting values and meanings.

This is where Paulston's account coincides with the literature from psychotherapy and counselling, but she makes a useful distinction between levels: the ability to adapt in behaviour but not necessarily in values and beliefs.

Our research with languages students spending a year in another country as undergraduates, who were then interviewed ten years later, also suggests that having two national identities is difficult. Consider one of our informants, whom we call Lynn. After the year abroad in France she said she no longer felt English, although even the short passage of time between 'when I came back' and 'now' – some three months – was already changing her:

> I would now say – I'm not sure now, but when I came back – I would say I was European rather than English . . . . I would love to be French, but you can't. I can never be French because you have to be born French. I could be a European. I couldn't be French though. There's no way you can become French. You could live in France, you could speak French, but you'll never be French unless you're actually born French.

So at this point she has a view and experience of identity which links national and ethnic identity, at least with respect to being French. European identity is, however, of a different nature.

When interviewed ten years later she was married to a Belgian, living in Belgium and had just had her first child, whose bicultural socialisation into two identities and languages will focus her attention on her own identities too. She describes learning from her parents-in-law something of the history of Belgium which helps to 'put down roots'. 'I haven't really got roots on that side but I'm putting down roots in that way by learning through them and I would like A [daughter] as well to learn from them as well' (p.7). She is thus describing the creation of a sense of belonging, of ethnicity, in which historical awareness is crucial and yet she does not have the right to vote, so citizenship and identity do not coincide. So, in answer to the question of whether she feels she belongs in Belgium, she says:

> As far as I can, yes – I will always not be Belgian – I will always be English – but then there are so many other people who are in the same situation in Brussels – it's not a gaping difference. (Lynn, p.7)

Similar to the historical awareness of her new Belgian roots, she and her husband renew the sense of belonging to England, by joining the National Trust, by watching the BBC news.

The option of a European identity is, however, no longer as meaningful to her. It is not strong enough to be a 'nationality' and remains largely an economic entity:

> You don't get so centred on the idea of being European, not particularly – obviously I am, and that's why I can work easily in Brussels and travel around very freely, but the whole concept of being European

doesn't come up to much – we are what we are and that's the way we are – I think being European is almost not negative but you lose the differences, and I think what is important about Europe is that there are all these different nationalities and different languages and different cultures – if you all become one mish-mash of something European, what does it mean? – you have to have the history, you have to have the roots, and that means all the differences – if you just have European, as one globular thing, I don't think so – I think it is good that Europe is becoming stronger and the economy is improving, and we're defending ourselves a bit better against the Americans – but as a whole entity, I think it is hard – everyone feels European but that will never be your nationality. (Lynn, p.8)

What we must not lose sight of in all this, is that the focus of attention is inevitably on difference and conflicting values and beliefs, but that there is also much in common. The question of how much is in common is not addressed by those who analyse from their own experience or by those dealing with people who need therapy. There are probably common concepts across all cultures (Wierzbicka, 1997) but it is less clear how universal are beliefs and values. Comparisons and, again, especially contrasts between 'West' and 'East' suggest that within each of these there is common ground, and much literature and practice in cross-cultural training is based on this assumption, but there is a need for much more research.

Second, this attention to difference leads to a presentation of cultural identities as dichotomous, whereas the existence of common ground suggests that being bicultural may be easier in some situations, where there is commonality, than in others where there is difference. As always, the degree of acceptance by others and not just the commitment of the individual, is crucial, and it is for this reason that being biracial in the USA or 'Kikokushijo' in Japan is more difficult than being Swedish in the USA.

It seems, in summary, that ethnic/national identity is one of any number of social identities an individual has, but is a particularly significant one, which, in Europe and the West at heart, can be reinforced by politicisation as a nation-state identity. Like all social identities, it is socially constructed and other-ascription is at least as powerful as self-ascription. When other-ascription and self-ascription conflict, individuals suffer, sometimes to the point of needing therapy. Therefore self-ascription to two ethnic/national groups can be particularly open to conflict with other-ascription, and becoming bicultural can be particularly difficult and painful. Nonetheless, when people experience primary socialisation in two ethnic groups, bicultural identity can succeed and we can be 'two people'.

However, people who experience primary socialisation in one ethnic/

national group and then, in adolescence or later, find themselves in another group, do not seem to be able to be 'two people' in the same way. The power of primary socialisation is such that another set of beliefs and values cannot be accommodated, although it is possible to practise other behaviours.

So, returning to the question posed at the beginning, whether becoming intercultural involves a change in identity as well as a change in attitudes, what this discussion of being bicultural suggests is that having two cultural/ethnic identities is difficult though not impossible. Even though being bicultural in this sense entails holding in one person conflicting values and beliefs, it can be done if the surrounding society allows it. However, the difficulty of being 'two people' has become evident and the less demanding option of being able to adapt to different behaviour is perhaps more common.

A further point to take from this for the language teacher is that many learners are involved in this difficult process of being or becoming bicultural. When they therefore meet a new language and culture they are in a significantly different position from learners who are monocultural in ethnic/national identity terms. The implications for pedagogy need to be worked out in detail but it is certainly important to do so and not to treat such learners in the same way as monocultural learners.

As Geneviève Zarate and I said in our first paper on intercultural competence (Byram & Zarate, 1997), to act interculturally is to bring into a relationship two cultures. At the time we were thinking of the cultures of nations and, in particular, of nation-states, since we were developing the concept in the context of foreign/modern language learning. One of the outcomes of teaching languages (and cultures) should be the ability to see how different cultures relate to each other – in terms of similarities and differences, and perhaps also in terms of origins, although we did not stress the latter – and to act as mediator between them or, more precisely, between people socialised into them. This also includes 'mediating' between oneself and others, i.e. being able to take an 'external' perspective on oneself as one interacts with others and analyse and, where desirable, adapt one's behaviour and the underlying values and beliefs. Thus at any given point in time, the individual is bringing into contact through themselves two sets of values, beliefs and behaviours, and in this sense there is almost always a binary relationship, but any individual may have a range of experience and competences which allow them to relate a variety of combinations of cultures.

We called someone who can do this, not necessarily perfectly but to some degree, an 'intercultural speaker' because in the context of modern foreign language teaching, there has been a long-standing assumption that the aim is to imitate the native speaker. This started with the aim of imitating the linguistic competence (including phonetic competence and the production of a native speaker accent). The native speaker is thus the model, the authority. This is then extended to the assumption that the native speaker is also the model and the authority when one is acquiring a new cultural competence as one acquires a new linguistic competence, i.e. a new language. We wanted to contradict that assumption in two ways. First, the imitation of the native speaker is not desirable – and certainly not fully attainable – because it implies the abandoning of one social identity in order to acquire another. Paulston (1992) likens it to choosing one of two citizenships and it is certainly the case that national/ethnic identities are perceived as mutually exclusive. Second, the authority of the native speaker needs to be challenged because they do not 'know' their culture any more than they can be said to 'know' their language. They cannot externalise it without help and they do not have competence in the whole of it. Furthermore, their supposed authority is challenged by critical analysis of their culture by an outsider from another culture, and language. Because of the nature of ethnic identity and its implicit call on members' loyalty – 'my culture right or wrong' – the native speaker would tend to brook no criticism; any criticism is taken as an *ad hominem/feminam* insult.

So the phrase 'intercultural *speaker*' can be paraphrased as an 'intercultural mediator', although I think the emphasis on speaker is useful because it keeps the link with language, and the implication that mediation pre-supposes some linguistic competence. The best mediators, I would argue, are those who have an understanding of the relationship between their own language and language varieties and their own culture and cultures of different social groups in their society, on the one hand, and the language (varieties) and culture(s) of others, between (inter) which they find themselves acting as mediators. The relationship between language and culture is then encapsulated in 'key words' or richly connotated words specific to one culture and the relationship to apparent equivalents in another (Wierzbicka, 1997), the learning and analysis of which is a crucial stage in becoming an intercultural speaker/mediator (Byram, 1997b).

Since being intercultural is an activity, I have tried to describe what could be the behaviours involved (Byram, 1997a). I have done so in 'behavioural objectives' terms since the description also served the purpose of proposing an approach to curriculum design. This implies what I will discuss more explicitly later that there is a particular role for education in the development of the ability to be intercultural, which there may not be in the case of being bicultural. However, I do not want to imply by the term 'behavioural objectives' that what is involved is some simple adoption of surface behaviour or a simple adoption of classic behavioural approaches to curriculum design. The issues involved are affective and cognitive as well as behavioural, as the following extracts from a description of intercultural communicative competence indicate:

- *Attitudes*: curiosity and openness, readiness to suspend disbelief about other cultures and belief about one's own (*savoir être*).
- *Knowledge*: of social groups and their products and practices in one's own and in one's interlocutor's country, and of the general processes of societal and individual interaction (*savoirs*).
- *Skills of interpreting and relating*: ability to interpret a document or event from another culture, to explain it and relate it to documents from one's own (*savoir comprendre*).
- *Skills of discovery and interaction*: ability to acquire new knowledge of a culture and cultural practices and the ability to operate knowledge, attitudes and skills under the constraints of real-time communication and interaction (*savoir apprendre/faire*).
- *Critical cultural awareness/political education*: an ability to evaluate critically and on the basis of explicit criteria perspectives, practices and products in one's own and other cultures and countries (*savoir s'engager*).

Let me now turn to the issue of the relationship between being intercultural and social identity. The link is again provided by socialisation theory, taking the concepts of primary and secondary socialisation one step further with respect to language learning. It has been argued that, when children are introduced to foreign language learning in schools, they undergo a further, tertiary, stage of socialisation (Doyé, 1992). In its simplest version, this occurs essentially in two ways. First, they are required to re-live some of their primary and secondary socialisation in a new way. For example they have to re-learn how to count, or what the names of colours are, and this usually means a new way of linking language to reality because the names of colours and numbers do not have a one-to-one relationship with the approximate equivalent in their first language. At a more advanced stage, they learn that their concepts of 'freedom', 'friendship'or 'homeland' are not universal and are understood differently elsewhere (Wierzbicka, 1997). Second, their experience of the world is extended, as it is constantly in schooling, but with a different set of beliefs, values and behaviours implicit in the new world they meet, whereas most of the rest of the curriculum is founded on the culture of secondary socialisation, simply extending it; history and geography have the potential however, like language teaching, to introduce new cultures. In short, there is a potential for introducing children to the culture of a new social group, a new national identity which, like other cases of ethnic identity, is not complementary but mutually exclusive with their own.[1]

The question now arises as to whether learners will in fact wish to take on this new identity. In the extreme case, this would mean 'alternation' as described earlier, with the implication that it means abandoning their existing national identity, but such a case is very unlikely. In a less extreme version, there can be a fear that secondary socialisation is 'contaminated' by the values, behaviours and beliefs of another culture, for example when the foreign language is of a higher status than the learners' own (the teaching of (American) English in developing countries may be a case in point (Ho, 1997)). However, professional experience and intuition suggests that language learning in the classroom is not usually sufficient to create a desire to pass into another national group, to take on another national identity and experimentation with students in upper secondary in Germany (Meyer, 1991; Kordes, 1991) suggests that they cannot reach a very advanced stage of being an intercultural speaker/mediator.

On the other hand, as 'Lynn' suggested earlier, those who spend a long period in the other group, such as university language students spending year abroad, sometimes feel they have shifted not to another national identity but to a transnational, or international identity, and there may be significant long-term influence.

A Comparison of Being Bicultural and Acting Interculturally

I started with the question as to whether an analysis of what it is to be bicultural can help in being more precise about what teaching intercultural competence means. It is also interesting to consider whether an analysis of acting interculturally throws more light on the being bicultural.

It has become clear that to become bicultural can be difficult and depends on how different the two cultures are as well as on the degree of acceptance by other people. Analyses may exaggerate the difficulties because the literature is largely focused on people who find the experience problematic and need help. More analyses of 'success stories' is needed and it may become clear that biculturals find some aspects of their experience less difficult to deal with than others. A simple conclusion from all this for teachers is that it would be extremely difficult to 'make' their monocultural learners bicultural, and even to make their bicultural learners tricultural through teaching a third language and culture.

What is remarkable for its absence in the discussion of biculturalism is any examination of if and how biculturals act as intercultural speakers/mediators between their two cultures. Nor is there any discussion of biculturals' attitudes to third cultures. Research on bilinguals – and most biculturals are bilingual – suggests that they have a greater meta-awareness of language and an ability to decentre, but this has not led to research on attitudes to other cultures. It is possible that biculturals are 'ethnocentric in two cultures', just as monoculturals can be ethnocentric in one. If this were the case, there would be a pedagogical task with biculturals although this should be different in procedure and methodology from work with monoculturals.

What makes acting interculturally different from being bicultural is the level of conscious awareness involved. The literature on biculturals who need therapeutic help suggests that part of the treatment is to make them aware:

> The therapeutic approach to work with these bicultural clients needs to focus on helping clients become aware of the complex process that occurs in the development of their self-identity and how this complex development affects their everyday interaction with the environment. (Valdez, 2000: 242)

The pedagogical literature, both theoretical (e.g. Zarate, 1993; Kramsch, 1993) and practical (e.g. Byram *et al.*, 2001), focuses on making learners aware of the relationships among cultures, and promotes methods of comparative study to do so.

Thus, returning to the question of whether teaching intercultural competence includes changing learners' cultural/ethnic/national identity or, rather, changing attitudes, it seems to be more important to change attitudes. Whether learners are monocultural or bicultural, they share certain social representations of other cultures with those in their own group(s). They also share attitudes towards those representations. For example they may believe with others in their group that another group's customs include arranging marriages for their children, and they are likely to share their own group's attitudes of approval or disapproval of the custom. It is possible, first, that the shared representations are inaccurate or incomplete and one task of the teacher is to ensure that learners understand the custom in full and as it is understood by those who practise it. This may already change disapproval to approval, or even *vice versa*, but then the teacher must decide whether they wish to influence the attitudes or simply make learners aware of their own basis for approval/disapproval, i.e. their own culturally specific values. One option for the teacher is to refer learners to internationally agreed human rights as a basis for making a decision, rather than attempting to impose their own views from their position as teacher (Byram, 1997a: 44–6).

Whatever position the teacher takes, it is clear that acting interculturally involves a level of analytical awareness which does not necessarily follow from being bicultural. It is also evident that the more experience of other cultures a learner has, the more easily they will see the relativity of their own culture or cultures. The introduction to a second culture for monoculturals or a third for biculturals is only a first step in this educa tional process.

Notes

1. This version is based on the assumption that there is no major disjuncture between primary and secondary socialisation, i.e. that the basic values are common to both, as is typically the case in a homogeneous society. In most societies this is a simplification since there is often a significant difference between the world of primary socialisation in the family and the world of school where much of secondary socialisation takes place. As previously suggested, most classes include learners who are, or are becoming, bicultural. Foreign language learning could therefore be yet another world with new values and it is an interesting question whether children who have already bridged one sociocultural gap are more likely to find the second one easier to deal with. This would, however, complicate the argument here too much and I have considered the simplification necessary for the purposes of the argument.

References

Barth, F. (ed.) (1969) Introduction. *Ethnic Groups and Boundaries*. London: Allen and Unwin.

Berger, P.L. and Luckmann, T. (1966) *The Social Construction of Reality*. Harmondsworth: Penguin

Bourdieu, P. (1977) *Outline of a Theory of Practice*. Cambridge: Cambridge University Press.

Byram, M. (1997a) *Teaching and Assessing Intercultural Communicative Competence*: Clevedon: Multilingual Matters.

Byram, M. (1997b) Cultural awareness as vocabulary learning. *Language Learning Journal* 16 Sept. 51–7.

Byram, M. and Leman, J. (1990) *Bicultural and Trilingual Education: The Foyer Model in Brussels*. Clevedon: Multilingual Matters.

Byram, M. and Zarate, G. (1997) Definitions, objectives and assessment of sociocultural competence. In Council of Europe *Sociocultural Competence in Language Learning and Teaching* (pp 7–43). Strasbourg: Council of Europe.

Byram, M., Nichols, A. and Stevens, D. (2001) *Developing Intercultural Competence in Practice*. Clevedon: Multilingual Matters.

Doyé, P. (1992) Fremdsprachenunterricht als Beitrag zu tertiärer Sozialisation. In D. Buttjes, W. Butzkamm and F. Klippel (eds) *Neue Brennpunkte des Englischunterrichts* (pp 280–95), Frankfurt am. Maine: Peter Lang .

Edwards, J. (1985) *Language, Society and Identity*. Oxford: Blackwell.

Egger, K. (1985) *Zweisprachige Familien in Südtirol: Sprachgebrauch und Spracherziehung*. Innsbruck: Innsbrucker Beiträge zur Kulturwissenschaft.

Farr, R.M. and Moscovici, S. (eds) (1984) *Social Representations*. Cambridge: Cambridge University Press.

Garrett, M.T. (1996) 'Two people': An American Indian narrative of bicultural identity. *Journal of Ameriucan Indian Education* 36 (1), 1–21.

Herring, R.D. (1995) Developing biracial ethnic identity: A review of the increasing dilemma. *Journal of Multicultural Counselling and Development* 23, 29–38.

Ho, M.-C. (1997) English language teaching in Taiwan. A study of the effects of teaching culture on motivation and identity. Unpublished PhD thesis, University of Durham.

Holcomb, T.K. (1997) Development of deaf bicultural identity. *American Annals of the Deaf* 142 (2), 89–93.

Hoffmann, E. (1989) *Lost in Translation. A Life in a New Language*. Harmondsworth: Penguin.

Kanno, Y. (2000) Kikokushijo as bicultural. *International Journal of Intercultural Relations* 24, 361–82.

Kordes, H. (1991) Intercultural learning at school: Limits and possibilities. In D. Buttjes and M. Byram (eds) *Mediating Languages and Cultures*. Clevedon: Multilingual Matters.

Kramsch, C. (1993) *Context and Culture in Language Teaching*. Oxford: Oxford University Press.

Meyer, M. (1991) Developing transcultural competence: Case studies of advanced foreign language learners. In D. Buttjes and M. Byram (eds) *Mediating Languages and Cultures*. Clevedon: Multilingual Matters.

Miller, J. (1999) Becoming audible: Social identity and second language use. *Journal of Intercultural Studies* 20 (2), 149–65.

Norton, B. (2000) *Identity and Language Learning. Gender, Ethnicity and Educational Change*. Harlow: Longman.

Oommen, T.K. (1999) Conceptualising nation and nationality in South Asia. In S.L.Sharma and T.K.Oommen (eds) *Nation and National Identity in South Asia*. New Delhi: Orient Longman.

Paulston, C.B. (1992) Biculturalism: Some reflections and speculations. In C.B. Paulston (ed.) *Sociolinguistic Perspectives on Bilingual Education*. Clevedon: Multilingual Matters.

Poston, W.S.C. (1990) The biracial identity development model: A needed addition. *Journal of Counselling and Development* 69, 152–55.

Seward, G. (1958) *Clinical Studies in Culture Conflict*. New York: Ronald Press.

Scollon, R. and Scollon, S.W. (1995) *Intercultural Communication*. Oxford: Blackwell.

Sherif, M. and Sherif, C. (1969) *Social Psychology*. New York: Harper & Row.

Tajfel, H. (1981) *Human Groups and Social Categories*. Cambridge: Cambridge University Press.

Taylor, C. (1971) Interpretation and the sciences of man. *The Review of Metaphysics* 25 (1), 3–51.

Valdez, J.N. (2000) Psychotherapy with bicultural hispanic clients. *Psychotherapy*, 37 (3), 240–46.

Wierzbicka, A. (1997) *Understanding Cultures through their Key Words*. Oxford: Oxford University Press.

Zarate, G. (1993) *Représentations de l'étranger et didactique des langues*. Paris: Hachette.

Chapter 5

Learning To Be Intercultural

LEAH DAVCHEVA

Introduction

This chapter seeks to examine the intercultural learning experiences of a group of 36 Bulgarian student-teachers of English who were involved in a joint teaching project with the School of Education, University of Durham, for the period 1997–2000. In aiming to provide a sharper focus I have chosen to analyse and evaluate the Bulgarian student teachers' developing interculturality in terms of their:

- intercultural vision and knowledge,
- teaching and learning disposition and classroom behaviour and
- professional relationships and participations.

The chapter starts with placing the Intercultural Training Project in context and examining the factors, which have made the setting up of the programme with its specific aims and objectives possible. It then outlines the key activities the students engaged in and goes on to discuss their impact on the participants' evolving theories of intercultural teaching and learning. Finally the chapter considers how the project experience has influenced the student-teachers' attitude to and understanding of what it means to be intercultural, both in and outside the foreign language classroom. The analysis that follows is based on three types of data originating from

(1) observation of the students' learning and teaching behaviour throughout the project,
(2) personal contacts and informal communication with them and
(3) a record of their ideas and reflections revealed in the journals, which they kept for the duration of the project.

The perspective presented here combines different voices. The strongest are those of the student teachers. They speak through the entries in their diaries and the opinions expressed in numerous conversations. In addition one can hear and trace the perceptions of the students' tutors, the programme evaluator and the project manager, all of whom gained enormously from working and collaborating with their younger colleagues.

In recent years there have been signs of interest and a certain willingness on the part of the Bulgarian general schooling system to promote the teaching of the cultural dimension of language in foreign language classrooms. In the circumstances of increased mobility and globalising communications it has gradually become accepted that mastering foreign languages and learning to communicate across cultures go hand in hand.

Through the pioneering work of the Cultural Studies Network of teachers, who wrote and published a syllabus for the teaching and learning of culture, *Branching Out: A Cultural Studies Syllabus* (British Council, 1998), English language education in secondary schools was the first to set intercultural communicative competence as the main goal of foreign language education. Moreover, the Network members, 60 teachers of English mainly from secondary English-medium schools, committed themselves to and successfully trained 700 of their fellow teachers to use the Syllabus in their own classrooms.

In higher education in the faculties of philology, where most of the language teachers receive their university degrees, a variety of British Studies and American Studies courses have been set up in the last decade. They have remained, however, knowledge-oriented, engaging their participants in culture-specific, specialised studies of literature, history and political and social life. Little attention has been paid in pre-service teacher education as well to exploring the cultural component of language study and encouraging future teachers 'to see themselves as brokers between cultures of all kinds' (Kramsch, 1998: 30). Until recently study programmes and training methods did not seem to go beyond an approach which focused on presenting background information about a dominant target culture. Similarly, there used to be hardly any indication in the locally published pedagogical literature of the growing significance of intercultural competence to foreign language teaching theories and practices.

Recent political, societal and educational factors, external to the universities, however, pressed for the initiation of intercultural awareness education for language teachers. Among them were needs arising from the country's enhanced international recognition and increased opportunities for travel and communications. A conscious desire for understanding and respect among the Balkan countries demanded skills for coping with prejudice, conflict and difference. The media developed an interest and engaged with discussing the role of language teachers in times of radical social change. Interest in Cultural Studies and education for citizenship expanded. Numerous pedagogic events, both local and international, stressed the significance of education for intercultural communicative competence and thus opened the way for recognising the merits of innovative teachers' practice. The Ministry of Education offered their unquestioned support in adopting *Branching Out: A Cultural Studies Syllabus* as a valid document for foreign language teaching in secondary schools. (Current plans to re-design the professional qualification scheme for language teachers include the development of intercultural teaching skills and critical cultural awareness.)

It was becoming evident that initial teacher education needed a stimulus to start developing its own expertise for intercultural teaching and learning. This led to the launch of the project, which involved four Bulgarian universities and the School of Education, University of Durham. In the sections that follow I outline each of the key stages and events in the project but I mainly concentrate on the learning outcomes of the lesson preparation stage and the visit to the UK. The two seem to have played an extremely important role in challenging the students' existing beliefs and attitudes and have enhanced significantly their evolution as intercultural learners and teachers.

The Project: Aims and Objectives

On a general level the purpose was to contribute to the integration of an intercultural training component in the foreign language teacher preparation programmes at four universities in Bulgaria. The project aimed at training students who, themselves culturally aware, would be capable of developing their learners' capacity for intercultural sensitivity through the study of foreign languages. The project enabled its participants to teach a series of culture-focused lessons in British and Bulgarian schools and in doing so the student teachers enriched their personal and professional intercultural learning experience.

In more specific terms the project objectives were to:

- build up the participants' conceptions of culture and intercultural education;
- assist them in choosing the sources and contents of their programme of lessons and in defining which aspects of Bulgarian culture would present better learning opportunities for their UK learners;
- provide the participants with possibilities for diverse intercultural experiences, e.g. the study of their own and other cultures, personal encounters with others, short-term immersion in a foreign cultural environment;
- equip them with skills to interpret processes of interaction, to reflect upon their own cultural habits and worldview, to interrogate the fa-

miliar, to communicate across boundaries and mediate between cultures; and

- help the student teachers identify themselves as innovators in their profession and encourage them to share resources, further develop expertise and sustain the intercultural aspect of their new identity.

The project thus aimed to provide a carefully structured learning programme which had the potential of empowering its participants to become agents of change in their academic environment and, later, in their teaching careers.

Key Events

The yearly cycle of the project included the following activities: participant selection, distance training, five-day intensive training seminar, lesson design, peer presentation and trialing of sample lessons and finally teaching practice in Durham and Stockton-on-Tees. The ultimate and most significant task of the student teachers was to teach English children about aspects of Bulgarian culture. A project evaluation process was set up from the outset.

Participant selection

The purpose of the rigorous selection procedure (interviews and lesson design tasks) was to identify students whose minds would be open to the less traditional, in the Bulgarian context, experiential learning mode. The candidates were also interviewed for originality and creativity, inclination to work in a team, skills of observation and critical analysis.

Distance training

Training was seen as crucial for the success of the project. Although highly competent in English and academically soundly educated the student teachers lacked in awareness of culture. They had never before had a reason, or a stimulus, to interrogate their experiences in becoming socialised into their native linguistic and cultural environment. They had always taken Bulgarianness for granted and were hardly conscious of their own ethnocentricities. In addition, the students' knowledge of the foreign cultures was mainly acquired through the academic study of historical and literary texts. Personal contacts with and guided practical investigation of otherness were almost non-existent. Without the opportunities which the training gave the students to develop in that direction they were going to find it extremely difficult, if not impossible, to cope with the main task of the project – to teach 11–14 year old students in several schools in England.

Taking into account the participants' profile the training process set out to encourage them to construct a meaningful picture of the relationship of language and culture teaching and learning. They were introduced to new terms and were asked to re-think the old ones. They were also assisted in re-examining and articulating their views on recent and more distant learning experiences.

Second, the training activities aimed to arouse the students' curiosity about their own native culture and provoke their interest in studying some of the cultural practices and concepts which were grounded in everyday life and had so far escaped their conscious attention. They were expected to practise and develop their skills of observation and analysis.

And finally, the trainees were preparing to empathise with their future learners and see their own cultural world through their learners' eyes.

Training seminar

The five-day training seminar had two important objectives. It sought to further the development of the participants' personal theories of intercultural teaching and learning. Furthermore, it attempted to create the right learning and decision-making environment for the team of student teachers to work out the rationale, goals and procedure of their teaching in England. It also had the difficult task of dealing constructively with the concerns and anxieties of the students who, by the time of the seminar, had come to realise the unusualness and responsibility of the new role they were going to play.

Lesson design, presentations and trialing

This was the stage when the participants presented the conceptual grids of the lessons they were going to teach in the schools in England. Some of the tasks were trialled through peer teaching, others in Bulgarian secondary schools. Self, peer and trainer evaluation took place.

Teaching practice in the UK

The visit to the UK was the culmination of the project for it was then that the student teachers were able to carry out in practice their developing conceptions of teaching for intercultural competence and also to immerse themselves in the culture most of them had experienced only vicariously. The stay provided them with a wealth of experiences related to teaching in British schools, attendance at lectures and workshops at Durham University and encounters with people and everyday life in England.

Project evaluation

To get insights into the learning promoted by the project an evaluation was set up. It sought to capture the continuous nature of the changes the student teachers were experiencing. It was conceived as participatory interaction and comprised two components – the process component and the outcome/impact component. Data were collected through journals, observation, questionnaires and documentation review.

In the sections which follow I present and reflect on the progress which the student teachers made towards becoming intercultural learners and teachers. The process was by no means linear and uniformly continuous but the data demonstrated that the participants' thinking and behaviour were clearly influenced by their involvement in the discreet events of the project. In view of the complexity of the programme effects it seems sensible to adapt a model drawn out by Finkelstein *et al.* (1998) and categorise major outcomes in terms of the students'

- developing knowledge and vision of culture,
- intercultural teaching and learning disposition and patterns of classroom behaviour and
- professional collaborations and participations.

Cognitive and affective changes occurred within and across events but it was possible to discern several more or less distinct aspects in the formation of the student teachers' interculturality. Their parameters were defined by the specifics of the tasks the students were striving to complete and by the nature of the pedagogical and personal decisions they were making, thus crossing cultural borders and learning to be intercultural.

Knowledge and Vision of Culture

In this section I address three features of cultural vision and knowledge the development of which enabled the participants to re-visit cultural experiences, explore new ones and discover deeper meanings. These are choice of focus, perceptions of self and images of Bulgarianness.

Choice of focus

The choice of conceptual focus was the first really intercultural challenge that the student teachers faced when they started preparing for their teaching. Looking for the *'why?'* and the *'what?'* of the interaction with their prospective learners they went through a process of interpreting and connecting their own meanings and experience to what they imagined the world of their learners was. They asked themselves questions like:

'What is Bulgarian culture?'
'Does Bulgarianness exist?'
'How is it constructed and represented?'
'How accessible can Bulgarian culture be without knowledge of the

Bulgarian language?'
'Would British children be interested to know about us?'
'Who are they and what do they already know?'
'How can we provoke their curiosity and coax them into venturing on a
long journey towards a distant and little known other?'

The search for a culturally unifying and productive notion led to the discovery of the 'mountain'. The mountain in its role of a cultural construct and in its universality served as a possible entry point into the multiplicity of Bulgarian culture.

Mountains occupy a special place in Bulgarian national, historical and regional cultures. They rise high in the opening line of the national anthem; they have been assigned the role of national heroes in the historic past of the country; and they have poems composed and songs sung to them.

Mountains are both real and imaginary. Children and adults roam their forests, ski down their slopes or observe and protect their wildlife. They also learn about them at school, see them in television programmes, read tales set in the mountains. Early in their childhood Bulgarians learn to attach a special significance to the mountain, to recognise its relationship to a range of human values, e.g. true friendship, loyalty, purity, justice.

The task of involving their English learners in the interpretation of cultural meanings attached to the image of the mountain intrigued the student teachers. They were consciously trying to imagine the space where they would meet their students' expectations and first perceptions of Bulgarian reality. They were gradually becoming aware of the necessity to map out their own journey and discover the route to this place of shared understanding.

Anxiety and hesitation marked the start of the road, the stage when the student teachers needed to feed substance to their newly formed vision and select the content of their teaching. The first journal references point to their fears and concerns:

> It's become obvious that all of us are concerned about how exactly we are going to teach Bulgarian culture to the British students. (Miroslava)

> We all wanted to know one thing, that is, how we are going to teach the British children the concept of Bulgarian culture with the help of our materials and our own background knowledge, and possibly our personal experience. I know this is a very responsible job and if we are supposed to manage successfully with it we shall need more advice, help and even instructions about what to do and what not to do, what is right and what is wrong. (Illiana)

This is the place to say that the trainees wrote their journals in English. At no one point in the project was the issue of the language of communication between trainers and students raised. Both sides had taken it for granted that in line with the Bulgarian academic tradition in language education all formal expressions of tutor–trainee verbal interaction would be in English. Journal entries and written tutor feedback fell into that category and neither of the sides thought of debating it.

The process of shared learning began when some of the trainees felt the need to start a conversation and articulate the beginnings of new ideas. They wanted to make sure that as a newly formed team of teachers they exchanged understandings of both Bulgarian culture and of the task ahead of them:

> If we have any ideas at all, they are vague and we need to talk to each other. We all think differently and have different views of the world. (Emanuil)

Another student sensed how important it was to accomplish the transition from intuitive and silent thinking to articulating and structuring one's views:

> We all seem to have the same problem: we have ideas about the Bulgarian mountains but we simply don't know how to articulate and present them. What aspects shall we deal with, where shall we start? (Daniella)

And later on, when the questions started generating answers, they were quick to register their new positive feelings and insights. First appeared a sense of confidence in their understanding of what was involved in teaching this kind of lesson:

> I am thinking, or rather trying to find the positiveness in our new experience. I expanded my knowledge on what a good cultural lesson is. Now I no longer wonder what to teach. (Marta)

Then there was a reflection on the effect that preparing for teaching had on their understandings of Bulgarian culture:

> I am quickly learning about Bulgaria – my native country . . . I didn't know that I can associate Pirin with so many rare flowers . . . and that there are so many historical monuments in Stara Planina. (Zhivka)

These journal entries show that the process of developing pedagogical theory is closely connected with the process of reflexivity, the conscious analysis of one's own reactions to the learning experience.

Perceptions of self

The student teachers' diary entries indicate an attempt to rationalise their choice of perspective. On the conceptual level they struggle with existing ideas of self and with stereotypes rooted in their own thinking. In particular the relationship of past and present and its effect on the individual becomes clear:

> I learned to think about what our mountains mean to me. I no longer associate them with history only. They can be modern, part of me. (Dessi)

Another student records new learning in that direction as well:

> The distinction between history and heritage is new to me, in the sense that I didn't know that heritage is active, experiential . . . . (Borislava)

They also seek ways to achieve a more sensitive and diverse portrayal of cultural views and beliefs. There is an increasing sensitivity to the nuances of the symbol which might have hitherto been little analysed but just taken for granted:

> It hadn't occurred to me that the mountain could be a place of conflict where various interests meet. (Mihaella)

There is also an increased awareness of how the symbol of the mountain can be refined and made more complex in iconic representation:

> I liked the session on paintings. It coincided with my idea of how we can use paintings to decipher cultural values.(Teodora)

Images of Bulgarianness

Another major issue which the student teachers addressed concerned the image of Bulgarian culture they should aim to present. The problem was voiced when they were considering the pedagogic worth of tourist brochures and magazines:

> Tourist materials are tricky. They represent only the best features (or may be not the best but the positive features) of our country and the mountains. But we, as Bulgarians, know that there are many negative features as well. Bearing in mind that brochures in particular and most tourist magazines want to sell the places they advertise, it is only logical that they would choose to show the positive side. I have learned from this session that we should not be afraid of negativeness because it exists. We can help the children find out the reasons and draw their own conclusions about brochures choosing to show positive images only. (Nadka)

This is evidence of the students beginning to grasp their role as mediators, as insiders who had been empowered to take an outsider perspective and thereby had become more critical. They realised that this critical perspective should become one of their objectives. It was not just a question of introducing a critical angle in their presentation, but rather of helping learners to discover a critical perspective for themselves.

It was evident that the gap between previously held conceptions and newly formed ideas was gradually widening. Here is another student-teacher who recognised the difficulty of working with tourist materials in an educational setting:

> The problem with tourist materials is that they are made to serve one purpose only – 'to sell' our country. This however is not our aim. There-fore it is difficult to design a true culture-based lesson with tourist materials. (Diana)

Rather than trying to find a route for escape she would continue to use tourist information subordinating the characteristics of the genre to the objectives of her lessons. In this way the students began to demonstrate their own awareness of how mutual perceptions among people of different countries were created – and needed critical analysis.

Intercultural Teaching and Learning Disposition

Throughout the project cycle the participating students went through a process of coming to terms with the parameters of the unusual teaching situation in which they found themselves. Unlike the familiar frame of their university programmes which had prepared them for teaching English as a foreign language to Bulgarian learners in their native country, the trainees were now going to face classes of young learners for the majority of whom English was a mother tongue. Hence, rather than draw on their carefully cultivated ability to interpret aspects of a shared linguistic and cultural otherness they needed to shift perspective, as we have seen earlier, and acquire skills enabling them to reflect on their own Bulgarian culture, and choose how to present aspects of it to their new audience. What added to the challenge was that teaching was conducted in English as it was the only language in which teachers and students could communicate. It was feared at the beginning that the necessity to decipher Bulgarian cultural meanings in the English language would forcibly sever the bond between language and culture. In conversation they shared that they were surprised to discover that this did not happen. On the contrary, the student teachers felt that the need to interpret their own cultural world in English and to plan their classroom activities accordingly helped them adopt a critical distance and question what used to be seen as natural and taken for granted.

There was a point in the training process when the tutoring team felt that the key to the success of the whole teaching and learning endeavour could be found in channelling the positive energy generated by the tensions in the students' emerging awareness of their multiple professional identities. The tension was between the convenient authority of their previous competencies as experts in English and British Studies and the attractive uncertainty of new culture teaching perspectives and skills. It was in the bridging of this gap or in resolving this tension that the trainers saw the opportunities for learning.

Several important themes emerged as a result of the analysis of the journal data: (1) novelty of intercultural teaching as a stimulus for professional growth; (2) design and ownership of materials; and (3) evidence of culture learning on the part of the English pupils.

Novelty of intercultural teaching

All the student teachers reflected on the novelty that culture teaching represented. They spoke of new horizons and changing attitudes:

> The lessons we prepared for England broadened my understanding of teaching and helped me get rid of the 'stale' framework of lessons imposed by our educational system. (Grozda)

They tried to negotiate a relationship between what they perceived as their old professional selves and the new role that intercultural teaching assigned to them. For example one of them pointed to the importance of promoting independent learning and learning partnerships, aware of the fact that she was preparing to act differently from the model traditionally accepted in Bulgaria:

> Before we went into the details of lesson planning I thought that teaching culture meant advertising or even selling the culture of your country. I gradually understood that the approach here is to ask your students to read critically and find out for themselves. And also, when I teach language I know that my students learn from me only. When I teach culture I will ask my students to do things drawing upon their own personal experience. More like guidance. (Victoria)

This student thus distinguishes between the openness of culture teaching and the closed relationship of language teaching in which learner is dependent on teacher, although in fact there are developments in pedagogy which extend the notion of autonomous learning to language learning too (Ellis & Sinclair, 1989; Nunan, 1988).

Another student drew attention to the mediating aspect of the role they were aspiring to master:

We are now learning how to present aspects of Bulgarian identity through images of the Bulgarian mountains. The more I think about our mountains the more I believe that we should try to make our English students aware of the role of *their* mountains, or perhaps something else, of similar importance in their own culture. (Maria).

Mediation is thus not simply a matter of enabling understanding of 'the other' but also creating reflexivity and self-awareness.

The trainees were unanimous in voicing their worries about lacking the skills to teach culture and not having personally gone through such an experience as learners:

Cultural teaching is a new area and I have never been taught in this way and therefore before the seminar I had no idea of what cultural teaching and learning was. It would have helped if we had been exposed to cultural learning at school.

Luckily I am beginning to understand the mechanism of making culture lessons and placing skills in the centre. (Maria)

Several of the participants reflected on the newly learned significance of skills, dialogue and interaction in the context of culture teaching and began to draw more general conclusions about the nature of teacher–learner relationships and the process and objectives of learning:

Culture learning proves to be tricky but at the same time engaging and requiring creativity. I expected that all I had to do was listen to teacher talk and absorb recipes. What happened was completely different. I had to master skills. Thinking, discussing, taking risks, agreeing, summarising are skills which I think I learned and can probably teach. I shall look for ways to open a dialogue with my students. The idea for a balanced interaction between students and teacher is new to me. (Teodora)

The majority of the trainees thus associated intercultural teaching with their growing awareness of an alternative to the transmission mode of teaching – the inquiry-based approach:

Intercultural lessons have to be structured in a way that gives the students the possibility to be explorers rather than observers or recipients of information. (Milena).

For some this principle came into conflict with existing beliefs:

With regard to the problem-solving, discovery-oriented way of teaching culture, I couldn't help thinking that this way of teaching gave a very vague idea of culture. Maybe because I'm used to giving and receiving information about a country rather than understanding it. My learning ideal is knowledge. (Elitsa)

While several others extended this principle to education in general and expressed their regret that

[I]n our Bulgarian education we still miss the point somehow and our students are overloaded with information, which is mostly of theoretical value. (Dessi)

Design and ownership of materials

Most of the student teachers identified as new learning the process of designing intercultural teaching materials. As it turned out their regular university training had not taken care of developing materials design skills:

The big difference here is that we are expected to design our own culture learning activities rather than use ones from ready-made textbooks. This is a responsible task. I am getting really involved. (Nadka)

They reflected not only on the nature and quality of the teaching materials they produced but also on the complexity of the process:

It is strange that we can't see our own mistakes sometimes. It is easier to examine somebody else's lesson plan, to discuss it, rather than make your own. It seems that we are better at criticising the work of others. However, we are now getting deeper and deeper into lesson planning and our awareness of constructing activities increases. (Zhivka)

The need to plan their own lessons collaboratively and devise activities stimulated the participants' creativity and eventually became a source of professional satisfaction:

I found the work today amazing. It was our creativity that was the driving force. What was really important to learn was the 'what', 'why' and 'how' of making intercultural lessons. For example, designing our introductory activity involved a lot of ideas, discussions, making decisions. It was hard to reach a consensus because each one of us had her own imaginations, her own interpretations of the mountain, but somehow we failed to reach clarity. We thought we knew what we wanted but were not quite sure how to get there. However, step by step we pushed forward, as if stretching a hand to our pupils. (Victoria)

It thus became evident that it was in the detail of planning that the issues of shared cultural understanding came up and the process and content were inseparable.

An important component of the materials design process was the framing of the intercultural teaching goals on the part of the student-teachers. Several of the participants commented on how they had come to realise the organising power of the teaching purpose. Here is a typical remark:

> Before the seminar I didn't know that the materials we decide to use should be subordinate to the aim of the lesson and that we could not use everything we come across. The purpose is the guiding idea. It helps me find the most appropriate materials and get more confident about intercultural teaching. (Borislava)

Another student admitted, reluctantly perhaps, that defining teaching aims helped reduce the uncertainty of the planning process and freed space for considering issues which were related to learning outcomes. Without actually giving it a name the trainee touched upon the importance of empathy in materials design:

> What was a vague idea of an activity slowly starts having a shape. While we design activities we should consider both sides – the learning and the teaching. I think that when we devise activities we shouldn't only think of aims and objectives but also of how the children will accept the lesson, of their way of perceiving the world. (Dianna)

The starting point had therefore to take into account not just the logical presentation of the content but also the existing perceptions and feelings of the learners.

Designing activities became so important that the success of the training seminar was measured against the quantity and the quality of the teaching materials produced. One of the teachers sounded optimistic when she wrote:

> The number and worth of the materials our team has produced impress me. We've managed to translate our ideas into the language of the classroom. We are getting deeper into lesson planning and our skills visibly improve. (Iva)

In evaluating the role of materials design for the development of the pupils' intercultural awareness it became clear that the process helped them re-consider their own conceptionss of culture, choose their sources and frame their teaching and learning objectives carefully and structure opportunities for cultural reflection.

Another theme which the student-teachers talked extensively about was working with a huge variety of texts and exploiting them for intercultural teaching. They discovered the possibility and indeed the fascination of using postcards, paintings, films, tourist brochures and illustrations from books. They learned how to judge the materials' worth in accordance with the overall teaching goals. The trainees became increasingly capable of detaching themselves from their personal likes and dislikes of a given type of material and seeing it through what they imagined would be the eyes and ears of their students. The folloing two extracts exemplify the capacity of the participants to articulate the reasons for the choices they were making:

> What was interesting for me to learn was that we are free to use any materials we like. As long as they satisfy our aims. The most important of all the criteria is our learners' interest and previous experience. There's also the specifics of culture learning, representativeness, realism, context . . . . (Mihaella)

The next example also provides strong evidence of the growing awareness of professional ethics and accountability related to the materials teachers select for teaching. This particular student teacher had come to realise the significance of being familiar with or constructing a theoretical frame supporting intercultural teaching and learning:

> I know that in the future I will always keep in mind the importance of being just to the materials I use and to the students who I teach. If you pay attention, it may turn out that some of the materials do not actually fulfil your expectations. All the teachers, no matter whether they teach maths, geography or English, should observe this principle. (Marta)

In reporting their work with film one of the teachers sought to define the distance they had managed to go beyond the traditionally employed 'thin' approach to film in the foreign language classroom. She talked of adopting a more in-depth perspective which held the potential for exploring issues of representation, national identity and attribution of meaning:

> We did films this morning and decoding images. All of us found it extremely difficult. One explanation for this is probably the fact that when you watch a film you don't necessarily focus on the relationships or search for ideas and interpretations. But it's worth doing. The lesson comes out alive. If we are to teach culture using film we must learn how to guide our students through at least some of the meanings. Another problem is that we don't know how the British children will respond to the film. It is mainly connected with Bulgarian history. But isn't our interpretation of history cultural? (Grozda)

What has been discussed so far is how, in the course of the project, the student-teachers learned to think, interculturally, about their task, about themselves and, in fact, behave and be intercultural. In the next section the time perspective shifts and the analysis is based on the student-teachers' reflection on their teaching performance and the responses of their learners.

Evidence of culture learning on the part of the English pupils

The student-teachers devoted plenty of time and journal space to registering their impressions of the behaviour and classroom performance of their English pupils. In the process of reflection and on the basis of the training they had received they were establishing their own criteria by which they could judge whether their pupils were learning successfully. Several such criteria can be traced in their writings:

- demonstrating curiosity and positive attitudes to Bulgaria,
- working with imagination and creativity,
- developing the skills of comparing and contrasting cultural phenomena.

Demonstrating curiosity and positive attitudes to Bulgaria

The trainees recorded their pupils' interest and enthusiasm with enormous pleasure. They also began to rationalise their own positive feelings by identifying the aspects of Bulgarianness which provoked their pupils' interest. One such area undoubtedly referred to the lesson themes and content:

> Our lesson made them interested in the Bulgarian mountains and Bulgaria in general. We could see their suspicion disappearing. It gave way to curiosity. Apart from their interest in the names of the places and the characters in the story they were genuinely interested in what the mountains look like in reality. They all said they would like to come and stay in Bulgaria. (Dessi)

Another area of interest was the Bulgarian language. The English pupils were keen to listen to Bulgarian and work out some of the meanings. This almost caught the student-teachers by surprise as in the course of their university training the marginality of Bulgarian had never been questioned:

> We spoke in Bulgarian. The students listened carefully for words they could recognise and they listened hard. There was silence while we spoke and then a spontaneous round of applause. They liked the sound of our language and they could even recognise some of the words. (Diana)

Having invested so much effort into preparing the mutuality of their intercultural experience the student teachers were rewarded with open expressions of their pupils' interest in them as persons:

On leaving the school they followed us to the front door and said they had enjoyed the lesson. I can't imagine them running after their own teachers and asking them so many questions. (Iva)

The trainees experienced disappointments as well. The pupils' reluctance to participate and the various misunderstandings were regarded as symptomatic of the failure to establish interaction:

Today's students didn't show as much interest in Bulgaria as the students we had yesterday. Maybe because yesterday we were seen to be their guests, today we were their teachers. They seemed reluctant to participate. It seemed to me that they didn't understand the questions. (Diana)

Working with imagination and creativity

Realising how little their English pupils knew about Bulgaria the trainee teachers learned to encourage them to fantasise and to value the power of their imagination. They trusted their professional intuition, which was telling them that coping with ambiguity and creating imaginary worlds was an important culture learning skill:

Our students were imaginative and creative. They responded quickly to all the activities and we achieved our lesson objectives with ease. (Milena)

Another student also articulated the link between lesson theme, the development of relevant skills and the sense of having achieved one's aim:

We taught the lesson on mystical characters living in the mountains. I think we did well – the kids were good at giving answers, they were really inventive. I think they had a nice time dealing with the improbable. (Tsvetelina)

Comparing and contrasting cultures; empathy

Developing the skills of comparing and contrasting rated high in the student teachers' evaluative reflections on the progress that the students were making.

I think that our students managed to establish a link between their own knowledge of fairy tale characters and the characters in the Bulgarian storybook. When they were given the pictures from the book they gave the characters both Bulgarian and English names, e.g. they would call the 'samodivi' pixies, the 'tsoglavtsi' giants. (Boryana)

And again, a sense of achievement was evident when the trainees discussed their pupils' emerging ability to understand difference:

> We achieved our aim. The kids concluded that Bulgarians associate the mountains with their history, culture, religion, values, while the British mostly connect them with scenery. (Victoria)

Some of the student-teachers managed to put a finger on how interculturality emerged. One of the journal entries seems to be giving an account from the teacher's perspective of how students gradually learn to reconceptualise familiar phenomena and give them new meanings:

> At the beginning our class didn't take the materials seriously. I think the reason was they hadn't thought about mountains before. By the end of the lesson they had already become aware that different people had different ideas and opinions and they could view one and the same thing in various ways. We managed to demonstrate to them how the place of residence determines one's view of the world. (Illiana)

The ability to recognise interculturality and problematise it can in its own right be regarded as evidence of developing one's own interculturality.

> Another student, in just one sentence, recaptures the essential aim of the whole teaching exercise – enabling learners to think empathetically and understand the significance of the Bulgarian mountains to Bulgarians and at the same time raise their awareness of their own cultural spaces: our lessons made them think about their local places of importance. (Detelina)

Detelina's observation convincingly brings together the beginning and the finishing stages of the project. It foregrounds the link between what the student-teachers set out to do and what they actually achieved. In conclusion I would like to go back to what Maria had said at the start of the project:

> We are now learning how to present aspects of Bulgarian identity through images of the Bulgarian mountains. The more I think about our mountains the more I believe that we should try to make our English students aware of the role of *their* mountains, or perhaps something else, of similar importance in their own culture. (Maria)

Professional Collaborations and Participations

This section is relatively brief and is based on activities which mostly happened outside the project framework and time span. Although marginal in time and planning to the key programme events they can be regarded as indicators of the project's success. They concern the extent to which the participants were inspired by the project to move beyond their direct responsibilities and to extend their experience and shared expertise to the larger professional community. A record of these outcomes can hardly be found in the students' journals as they had been asked to keep them only for the duration of the programme. Much to the regret of the project team we had ignored the request on the part of some of the participants to give them their diaries back. We did not listen carefully when they voiced their intentions to keep on reflecting and we may have thus lost major evidence of changing attitudes.

The nature of the outcomes is extremely diverse. Some of them can be regarded as immediate results, while others will need longer to mature. A number of the effects have taken on material shape while others have developed in the sphere of human relationships. I will list them in the order in which they have occurred but it should be remembered that the process of professional learning is extremely complex and will not succumb to the enumeration of a few bullet points:

- a publication of the lesson plans where each plan is prefaced by a brief account of the participant's classroom experience (Tarasheva, 2000);
- development and design of own culture teaching syllabuses to fit individual teaching contexts;
- on-going collaboration among project participants and a growing sense of belonging to an innovative professional group;
- sustaining relationship with project tutors and evaluator, seeking advice, sharing experience;
- writing end-of-course dissertations on culture-related research topics;
- enrolment in postgraduate level courses specialising in intercultural communication;
- membership in the Cultural Studies and Intercultural Communication Special Interest Group;
- numerous conference presentations; and
- vigorous attempts to think and behave interculturally in their new teaching environments in spite of institutional resistance.

Conclusion

Now that the Intercultural Training Project for Student Teachers of English is complete one inevitably tries to formulate the lessons that have been learned. It has become obvious that, for its participants, the project mapped out a learning path which was quite out of the ordinary. Both student-teachers and tutors benefited from working together and ensured the success of the programme.

'Success' in this context meant that the project participants made their first tentative steps in becoming intercultural learners and teachers of language and culture. They had their first taste of theoretical readings in the field and groped their way through the specifics of the terminology. For the first time in their learning careers they faced the challenge of doing ethnography tasks and ran the risk of questioning the 'familiar'. They designed their own intercultural lessons and taught them in a foreign setting. They wrote their first professional journals and talked about what they thought, what they did and who they were.

The question arises then whether the project has succeeded in setting up a model for training student-teachers of foreign languages to teach interculturally; a learning model which can be further developed to suit the regular teacher education programmes at Bulgarian universities.

References

British Council (1998) *Branching Out: A Cultural Studies Syllabus*. Sofia, Bulgaria: British Council.

Ellis, G. and Sinclair, B. (1989) *Learning to Learn English*. Cambridge, England: Cambridge University Press

Finkelstein, B., Pickert, S., Mahoney, T. and Douglas, B. (1998) *Discovering Culture in Education*. Washington, DC: ERIC Clearinghouse on Assessment and Evaluation.

Kramsch, C. (1998) The privilege of the intercultural speaker. In M. Byram and M. Fleming (eds) *Language Learning in Intercultural Perspective* (pp.16–31). Cambridge, England: Cambridge University Press.

Nunan, D. (1988) *Learner Centered Curriculum: A Study in Second Language Teaching*. Cambridge, England: Cambridge University Press.

Tarasheva, E. (ed.) (2000) *Lessons of the Mountain: A Collection of Lessons Designed and Taught by the Participants in the Intercultural Training Project*. Sofia, Bulgaria: British Council.

Chapter 6

Intercultural Experience and Drama

MICHAEL FLEMING

Introduction

This chapter will explore whether it is productive to view teaching and learning in drama as a form of intercultural education. The links between theatre and interculturalism are not new. As early as 1885 *The Merchant of Venice* was produced in the style of Japanese Kabuki theatre, followed a few years later by *Julius Caesar* and *Hamlet* (Pavis, 1996: 30). There are numerous examples of theatre translating across cultures or employing different cultural traditions in production and it is not difficult to imagine how these could be used in the classroom as a way of learning about other nations and traditions. However, the wider view which I want to explore, that *all drama* education can be seen as a form of intercultural education, is one which runs the risk of being true at the expense of being of any practical value, of being acceptable simply because it is vacuous and makes no meaningful distinctions. In order to make the assertion worthwhile it will be necessary to ask whether there are any special characteristics of drama as an art form which justify its claim to be viewed as a form of intercultural education and whether, in turn, there are any consequences of viewing the subject in this way. It is a more fundamental perspective than one that argues for the value of using drama techniques as a method of teaching intercultural awareness.

The first part of this chapter will be structured around five approaches to using drama to promote intercultural awareness, starting with more obvious examples before considering those which are more oblique. This discussion will be followed by an examination of the unique contribution which drama can make to the education process by virtue of the way it works within fictitious contexts.

Drama for Intercultural Awareness

Exploring other cultures through their drama and theatre traditions

It is at the 'crossroads of culture' (Pavis, 1992) that drama and interculturalism are most closely associated. Drama can be used in a very focused way to learn about other cultures which is at least the beginning of a form of intercultural education. This can happen through examining how familiar plays have been performed and transformed into other cultures or through exploring theatre traditions which are different from one's own. Brachmachari (1998) contrasts the rather limited anti-racist role-plays in drama lessons of the 1970s and 1980s (which she suggests never seemed to transform pupils who had racist views) with the richer possibilities of investigating the particularities of peoples, histories and artistic practices through drama. She argues that giving pupils experience of theatre from different countries (particularly non-western traditions) is likely to promote values of tolerance, sensitivity and understanding as well as widening pupils' predominant conception of drama as pure naturalism.

Although this is perhaps the most obvious approach, it is by no means the most straightforward because it is not easy to avoid fostering the notion that other theatrical traditions are simply exotic or bizarre. In the drama classroom it is often a challenge to move pupils beyond a very narrow conception of drama as 'kitchen sink' naturalism, drawn from their experience of television. It is necessary to widen their conception of drama forms even within their own culture. The result of introducing them to other theatrical traditions, however well intentioned, might be to reinforce their conception of these as being simply weird or exotic. An overemphasis on knowledge may have little impact on the transformation of attitudes.

Participating in theatre in other languages/using drama in the modern language classroom

An impressive example of participating in theatre in a foreign language is described by Schmidt (1998). The project involves the devising and producing of a play in English and other languages in the suburbs of Paris. It is coordinated by a professional theatre director, a French teacher of English and French students of different ethnic backgrounds, ensuring a balance between the artistic, pedagogic and cultural objectives. The fact that the participants themselves devise the play is a key aspect of the intercultural dimension because the participants have to transpose the action into a foreign culture.

On a much smaller scale, foreign language teachers often ask pupils to create dramatic situations in the target language in the classroom. When students are simply repeating sentences or answering questions in the target language it could be argued that they are using a form of role play because the intention is that they do so *as if* the situation is happening in real life. These exercises can be taken a step further, extending the make-believe context by creating simple scenarios to be acted out, e.g. buying an item in a shop, ordering a meal in a restaurant, making conversation at the breakfast table, checking in at an airport. Such approaches can increase motivation because they embed the language in concrete contexts and capitalise on pupils' willingness to engage in forms of dramatic play but they represent a limited use of the dramatic art form.

This type of role-play exercise tries to replicate real life situations but does so often in very functional ways and tends to contain a minimum of human interest or dramatic tension. Buying a loaf of bread in a simulated situation in the classroom tends to be viewed as a substitute for the equivalent real experience. It might be thought that the dramatic art form can be exploited more by heightening the level of realism, by using more props, costumes and a more realistic set. Irrespective of the impracticality of importing such elements into the classroom, such an approach is increasing the 'theatricality' of the role play without necessarily deepening the use of drama.

A drama teacher might approach the simple situation of buying a loaf of bread by including an extra layer of meaning, adding a sub-text, enriching the context. Imagine a simple exchange of dialogue.

A: A loaf of bread please.
B·   Is this one o.k for you?
A: Something smaller?
B: What about this one?
A: Fine – how much?

This situation can be deepened in different ways by creating different contexts but using the same words: A has run away from home and is scared of being caught; this is a preliminary exchange before A conducts a robbery in the shop; A is a parent with a family to feed who can barely afford the purchase; it is B's first time in the job and is very nervous; A and B are both spies and this is in fact an exchange of a code or password; A is very upper class and is condescending to B; B is always rude to customers; A used to be B's boyfriend; it is A's first time in a foreign country, using the language in a real situation for the first time; A is an escaped prisoner who must not give away the fact the s/he is from another country. The possibilities are numerous but the different contexts require different experimentation with actions, tone, volume, speed of delivery, use of pause. This type of exercise can be developed by having two pupils speak the words aloud while two others repeat the actual thoughts of the characters after each line. From a pragmatic point of view, learners are likely to be motivated to keep repeating the same lines in the second language in different ways thus committing them to memory. But it could also be argued that probing the context and meaning is a way of probing the cultural context, defined in its broadest sense .

Of course a simple situation such as buying a loaf of bread lends itself to comparisons across national cultures. What is different about buying a loaf of bread from one country to another? Is the French word 'pain' exactly equivalent to 'bread'? What are the different local words for types of bread? The theme of buying bread can be continued in drama but this time exploring contexts in different countries, perhaps with the teacher taking a role in the exchange. There is an important difference then between using *drama* activities and the more common role-play exercises often used in foreign language lessons. A simple distinction here is that between 'role' (the participants are defined simply by their actions e.g. buying an item in a store, asking directions, arriving at an airport) and 'character' including attitude (e.g. 'I am buying this item in a store even though my family cannot really afford it'; 'I have been sent out to buy bread in this country and I am nervous'; 'I know I am amusing them in this shop by what I have said but I don't know why'). The drama approach has more potential to explore subtexts and underlying cultural dimensions.

In the drama classroom spontaneous improvisation was at one time the dominant way of working. However, teachers now embrace a wider range of approaches such as teacher in role (in which it is the teacher who adopts the fictitious role, perhaps using the target language), tableaux (in which groups create a still image to which can be added dialogue or thoughts), questioning in role (in which a fictitious character is questioned by the class to explore motivation), all of which exploit the power of drama more fully. Likewise, the use of script has been neglected because it was assumed that it had to involve pupils acting out entire plays, with all the skill and preparation that involves. However, the approach described here which takes just a small scripted exchange and probes its meaning in different ways is both more accessible and potentially richer than simply acting out the lines in a one-dimensional way. These approaches have the advantage for the teacher of foreign languages that they do not require pupils to have the fluency in language required by spontaneous, improvised work.

Exploring cultural differences through drama activities

For an example of this kind if work I will draw on a drama workshop with a group of Norwegian student teachers and a small group of British 15-year-old pupils. The specific brief for the session which was held in Durham was to explore some drama teaching techniques with the trainee teachers rather than work specifically on cultural issues but this seemed an obvious focus given the presence of the two nationalities. Both groups were experienced in drama. The first ice-breaking activity was a simple game (each participant tried to communicate the name of a country to a partner by mime alone) designed to initiate a discussion of stereotypes. One of the dangers in using drama directly to explore cultural differences is that it invites the reinforcement of stereotypes; the warm-up activity raises this question for explicit discussion. The pupils were very interested in the image of Britain held by the Norwegian students (as represented for example in their depictions of tea drinking) and *vice versa*.

For the next activity the participants were asked to create a still image or tableau in small groups which depicted a scene in which a foreign visitor is unwittingly made to feel uncomfortable for some reason. For this part of the workshop the British pupils worked as one group. After viewing, reading and discussing these still images, new groups were formed with British pupils now working with Norwegian students. The brief now was for them to explore similar situations, not this time using tableaux but employing fuller dramatic improvisations. They produced dramatisations of simple everyday situations of their choosing (buying an item in a shop, going to someone's house for dinner, asking directions of people on a bus, going to a football match) which provided a vehicle for exploring aspects of cultural differences. One of the social conventions which they focused on was the practice of taking off one's shoes when visiting someone's house. The dramatic context transformed the social convention from mere knowledge of customs because the participants were acting out the different scenarios and reflecting on their own reactions within the drama.

Exploring aspects of one's own culture through drama

One of the scenarios created during the project with the British and Norwegian students brought an interesting difference of opinion in the discussion afterwards. The dramatic enactment depicted a group of Norwegians planning and taking their British visitor friends to a football match, showing the different attitudes of each group. The British visitors, to the amusement of their more reserved hosts, unashamedly brought their own customs to the experience of going to a football match in Norway, including chants, songs, mild but unjustified abuse to the referee and meaningless partisanship (arbitrarily adopting the 'red' team as if it was matter of life and death). When the drama was enacted some of the Norwegian observers disputed the implicit assumption that Norwegians are actually quieter at sporting occasions than British supporters and whether this was more a questions of class difference. This was an interesting discussion for the British pupils to hear but the main value for them lay not just in learning about the customs of a different country but in examining familiar situations from home with a fresh eye. This was of course made easier and more purposeful by the presence of people from another country but there was an element of defamiliarisation intrinsic to the process of creating the drama.

In order to enact 'going to a football match' the pupils cannot simply act out what they would do in real life. They have to construct a representation, implicitly adopting the semiotics of the theatre using voices, physical positioning, use of space, props, selection and focus in order to convey meaning. Even the enactment of a very simple scenario of this kind carries an aesthetic dimension. The pupils, if the drama works well, will be emotionally engaged in the experience because they 'live through' it in real time in the present. At the same time, however, there is a necessary element of distance in the construction; everyone knows that this is not as real situation. The pupils had to distance themselves from familiar behaviours in order to parody them.

The simple scenario which was entertaining and well acted raised more questions than the participants intended. Was the behaviour of these British football supporters going to a match in Norway mainly a function of their nationality, gender (the group happened to be female but they acted the part of males) or class? Or was it more a function of them feeling alienated in a foreign culture, defiantly asserting their own group identity? What started as a simple scenario about different customs in different countries raised more complex questions about social identity. The drama works as aesthetic experience only if the consequences of actions are taken seriously (we feel 'real' embarrassment for the Norwegian hosts) but ultimately we know that this is 'play' where actions have no real consequences.

Exploring the concept of 'other' in drama

The final example is taken from a drama project with a small group of 11-year-olds which I have described in more detail elsewhere (Fleming, 2001). The stimulus was a child's rhyme taken from the final scene of Brecht's *Galileo* (1947):

> One, two, three, four, five, six,
> Old Marina is a witch.
> At night, on a broomstick she sits
> And on the church steeple she spits.

A group of seven eleven-year-old pupils (three boys and four girls) were given this verse and asked to use it as a basis for drama. They were extremely well motivated and applied themselves to the task with enthusiasm and considerable imagination. Their initial suggestions were wide ranging ('It could be set in ancient times and everyone would be thinking she's a witch'; 'They don't know she's a witch'; 'There is a house in the background with all these kids walking by saying nasty songs and pointing'; 'One, two three, four, five, six could be bells on the church at night'; 'It's the time she's about to come out'; 'The children echo it and on six she turns into a witch'; etc.).

With help from the teacher they focused on the idea of Marina transforming into a witch because of her treatment in the village as the main theme of their drama. The nature of the teacher intervention consisted in some focused questioning (to use their ideas to create a narrative and dramatic plot), some help in constructing different scenes and the use of a 'whispers' convention to simulate the spread of gossip. Marina was an old woman who had helped when a young child had become injured in the park. Marina's gossip in the neighbourhood (talking for example about the parents' neglect of their child) turned the community against her and rumours spread that she was a witch. The local antagonism and teasing (children knocking on her door and running away) resulted in her actually turning into a witch (enacted at the end in very stylised way). The pupils had created a simple narrative which derived its depth from its metaphorical content (a person's behaviour and personality is often a result of the way they are treated) which had certain resemblances to a folk tale or myth.

This project was not planned or conceived specifically in terms of interculturalism but it can be analysed in those terms and it is appropriate to ask how might it have been focused and adapted if intercultural objectives were more to the fore. The pupils had created a narrative in which an 'outsider' was created because of that person's transgression of the norms which defined the social group. Marina was not interculturally aware because she did not show enough sensitivity to the prevailing social conventions. The villagers similarly lacked cultural sophistication because they did not make allowances for her transgression; they created an insular group which rejected her, symbolised by her transformation into a witch. The subsequent reflection with the pupils on what they had created would have been richer and more purposeful, probing beneath the surface of the metaphor, had it been conceived in terms of its cultural content. The situations in which Marina inadvertently turned the villagers against her could have been re-enacted in the drama but this time with the inclusion of Marina's actual thoughts to reveal that her transgressions were innocent and not intended. The pupils could have been asked to brainstorm and re-enact other simple situations which might have caused tensions between Marina as the outsider and the villagers. Discussion could then have focused on how the misunderstandings could have been avoided – should the villagers have been more understanding and flexible? The whole project of course can be conceived as a metaphor for the growth of racism but working through analogy distances the theme and avoids the danger of crude stereotyping. However, the drama may open the way for such themes to be addressed more directly, revisiting the narrative but this time considering Marina as someone from another country. The project may have prompted such questions as whether approaches and attitudes to bringing up children differ across cultures.

The drama worked because it created a closed world or 'form of life' with it own internal cultural rules. It did not matter that the whole tale was far-fetched – that a simple piece of gossip should result in someone changing into a witch – because it had created its own context, reflecting reality but at the same time bracketed off from the real world. When viewed as a metaphor the transformation has more meaning. The extent of the retribution (the transformation into a witch) may seem excessive but *King Lear* provides another example of someone more sinned against than sinning.

Drama and Interculturalism

It is the power of the fictitious context and the particular effect it has on the uses and meaning of language which I want to explore and that is where I find the writing of Wittgenstein helpful. His writing on language and meaning has had enormous impact on contemporary thought and his concept of language games and family resemblances are well known and very influential in a variety of fields. His concept of 'forms of life' has been less widely employed and that is not surprising; it is not exactly clear to what he referred to by using the term in that he did not give specific examples.

The concept of 'forms of life' is best understood in the context of the contrast between the two philosophies which Wittgenstein advanced in his life-time which both sought to give an account of how language has meaning. In *Tractatus* he sought for a logical 'calculus' explanation of the relationship between language and reality. He had assumed that because we use language to talk about the world it must be related to the world in a strict logical fashion and that there must be a simple correspondence between language and what it represents. His later philosophy rejected that systematized approach in favour of a more organic view; language has meaning not by any simple correspondence with reality or with ideas in someone's head but through shared human contexts. The logical view in *Tractatus* is reflected in the austere and economical style of his earlier publication as much as through the content:

> Logical pictures can depict the world . . .
> A logical picture of facts is a thought . . .
> In a proposition a thought can be expressed in such a way that elements

> of the propositional sign correspond to the objects of the thought . . .
> A proposition is a picture of reality.
> A proposition is a model of reality as we imagine it. (Wittgenstein,
> 1922: 10)

In contrast the more discursive, conversational style and loosely structured format of *Philosophical Investigations* (1953) reflects not just a greater tolerance of loose boundaries, ambiguities and uncertainties but sees these as central to the way language has meaning. Some writers have seen in Wittgenstein's early writing an expression of the spirit of modernism, in contrast to his later work which has more affinities with post-modernist thought (Peters & Marshall,1999). Doll (1993) applied the same polarities to curriculum planning, contrasting the modernist paradigm (closed, linear, easily quantifiable) with a post-modern approach (complex, pluralistic and unpredictable). The relevant point is that it is through forms of negotiation within cultural contexts that meaning is established, not through making simple connnections of correspondence between language and reality.

Wittgenstein set out to show how common philosophical views about meaning, the nature of concepts and various mind/body problems derived from an inadequate grasp of the way language functions. He uses a quotation from Augustine at the start of *Philosophical Investigations* to convey the particular mistaken view with which he is concerned:

> The individual words in language name objects – sentences are combinations of such names. In this picture of language we find the roots of the following idea: every word has a meaning. This meaning is correlated with the word. It is the object for which the word stands. Augustine does not speak of there being any difference between kinds of word. If you describe the learning of language in this way you are, I believe, thinking primarily of nouns like 'table', 'chair', 'bread', and of people's names, and only secondarily of the names of certain actions and properties; and of the remaining kinds of word as something that will take care of itself. (Wittgenstein, 1953: 2)

The mistaken view is to assume that 'if anyone utters a sentence and means or understands it he is operating a calculus according to definite rules' (Wittgenstein, 1953: 81)

Wittgenstein's views have sometimes been mistakenly viewed as being behaviourist because he rejected the distinction between 'internal' and 'external' dimensions of experience. Words like 'understanding', 'feeling' and 'imagining' appear to be describing some inner mental state but in fact it is not from any inner state that they get their meaning. As Wittgenstein (1958: 3) comments,

It seems that there are certain definite mental processes bound up with the working of language, processes through which alone language can function. I mean the processes of understanding and meaning. The signs of our language seem dead without these mental processes; and it might seem that the only function of the signs is to induce such processes, and that these are the things we ought to be interested in.

Wittgenstein's insight is that to seek to imagine an inner process as a way of explaining the meaning of 'understanding' is wrong. When we say that someone has understood something we are not pointing to an internal change but to observable aspects of people's lives. We do not determine whether or not someone has understood something by looking inside them but by observing what they do and say.

It is in order to provide a more accurate representation of language and meaning that Wittgenstein (1953: 88) introduced the concept of a 'form of life'.

To imagine a language means to imagine a form of life ...
The speaking of language is part of an activity, or of a form of life ...
[Human beings] agree in the language they use. That is not agreement in opinions but in form life.

This idea provides a striking contrast to the views he expressed in *Tractatus*.

The idea of language as a form of life is in total contrast to the idea of language simply as a system of signs but emphasises instead the fact that language is embedded in the significant behaviour (including non-linguistic behaviour) of human beings.

Grayling (1996: 84) interprets Wittgenstein's use of form of life as follows:

It is the underlying consensus of linguistic and non-linguistic behaviour, assumptions, practices, traditions, and natural propensities which humans, as social beings, share with one another, and which is therefore presupposed in the language they use; language is woven into that pattern of human activity and character, and meaning is conferred on its expressions by the shared outlook and nature of its users ... . The form of life is the frame of reference we learn to work with when trained in the language of our community.

What is the relevance of this to the theme of interculturalism? The notion of a 'form of life' has cultural connotations. It is not just that language has different meanings in different cultural contexts (which is the case) but language *only* can have meaning in contexts of shared judgements and shared practices. The history of much western philosophy can be seen in Wittgenstein's terms as an attempt to detach language from its everyday employment and create problems where previously none had existed.

Finch (1995: 51) interprets Wittgenstein as saying that a form of life is necessary to give full sense to a language activity:

> Suppose, for example, that an anthropologist sees a group of women down by the water in the morning arranging themselves in a particular order while carrying what appear to be clothes. Is this laundry or a religious purification or both or neither? We need to know not only what they are doing but also a wider context of how it fits into other activities in their lives if we are to understand the language that accompanies their activities. The form of life does not explain the language game, but it does make it comprehensible. It distinguishes, for example, a ceremony from a daily chore, even though the two may at times overlap.

Lurie (1992: 193) sees in the work of Wittgenstein a reassertion of a concept of man as essentially a cultural being. This was a view which the Greeks had held but which was abandoned in the Enlightenment when man was seen as a being whose essence consisted in the possession of reason. It is not the 'intellectual power of mind to abstract' that enables man to form or acquire concepts (p. 194). Rather it man's capacity to adopt 'shared responses', to develop common judgements in specific contexts which leads to the formation of concepts:

> On this way of looking at the matter intellect does not explain the emergence of linguistic behaviour. It is the other way around. The adaptation of certain shared responses and common judgements (by means for example of linguistic practices) is the emergence of what is recognised as intellect. (Lurie, 1992: 198)

The insight that human life begins in doing not thinking has implications for education. It suggests that exploration of interculturalism is likely to require more than intellectual enquiry, reasoned argument and acquisition of knowledge. Drama can provide concrete contexts and affective engagement for the participants and by its very nature can be seen as a form of intercultural education.

The kind of explanation of meaning Wittgenstein gives is convincing. But if language is so deeply bound up with specific contexts it does raise problems of how we can look at those contexts 'objectively' which seems to be an important aspect of intercultural education – how we gain a perspective on our own cultures. This is where I think it is useful to return to the creation of fictitious contexts in drama. In our normal everyday life our use of language is 'saturated'; it is full of resonance and subtleties which derive from the form of life in which the language is embedded. The creation of a fictional context, however, strips away some of that complexity – a drama is bound by certain limitations by virtue of the fact that it not real. In a dramatic representation human motivation and intention can be simplified and examined more explicitly. On the surface, the dramatic representation seems to replicate reality particularly if it is using naturalistic conventions; however the characters who exist in the drama occupy the narrower more confined fictional world which is created.

Paradoxically it is the use of more crafted, stylised, theatrical devices which come closer to exploring human situations more realistically and in more depth. Language can be explored in human contexts in ways which go beyond the surface meaning of the words spoken. Drama of this kind can examine cultural contexts more explicitly and thus has greater potential for promoting cultural awareness. The fictitious family around the breakfast table and the visitor can voice their inner confusions and misconceptions while replaying the scene with different outcomes.

This view is the opposite of the way art is often conceived. The 'common sense' view is that language operates in much the way described by Augustine which is close to what Wittgenstein sought to reinforce in *Tractatus*; it has meaning in a fairly simple way by virtue of that to which it refers. Language in the context of art is more dense, metaphorical, compressed. What I am suggesting is that with regard to drama as an art form the reverse is the case. In the process of creating a drama (and this may be true of other art forms) there is actually a process of simplification because the context is more defined and controlled.

In the project with the visitors from Norway, paradoxically, the simplicity of the enacted scenes provided access to the more complex questions because it created a very reduced and condensed sequence rather than a complete narrative. In the improvisation about going to a football match we did not need contextual clues about who the people were, why they happened to be in Norway etc. which would be more likely of concern in a written narrative. Drama allows us to alight on a situation *in media res* – an audience often simply enters into a conversation at the beginning of a play as if it is in full flow. The fiction also provided a context in which the participants were free from any real responsibility for their actions.

When drama is used as an art form it offers something unique to the education process, resolving contradictions in ways which facilitate learning and which makes it reasonable to define drama education as a form of intercultural education. At its best it allows participants:

- to be emotionally engaged yet distant

  A participant who takes a part in a play whether scripted or improvised becomes another person. It is not a purely cerebral activity but
  involves the whole self – physical and emotional. When Marina is per-
  secuted in the play she reacts with feeling but all the participants are
  safe in the knowledge that they are working within a fiction.

- to be serious yet free from responsibility

  Such is the ferocity of the villagers' taunts that Marina transforms into
  the ultimate outsider. The pupils as participants in the drama have
  caused this to happen and they have to face up to the consequences of
  their actions but the fictitious context frees them from any responsibility for what they have done.

- to be participant as well as observer

  Traditionally, roles in drama have been distinguished between those
  who participate as actors and those who observe as audience. More
  recently, there has been recognition that the educational value of
  drama in part derives from the fact that one can actively engage in
  drama while at the same time keep one's actions under review.

- to be open to the new while rooted in the familiar

  Participants bring to the fictitious context their real-life experiences.
  In the Marina example pupils draw on their knowledge of social conventions and behaviour. But the quest to create a dramatic plot takes
  them to the creation of new meanings captured within the symbolic
  action of the drama.

- to simplify situations in order to explore their complex depths

  Each of the dramas 'bracketed off' extraneous details which clutter
  our experience of normal life. In effect the participants create a 'closed
  culture' or 'form of life' which allows an exploration of complexity
  because it is a simplification. They have no prior history other than
  that given to them within the drama

In order to become open to other cultures it is necessary to suspend disbelief. This is the *sine qua non* of drama. We enter a fictitious world which
we 'believe' is real but we also enter into a world which is objectified and
subject to scrutiny. Drama can be seen as a form of intercultural education
in as much as it provides an opportunity to create, observe and practise
forms of social behaviour with the safety of the fictitious context.

Wittgenstein's reminds us that we do not have to look inwards in order to find appropriate explanations of art, aesthetic experience and meaning but outwards into the cultural contexts in which we operate.

References

Brachmachari, S. (1998) Stages of the world. In D. Hornbrook (ed.) *On the Subject of Drama*. London: Routledge.

Brecht, B. (1947) *Galileo*. English version by Charles Laughton. Indiana: Indiana University Press.

Doll, (1993) *A Postmodern Perspective on Curriculum*. New York: Teachers College Press.

Finch, H.L. (1995) *Wittgenstein*. Dorset: Element Books.

Fleming, M. (2001) *Teaching Drama in Primary and Secondary Schools: An Integrated Approach*. London: David Fulton Publishers

Grayling, A. (1996) *Wittgenstein*. Oxford: Oxford University Press. First published by Oxford in 1988.

Lurie, Y. (1992) Culture as a human form of life: A romantic reading of Wittgenstein. *International Philosophical Quarterly* 32 (2, 126) 193–204.

Pavis, P. (1992) *Theatre at the Crossroads of Culture*. London: Routledge.

Pavis, P. (ed.) (1996) *The Intercultural Performance Reader*. London: Routledge.

Peters, M. and Marshall, J. (1999) *Wittgenstein: Philosophy, Postmodernism, Pedagogy*. Westport, CT: Bergin and Garvey.

Schmidt, P. (1998) Intercultural theatre through a foreign language. In M. Byram and M. Fleming (eds) *Language Learning in Intercultural Perspective: Approaches Through Drama and Ethnography*. Cambridge: Cambridge University Press.

Wittgenstein, L. (1922) *Tractatus Logico Philosophicus*. (C.K. Ogden and F.P. Ramsey, trans.). London: Routledge and Kegan Paul.

Wittgenstein, L. (1953) *Philosophical Investigations*. (G.E.M. Anscombe, trans.). Oxford: Basil Blackwell

Wittgenstein, L. (1958) *The Blue and Brown Books*. Oxford: Basil Blackwell.

Chapter 7

An Experience of Interculturality: Student Travellers Abroad

ELIZABETH MURPHY-LEJEUNE

Migrants of all kinds share a special position, that of strangers who, on the boundaries of sameness and otherness, provoke a sometimes unsettling awareness in their interlocutors and test the permeability of borders. Part of the experience of strangeness appears common to various types of travellers as they pass from one group to another and it can be assumed that 'on one level, exile is a universal experience' (Huston, 1999: 39). Another part is unique. Indeed, the kaleidoscope of the stranger embraces many different narratives, emanating both from within and outside national boundaries. The migrant within refers to cases of social mobility or marginality. The migrant outside suggests different individual trajectories, which vary depending on issues such as relative distance or proximity between home and host cultures, purpose and expected duration of the stay, host members' attitudes as well as travellers' attitudes regarding their hosts, status upon entry as political refugee, asylum seeker, labour migrant, professional expatriate, international student or foreign resident and, above all, force and choice in migration (Van Hear, 1998). People meet others as strangers in many diverse situations, at home or abroad.

However, strangers abroad are thrown, somewhat unwittingly, into direct contact with otherness. The sheer force of an unmediated holistic contact, particularly with linguistic otherness, must not be underestimated. This particular intercultural experience involves at first disorientation and loss, a confrontation with a foreign environment which may violently jolt individuals and perturb their taken-for-granted world. It places individuals in a situation where adaptation and transformations are necessary if they are to maximise life in their new conditions. In other words, life abroad represents an extensive natural learning situation which stimulates many more aspects of learners' personalities than are usually catered for in educational institutions. It can be understood broadly as an interaction between an individual and a new environment where the former is unsparingly put to the test as a whole person.

In this chapter, we look at one specific experience of interculturality, that of student travellers who spend a year in a European country other than their own, on the basis of interviews with 50 students (Murphy-Lejeune, 2002). The main research interest is to explore the specific features defining European student mobility and to focus the analysis on the individual traveller, in a phenomenological perspective, so as to account for a definition of the experience by those concerned. Here, we present the findings related to the learning process the experience generates. These findings may be presented as a tentative model for learning abroad, which sums up the main outcomes of the year abroad outlined by our students.

A Model for Learning Abroad

This empirically-driven model is descriptive and does not pretend to represent pedagogical guidelines. Its substance is grounded in what the actors said they learnt while living abroad. Whatever pedagogical implications may be inferred from the data belong to another investigation.

(1) Knowledge

- factual knowledge: history, geography, economics, politics, literature, etc,
- sociocultural realities: understanding contemporary society, its structures and rules,
- study/work-based knowledge in a professional milieu and
- language proficiency and communicative competence.

(2) Strategic skills

- autonomy: to live on one's own (previous experiences, organisational know-how) and
- self-confidence: learning 'how to cope'.

(3) Social competences

- communicative and social confidence: sociability, sociocultural participation and
- relational ease or how to get on with people: establishing new social relations.

(3) Personal and interpersonal attitudes

- openness: curiosity, tolerance, flexibility and
- critical awareness of self and others: learning culture as interculture.

The four general areas of development – cognitive, strategic, social and personal – do not carry equal weight. Some aspects, e.g. what cannot be learnt at home, are considered as more important than others by students aware of the specificity of learning abroad. This variable rating is also linked to the issue of learning modes, whose importance varies over time. Learning abroad takes place primarily through observation, participation and communication (Schild, 1962).

Cognitive and Linguistic Development

Cognitive and linguistic development refers to the educational component known as culture-and-language within language education pedagogy. But, what kind of culture and language knowledge do students acquire *in situ*? Four aspects are mentioned in our data: factual knowledge, sociocultural and work-based knowledge and language development.

Factual knowledge refers mainly to information related to the cultural environment and conveyed through different media; press, books, television, cinema, theatre, music or visits. If students' knowledge about the host country is enlarged, this dimension appears incidental to them. They regard it as secondary in relation to other more crucial discoveries. They also sometimes consider that this type of activity involves them as tourists, isolated consumers of guidebook references, while they came to learn more directly through face-to-face interactions.

By contrast, the discovery of sociocultural realities through observation of everyday actions and practices is not 'knowledge about' made explicit by an external discourse, but more 'understanding of' gained from private experience. In this respect, the cultural intermediaries who 'translate' their culture and lead travellers through potential interpretative hazards and enigmas give those who benefit from such guidance the opportunity to rationalise their live experience. Similarly, work-based knowledge such as university life for an Erasmus student, school life for a language assistant or professional customs for a *stagiaire* on work experience rests on personal involvement. Such exposure generally engages students in comparative speculations and interpretations of local conventions where the new and the familiar are contrasted and questioned. The ensuing learning is considered as 'natural': 'I did assume that it would happen naturally living in the country . . . which to some extent it has', says Elena who adds that one can 'never understand everything'. But many different degrees of understanding are attainable, from the outsider's superficial knowledge to the deeper insider's perspective. Philip started 'to get an insider's view of French society' when he studied for a *concours* into a *grande école* because he understood 'how people think from that perspective'. This kind of entry into local life, which touches upon ways of thinking, is rarely achieved after one year abroad.

Language development during residence abroad can hardly be measured purely in terms of linguistic proficiency. Life in between languages means discovering language as a social practice in the context of social interactions and as a personal stake which extends one's identity (Hoffman, 1989). The role of language is manyfold. It acts as a core motivation in the decision to go and corresponds to a desire for a live relationship with the language and with otherness. It is the key to intercultural contacts and its mastery represents a crucial element, particularly at the beginning when communication is tiresome and difficult. Strangers with insufficient language skills are left outside, marginalised longer than others. In the end, gaining a new linguistic territory may induce an expanded identity, a feeling of self-elation described as 'jubilant' by those who can play with different linguistic identities.

Strategic Skills

Two skills stand out as distinctive learning outcomes of life abroad: autonomy and self-confidence. They are strategic in that they derive from combined efforts to reach the goal of managing one's life in a new cultural environment. They are the means by which success abroad is attainable.

Autonomy: To live on one's own

Autonomy is a quality which students gain from having to survive in an unfamiliar environment. In this respect, previous experiences play a crucial precursory role. When experiences of adaptation precede experiences abroad, the adaptation capital boosts the mobility capital. It confers the ability to adapt with greater ease a second time.

Experiences of adaptation arise from situations where individuals are confronted with an unknown world whose social rules they do not master and which grants them the status of temporary stranger. The situations students identified as requiring an effort to adapt included intracultural situations such as a change in school or university, military service or family relocation. But for most, the main adaptation experience was their first stay abroad. The hallmark of transnational mobility is that language discontinuity is added to sociocultural dislocation, as Nicolas explains when he compares living abroad to moving houses:

> Moving country is like moving houses, I mean you find yourself in a totally new place, you have to adapt to the weather, new accommodation, new neighbours, a new culture.. to the new language, the new

customs. Yes, it's like changing countries in the end with just language being the same!

Student travellers learn to go through three rifts: relocation (*déménagement*) since travellers leave a geographical territory, disorientation (*dépaysement*) since they leave a social and cultural territory, and uprootedness (*déracinement*) since they leave an affective, personal and linguistic territory.

For the students, an 'experience abroad' requires four conditions to be considered as such: duration (ten-day trips are excluded), quality of contacts with the natives – considered as the distinguishing line between tourist and sojourner experiences – language immersion and travelling on one's own. Previous experiences of mobility in the case of our students generally started early and were repeated at regular intervals. For example, Julie went on her first language exchange at the age of 12 and every year from then on, alternating between France and Germany. Mobility experiences represent a budding capital, after which the year abroad appears as a more advanced stage in a spontaneous development. Learning mobility proceeds at a steady but cautious pace with progress, as students grow older, in the type of travel (family holidays, then language courses, then student trips or summer jobs), in the traveller's degree of autonomy and in the choice of gradually more distant destinations. In short, the travellers learn to live outside home for longer periods, in close contacts with individuals from different origins, using a foreign language, and on their own.

Newcomers face practical demands of all sorts which put pressure on them. The material side of autonomy is self-sufficiency or being able 'to solve all the common problems', says Josef. One of its most immediate facets is the way travellers organise their living space in its physical, personal, professional, cultural, social and mental aspects. It means discovering new spatial conditions and staking out one's habitat. For the organisation of a personal space one can call home represents the first step towards a feeling of belonging. The choice of accommodation is doubly crucial – as a personal refuge offering security and as the locus of interpersonal relationships, a basis for social relations. In the end, mobility is an experience which calls for a reappraisal of space and sometimes teaches students how to multiply their living space in the sense of being able to belong to more than one place.

Self-confidence: Learning 'how to cope'

Previous experiences produce a mental background regarding the countries visited, but also regarding language immersion, life abroad and the process of adaptation. Young travellers acquire skills which facilitate subsequent experiences. Caroline identifies two 'jumps': the language jump and the mental jump. Not being afraid of speaking in the foreign language represents the language jump. The mental jump stems from living outside one's home: 'I learnt how to cope . . . not to think too much about home . . . yes, to live independently'. Autonomy is defined here as a twofold competence, the ability to manage without family assistance and without a mental clamp connecting travellers to the home environment.

Amin identifies another important outcome: the ability to 'get through tough times by yourself', particularly through language difficulties. His advice to potential travellers is to 'be prepared that it's not going to be a rose garden', because entry into a new cultural world is comparable to a rite of passage. A new socialisation process must be engaged in and this effort makes the arrival, in particular, a trying period. Accepting its potential side-effects – homesickness, communicative strain, sense of loss or social isolation – and being aware that these are usually but a phase in the process of adjusting to the new milieu facilitates passage into the new world. When travellers are acquainted with these at an early age, the headstart smoothes the way later and lessens the risk of culture shock. For expert travellers, adaptability means independence and mental strength. They learn not to be afraid, as Juan explained: 'all those experiences, they help me . . . build strength . . . and I am not afraid to go to another country and talk to people and I feel I could go anywhere'. Acceptance of uncertainty as a challenge comes as more natural.

The strategic skills gained contrast with the anxiety and fear of the unknown which predominate in the introductory period. Overall, autonomy and self-confidence are skills closely associated with living abroad. Maria says that travellers 'feel at ease' when they 'no longer suffer from insecure attacks'. The sense of security induces the self-confidence required to communicate and go about meeting people. If the experience produces more self-confidence, Mathew says, it is because 'if you can solve complex problems in a language and in a country which are not your own, you can certainly do most of what life requires'. The learning outcomes are large enough to be transferable to other life situations.

Social Competences

Social competences are paramount in face-to-face intercultural encounters. Students highlighted two competences which influenced their process of social integration: communicative and social confidence, associated with sociocultural participation, and relational ease which results from social interactions.

Communicative and social confidence

Among the personality features of the potential wanderer, sociability is a core element. The aptitude to connect easily with individuals one encounters usually goes together with the desire to communicate. Lucy identified this social attribute as 'to like meeting new people' and explained:

> my mother noticed that about me, any time (foreign) students came into our house, it was always sort of me, I made friends with them more than anybody else did ... my sisters would fairly much ignore them, be polite or whatever, but would not take them into their lives at all ... I think it's just a sociable thing'.

She linked this sociability to a certain 'flippancy' in relations, described as the ability to entertain a friendship for a while without being too demanding in the long term. Her talent to open up her world to others, even for a short time, prepared her to accept the precariousness of relationships with foreigners. She understood early that travellers lose some friends, gain others and that 'friends come and go'.

Communicative and social confidence increases as students become acquainted with the new social setting. Starting with the choice of a place to live (who to live with), their social progress is pursued with their new professional role which introduces them to new ways of doing and being. Since participation in local life may be restricted for strangers because of their peripheral social situation, adopting a professional role similar to the natives' represents a valuable entry into a foreign culture, potentially leading to genuine intercultural exchanges and to the discovery of a certain social diversity otherwise unattainable. For Thomas, work experience constituted a powerful way of conquering linguistic and social distance. He noticed that 'just talking French eight hours a day with ... the secretary or the chief ... always it was integration and what they were interested in ...'; and he mentions learning about local topics of conversation, eating habits, business practices. But he adds: 'You have to make the effort'. Special faculties of creativity and enterprise are needed so that travellers can work out strategies allowing them to move in and take part in the new social setting. Individual initiative is mandatory.

Beside their professional context, student travellers have access to other activities which lead to diverse social contacts and learning situations in an informal context. Sharing activities with others, natives or otherwise, produces a fraternity based on the discovery of a certain commonness which Hugo clarifies: 'because of the experiences you have together, ... sports or going out in the country (...) you have this experience at home and a similar experience here... and the people are the same'. A bridge across social distance is provided. Sharing experiences contributes to the emergence of a common history. Integration into a group or the fact that travellers have become part of their friends' life may be gauged, according to him, from the fact that the new friends make plans together for future projects.

The nature and quality of social integration depends largely on the various modalities one selects as a way of getting inside society. Shared accommodation and shared activities with native people generate closer contacts and usually hasten the process. Participation in a local structure can be either seized to open doors wider or ignored as an opportunity. Shared activities may remain at the functional level of relationships between acquaintances. They may also serve as a valuable stepping stone into more personal communication among friends. In the end, students define adaptation as feeling 'comfortable', 'at home' and acquiring 'a history' over time. These words concretely mean that students would be happy to continue living for a while in a country which has become familiar to them. They have acquired the communicative and social confidence required.

Relational ease: 'The keys to get on with people'

Social relationships in the case of strangers are asymmetrical to start with. The challenge is then to build a social fabric of their own, so as to restore some kind of symmetry. To do so, they must rely on their own power of social seduction: mere physical proximity in no way guarantees personal proximity. The relational dimension of the stay is uppermost in the students' eyes as a major incentive and expectation. However, travellers leave a familiar social scene to be confronted with a relational void, where at times even the simplest forms of interaction may result in misunderstanding. Moreover, even though the strangeness is mutual, the natives do not perceive themselves as strange and will not usually alter their ways. The onus is on newcomers to adapt and to charm their entry into the ordinarily closed circles of established groups.

The construction of a social fabric is similar to a conquest, a triumph over distance between self and others, which is more or less successful depending on individuals, their starting point, their motivations, their previous experiences, their personal ambitions and talent, the context of entry into the local society, their knowledge of the language and country, and the links they maintain with their original context. This complex process stages a variety of individuals, natives or others, who create a given social landscape from which travellers will, if they choose, construct their personal social milieu. The undertaking implies identifying and seeking those contacts one wishes to create, having recourse to specific and reasoned strategies, and transforming distant external relations into close ones within the time constraints imposed by the stay. The necessarily limited duration of their stay gives prominence to the challenge represented by the venture. Students try to overcome this constraint differently, by playing the international game, by announcing continuity in their friendships or by creating a family-like relationship with a few chosen individuals.

For most students, the emerging social fabric is motley and comprehends an assortment in variable quantity of secondary and primary contacts with other strangers or with natives. If the diversity and quality of their social contacts influence their appreciation of the stay abroad as a whole, these social contacts extend beyond the native group. The international group, which promotes relationships among 'equal' strangers, usually represents the main interactional resource in the student experience, others playing lesser roles.

The type of social learning gained in these circumstances grants a specific social competence, relational 'ease'. It gives, according to Marina, 'the keys to be able to get on with people ... really, we are given the tools and the key, how to behave with others so that it works ... with other nationalities'. The special intercultural situation which social contacts abroad entail places them in a maximal learning position: 'as if I had jumped four steps at once', she adds. But Christine stresses that 'in order to meet a maximum amount of people, to speak, to learn, to read, to share, you must not have a passive, but an active behaviour'. An introvert with a tendency to close in on her/his own world has less chance of succeeding. Contacts, particularly with natives, are essential because, Ana says, 'you learn so much from others' in this setting: experiential learning takes place from observing, sharing and interacting with people. This relational competence represents a test for students, but also a great source of satisfaction. Through learning how to manage a great variety of contacts, travellers acquire social tools which open up a larger world of possible contacts.

Personal and Interpersonal Learning

The enrichment which students derive from living abroad comes from a deeper sense of who they are and what resources they can avail in unusual social circumstances. This double edge may be summed up as twin gains – the discovery of self through the discovery of otherness. Successful adaptors will develop personal qualities, notably openness in its different forms. They will also travel mentally and go from a distant, stereotyped outsider's knowledge of others to a more intimate, personal insider's knowledge.

Openness: Curiosity, tolerance, flexibility

Openness and its various facets – curiosity, tolerance and flexibility – are repeatedly identified as core qualities in the students' comments, as well as in assessments of intercultural adaptability (Kelley & Meyers, 1992) or competence (Byram, 1997).

Curiosity or the desire to learn new things is an attitude which characterises student travellers before their departure, its opposite being indifference or intellectual apathy. Christine explained that she 'loves accumulating experiences' and is fascinated 'by civilisations, by people'. Régine found that she was 'rather lazy' except when 'in travelling mode': 'to get out of my laziness, I need a big jump, to go somewhere else ... because it's liberating'. For her, curiosity is both the condition and the outcome of travelling. Amin defines it as a 'broadness of perspective' which allows one to question the familiar and counterbalance the tendency to intellectual stability and compliance. A curious mind is ready to ease the supremacy of the ready-made wisdom received through early socialisation. As a cognitive disposition directed towards the outside, it frees and energises.

Tolerance is primarily defined as a mental attribute, a function of knowledge according to Régine. As such, its opposite, narrow-mindedness, is synonymous with ignorance: 'When you want to say that someone is narrow-minded, you say that s/he is ignorant, and the term "ignorant" means both that you are stupid and narrow-minded while it really means that you don't know something'. Maria found that the mere fact of having to extend one's relational circle outside one's social cocoon brings on tolerance. The experience expands sociocultural knowledge, in the dual sense of cultural information and social relations, and broadens horizons. Christine and Hugo related it to arrogance which proceeds from being on the defensive and troubled. Tolerance occurs when your fear of others has been mastered and you are ready to launch into adventure. In all cases, whether it refers to intellectual, social, personal or relational openness, tolerance contains the notion of difference. What the students indicate is a broadening of their mental horizon in the way they approach others, which allows them to break free from their own frame of reference to try and penetrate others'. Tolerance is oriented towards others, even if it implies working on self. In this sense, it is a true adventure.

Flexibility is oriented towards self. It refers to the way individuals respond under the impact of changing circumstances. Life abroad represents a radical social change which disturbs one's taken-for-granted habits. When Damien says that 'you bend, but you don't break', he conjures up the flexibility required to adapt to newness in a foreign context. It has two sides. Faced with the difficulties inherent to the new situation, foreigners must bend without letting those difficulties take them down. In the process, they learn how to become flexible which means taking up or learning new characteristics while remaining true to themselves. By contrast, those who do not adapt are rigid. They are 'in a system' and refuse change, says Damien: 'Bad adaptors, they are just set in their ways, they're in a system, they're systematic people who cannot change'. Maria quotes some students who 'weren't willing to change their way of portraying themselves even though it was going to work to their advantage'. They closed in on their own ethnic group. Refusing to bend is often due to people clinging to their own values, Mathias suggests. Lacking the plasticity to integrate external differences into their own life-world, they remain in their original position. The mental journey is null and void in this case.

To be open means to be willing to allow some flow of communication between self and the outside so that bridges are established, making social exchanges possible.

Critical awareness of self and others: Learning culture as interculture

Crossing cultural borders changes one's position in society and implies a social learning process. Caught in between groups, one's social and personal identity becomes unclear and must be redefined. The movement is dual, from self to others and from others to self: 'You have to ask for acceptance, also other people . . . you have to be in the environment before you can actually adapt to that environment. So you have to be open to the environment, you have to go out trying to meet people. I mean it's quite a difficult thing to do', says Lucy. Accepting and getting accepted implies developing critical awareness of self and others and the personal limits of individual perceptions and understanding.

Accepting the limits of one's perceptions again involves flexibility as an antidote to the prejudices and expectations which often mar the game prior to direct contacts. Abroad, Elena stresses, travellers should be less inclined to produce distance-maintaining judgements because they are not familiar with local rules and symbols related to social identification: 'I think being flexible, ready to change yourself as well and not come over with these preconditions, you know, *"someone wearing that sort of clothes, I am not going to talk to him"*, it's so easy to do (at home)'. Lack of familiarity should lead to suspension of judgement whereas in one's home environment, social signs constitute screens which filter interpersonal contacts. This characteristic affords foreigners a certain social elasticity. Anonymous in the sense that their origin is not well known, strangers may benefit from their social wandering and gain 'a certain ease to roam about in the social structure' of the new group (Tiryakian, 1973: 47).

The process requires time because it means moving from culture to interculture. From establishing a familiar environment, strangers move on to try to be 'accepted by the people as part of their environment' (Hugo). At this stage, discussing cultural differences is regarded as futile, according to

Marina: 'You're no longer that interested in other people's differences. You tend to take people not as Germans or less as Germans, French, Irish, I don't know, rather as individuals'. Categorisation becomes less potent as culture learners uncover the personality behing the national mask. Personal relationships lead to shared moments, shared memories which create a common past binding individuals together. This new interactive space based on interpersonal communication moves partners beyond categorical or stereotypical thinking about others into an area where the boundaries between self and others may be flexible, dynamic, under constant review (Barth, 1969). In this interactive space, partners are aware of the natural gap between strangers, but are also aware that intersubjective communication 'in real time' can bring them closer and reduce distance if one accepts to play the game. Learners come to recognise that the symbolic distance between them and others does not correspond to an objective boundary but rather to a subjective limit to one's perception. From that realisation, life abroad is experienced as an untried and refreshing meeting place, and culture can be conceived as interculture.

At the same time, individuals who leave their home environment learn to see it with a kind of detachment which makes them suspect in the eyes of the sedentary natives. Social conventions are broken twice in this process of secularising two sets of customs. The kind of objective viewpoint which strangers gain on both cultures confers on them a particular social role, that of being both inside and outside. For the individual stranger, crossing social borders may be experienced as an exhilarating trip into a new social territory or as a threat to one's identity if the discrepancy between self-identity and identity ascribed by others is too disturbing.

Adaptation or Learning Abroad

All of these are part of the process of adaptation which is defined by students as the capacity to change one's behaviour under the pressure of outside events in an effort to overcome strangeness in the environment. Changes are required in order to 'fit' into the new given framework so as to make one's presence less glaringly visible. Adaptation means picking up small things borrowed from the natives – clothes, gestures, actions, habits – so that, John explains, 'I was still a foreigner, but to a native one could see *I wasn't a foreigner who'd arrived yesterday*, that I was living there for a while, that *I'd picked up their . . . their sayings, their . . . movements and actions*'. The social cloak one puts on fits the local scene. Adapting also means directing one's life as a play in which one performs a new role, using different masks. Chameleon-like, strangers adjust to their surroundings and may end up feeling comfortable enough to maybe want to stay on for a while because they no longer feel so strange. Rather than a total personality change, this process takes on the shape of a personal expansion, an opening of one's potential universe.

The process of social construction of one's personal environment wherever one lives is felt as a maturing process. To relativise one's childhood environment, as Jose and Hugo do, implies a step towards greater independence or emancipation. Then space no longer conveys an intimidating strangeness, but promises of exciting experiences to come. Liberation from one's origins is no longer considered a loss, but more a step towards 'a new space of freedom' (Sophie). Identity may then rest 'on becoming rather than being, biographical (or historical) experience rather than the fatality of origin, derived from something more like a curriculum vitae than a birth certificate' (Wollen, 1994: 189). Space redefined, where we live no longer matters once being a traveller or a migrant is not summed up in a postal address, but implies a certain way of thinking of one's life space as mobile and changing. The road travelled by our students may be gauged by the social position they grant themselves at the end of the year.

References

Barth, F. (1969) *Ethnic Groups and Boundaries. The Social Organisation of Culture Difference*. Boston: Little, Brown & Co.

Byram, M. (1997) *Teaching and Assessing Intercultural Communicative Competence*. Clevedon: Multilingual Matters.

Hoffman, E. (1989) *Lost in Translation. A Life in a New Language*. New York: Penguin Books.

Huston, N. (1999) *Nord perdu*. Arles: Actes Sud.

Kelley, C. and Meyers, J. (1992) *The Cross-Cultural Adaptability Inventory*. Yarmouth, MA: Intercultural Press.

Murphy-Lejeune, E. (2002) *Student Mobility and Narrative in Europe. The New Strangers*. London: Routledge.

Schild, E.O. (1962) The foreign student, as stranger, learning the norms of the host-culture. *Journal of Social Issues* 18, 41–54.

Tiryakian, E. (1973) Sociological perspectives on the stranger. In S. TeSelle (ed.) *The Rediscovery of Ethnicity* (pp. 45–58). New York: Harper and Row.

Van Hear, N. (1998) *New Diasporas*. London: UCL Press.

Wollen, P. (1994) The cosmopolitan ideal in the arts. In G. Robertson *et al.* (eds) *Travellers' Tales. Narratives of Home and Displacement*. London: Routledge.

Chapter 8

Ethnography and Cultural Practice: Ways of Learning During Residence Abroad

CELIA ROBERTS

Introduction

In this chapter I will draw on anthropology (and to some extent cultural studies) to discuss how the practice of ethnography can contribute to learning during a period of residence abroad which is part of a university course. The students in question are on a course of language studies in higher education, but the concept of a period of residence abroad is integrated into many university courses in Western Europe and beyond. In considering how such courses might be developed, I want to take the notion of *learning ethnographically* and relate it to two things: (1) what we seek to find out in terms of the meanings, norms and patterns of others' worlds; (2) what impact this seeking has on learners in terms of, first of all, their conceptualisation of self and other and, second, on their reflexive knowledge of social and cultural practices.

The assumption on which these ideas are based is that the period abroad offers a unique experience in intercultural living but that intercultural learning is not an automatic outcome of this experience. Students do not necessarily need courses in intercultural communication or learning. But they do benefit from both intellectual and practical preparation before they go abroad so that their encounters with 'others' and with 'otherness' can contribute to their understanding conceptually, analytically and emotionally. Learning to be ethnographic about these encounters offers students some ways of structuring their experiences while still encouraging their sense of themselves as active agents in managing the period abroad.

I am borrowing from Dell Hymes' notions of ethnography here on a number of counts in order to argue for its value in intercultural education:

[Ethnography] is continuous with ordinary life. Much of what we seek to find out in ethnography is knowledge that others already have. Our ability to learn ethnographically is an extension of what every human being must do, that is learn the meanings, norms, patterns of a way of life. (Hymes, 1980: 98)

So using ethnography is to use common sense ways of learning. Through observation and interaction, we gradually build up an understanding of how things get done, what meanings they have and how there is coherence and indeed patterns in the flux and apparent random aspects of ordinary everyday life. This way of learning is a process we go through from our earliest days and it is a process students live through when they are confronted with new social and cultural practices. In experiencing the 'other', they are also having to think about their own identity and its social and cultural basis. In engaging with themselves as cultural beings at the same time as meeting what is strange and not yet understood in others, they are forced to be reflexive – to acknowledge their role in understanding others.

Hymes is not suggesting that we should all strive to become professional ethnographers but rather that we should use ethnography to pursue our particular interests and careers. In Hymes' vision of a democratic society ethnography would be seen:

as a general possession, although differentially cultivated. At one pole would be a certain number of people trained in ethnography as a profession. At the other pole would be the general population, respected . . . as having a knowledge of their worlds, intricate and subtle in many ways, . . . and as having come to this knowledge by a process ethnographic in character. In between . . . would be those able to combine some disciplined understanding of ethnographic inquiry with the pursuit of their vocation whatever that might be. (Hymes, 1980: 99)

Students spending a period in another country as ethnographers are in this 'in between' category. They can develop an ethnographic way of looking and working and combine it with whatever line of work they choose to follow. So, ethnography is not just useful for the period of residence abroad. It has a more lasting effect.

The idea of learning ethnographically[1] is not a new one. Within the North American tradition of educationally based anthropology, school pupils have been encouraged to undertake ethnographic studies of their own culturally and linguistically diverse communities (Heath, 1983; Egan-Robertson & Bloome, 1998; Heller, 1994). These innovations in the curriculum not only sensitised young people to the differences and varieties in their own communities, they also contributed to an improvement in their academic abilities more generally. Similarly, the course in Britain which was developed originally for students of languages also had a broader, ambitious educational aim: to provide a new kind of consciousness which would be reflected in the way in which students encountered others and the way in which they wrote about otherness.

The Ealing Ethnography Programme

The original programme comprised three parts: a taught module, an ethnographic study and a written ethnography on return to the home university:

(1) A taught module of 45 classroom hours in the second year of a four-year languages degree combines basic anthropological and sociolinguistic concepts with a methodological component introducing ethnographic techniques. Weekly assignments – data collection and analysis. Students write a 'home ethnography' as part of the assessment of this module

(2) An ethnographic study while abroad. Students go to two different countries, each for about five months and do an ethnographic study in one of the two, usually the first. Undertake extensive fieldwork, produce a highly focused textual account of a particular group or set of practices in that country. Visited by Ealing lecturer.

(3) Writing up the ethnographic project (in the foreign language) on return from abroad (5–7000 words). Tutorial support given. Project counts as part of the final degree.

(Jordan & Roberts, 2000; Roberts *et al.*, 2001)

Social Identity, Ways of Learning, Ways of Knowing

Linking ethnography with language and cultural learning involves the learner in thinking about their own social identity and their ways of learning and knowing. Table 1 summarises these aspects of the language learner as ethnographer. In the left-hand column is the time span of the period abroad including the preparation before and the process of reflection and writing up afterwards. The middle column represents the pedagogy and learning process and the right-hand column the theory and conceptual underpinning of the learning process.

This framework interweaves some of the classic assumptions about ethnography with a more recent post-modern consciousness exemplified by the writing of Stuart Hall, Homi Bhabha and James Clifford within a cultural studies tradition. This post-modern consciousness is rather nicely summed up in the idea of culture as 'travelling'. Of course, this is what the

Table 1

Time		Learning Processes	Underlying Concepts
Before	T	Who you are: a 'Professional Stranger' (Agar, 2000)	Social construction of reality (Berger & Luckmann, 1966)
	R	Skills of participation and observation	
During	A	How you learn: participation is learning (Lave & Wenger, 1991)	Holistic: the experience of being both a participant and an observer. Smallness and slowness (Silverman, 1999); the local and everyday. Unit of analysis: (Erickson, 1977). Narrative: (Rosaldo, 1989; Georgakopoulou, 1997)
	V	New focus on the participant in ethnography (Agar, 2000)	
	E		
	L		
After	L	What you know / write: representing the 'other' (Clifford, 1988; Clifford & Marcus, 1986; Hallam & Street 2000)	The personal politics of ethnography
	I		
	N	Representing the other is abouth representing the self	
	G		Generalisation: (Mitchell, 1984) the 'telling' case

students on their residence abroad literally do but as cultural beings they are also travelling before, during and after this period.

The notion of culture as travelling suggests some place in-between, not 'there', of being in motion rather than static. Social life is blurred not crystal clear, fragmented not whole. Worlds are constructed through the traveller's gaze rather than existing and waiting prone to be discovered. As Rosaldo (1989: 217) says:

> A renewed concept of culture thus refers less to a unified entity ('a culture') than to the mundane practices of everyday life. . . Ethnographers look less for homogeneous communities than for border zones within and between them. Such cultural border zones are always in motion, not frozen for inspection.

Students as ethnographers are not only travelling themselves but find that the groups and activities that they are studying are also 'in motion'.

This post-modern consciousness of culture can sit quite comfortably with the students' experience of being both part of 'home' and domestic university life and part of 'abroad' – travelling between the two – not just during the year away but in leading up to it and in the period after it. Before they leave Britain, they are already stepping out beyond their own cultural zones. While they are away, they remain still part of the institutional life they have left behind (through emails, visits from tutors, trips home and so on) and when they return to their British university and while writing up their project, they are still in-between two worlds:

> If we rethink culture and its science, anthropology, in terms of travel, then the organic naturalizing bias of the term culture – seen as a rooted body that grows, lives, dies etc. – is questioned. Constructed and disputed historicities, sites of displacement, interference, and interaction, come more sharply into view. (Clifford, 1992:101)

So the student who spends a period of time resident abroad is a traveller, twice displaced and no longer rooted in one 'culture'. The ethnographic experience helps him or her to analyse and reflect on being 'in-between' and to think about the social, emotional and intellectual experience of being 'in transit'. As Clifford (Clifford, 1992:109) suggests: 'Everyone [is] more or less permanently in transit . . . Not so much "where are you from?" but "where are you between?"'.

These notions of being 'in-between', of having no fixed and unifying ethnic identity, are part of the new politics of cultural difference that Hall, Bhaba and Clifford, among others, have discussed. They are post-modern concepts used to critique the certainties of social order of the modern period. As I have suggested, in one way, they fit quite snugly with the experience of being and learning abroad. Students who undertake a participant observation project may increasingly feel that their 'English' or 'British' identity is being transformed, that they can pass themselves off as being someone else, that their sense of cultural and national identity (as British, Scottish etc.) is not quite so obviously at the centre of their view of the world as it used to be. This may begin the process of what post-modern thinkers see as the 'de-centring' of the subject – an uncoupling of the self from some solid, unproblematic stance from which everything is seen. This de-centring may also encourage a movement towards seeing the self as others see us, as the very act of becoming less of a stranger and more a member of a group creates awareness of who we are in relation to others.

However, in other ways the experience of being abroad may produce a hardening of the boundaries between self and other. Idealistic versions of the inhabitants of the new country may soon become eclipsed by negative experiences and a stronger sense of the rightness of one's own national and cultural identity. Indeed, there have been suggestions that the period of residence abroad creates more rather than less negative stereotypes. This is where the reflexive practices of ethnography can be called up, as I discuss later. Rather than knee-jerk reactions to difference in everyday practices, reflexivity propels the individual towards an awareness of the relationship between themselves and others and how each is constructed in and through social and discursive contact with the other.

The idea of travelling, in the many senses of the word suggested here, frames the whole ethnographic project as I have charted it. I will use Table 1 to structure the rest of this chapter, starting with the period before the residence abroad.

Before

In the ethnographic module that students take, usually but not necessarily, in the second year of their degree, they begin the process of learning to be a 'professional stranger' (Agar, 2000). Agar's term is a kind of oxymoron, reflecting the paradox in ethnography between just being an outsider – someone defined by their lack of knowledge and familiarity, and being a professional – someone defined by their knowledge and skills. The professional stranger is not part of the cultural group s/he is studying, although ethnography assumes that s/he will participate, in at least some measure, in that group's activities. Nor is s/he simply a stranger. The ethnographic method students have learnt gives them a new identity as people who can do 'being a stranger' in systematic and constructive ways. They are learning a new role through an introduction to a new form of consciousness.

Hymes (1980) says we are all born ethnographers but we lose the habit of being one. The role of any introduction to ethnography course is to recreate the habit. But whereas the young child learns only from participation and observation, the adult learner has to grasp the ethnographic approach intellectually and analytically. So, learning ethnographically means learning a new way of looking at the social world and this involves understanding the notion that reality is socially constructed (Berger & Luckmann, 1966). The real world does not exist out there as a set of objective facts. It is constructed by us as social beings in our everyday lives and language is the chief instrument for doing this.

The idea of socially constructed reality is one of the hardest concepts for students to grasp. Most of their education has been based on epistemological certainties. For example, the idea of the nation-state is a fact rather than a set of political constructs which history, the media and folk notions of a 'people' sustain through discourse. Similarly, the idea that gender differences or the 'family' are socially constructed is often seen as defying common sense. And even though these students are language specialists the role of language and discourse in this reality construction has rarely been considered by them.

The discursive turn in anthropology (and sociology) brings anthropologists and linguists closer together – it is to the voices of informants as much as to their other practices, that the ethnographically informed language learner now orientates. While undertaking the Introduction to Ethnography course, students do small tasks 'out in the field' which direct them to documenting the ways in which talk constructs roles, relationships and knowledge. For example, participant observation in a pub leads them to see the patterns of ordering at the bar and to what extent these patterns are gendered. The social constructivist and discourse lens through which students are encouraged to observe is part of the process of de-centring mentioned earlier. The natural, assumed stance that we see everything from one unified point of view – our point of view – begins to break down. We can see some of this learning in the following quotes taken from student evaluations:

> The course tackled fundamentally significant issues, helping us to question and re-examine taken for granted aspects of social life.

> An excuse to analyse things you talked about casually already and I found there was some depth behind nearly everything that is going on.

> it had never occurred to me before the project to look at things from other people's point of view. That's one thing I overcame through this ethnography project, not to use your own vision, your own terms to describe things as a first resort. It was a huge step not only to see and speak to people but communicate with them in their own terms which was an excellent thing and one of the long lasting effects.

Students began to orientate towards a more analytic stance, challenging what up to that point had seemed natural and normal and beginning to see that it was socially constructed. They learnt to combine conceptual understanding with a more explicit realisation of the affective side to intercultural learning evident in the following:

> I didn't know I could be so nosy with a proper reason! And when interviewing informants I really felt they enjoyed someone else being obsessed with the detail of their knowledge or thoughts . . . Sometimes now I find myself aware that I'm maintaining a conversation . . . whereas in the past, I'd just be bored!

The nature of the material and the frankness of the staff encouraged if not obliged the students to open up to themselves and to the rest of the group . . . a feeling that everyone wanted to be there, a feeling of group identity perhaps or at least a shared experience of intellectual gymnastics, not unlike bonding.

The students quoted here were reflecting on different aspects of the course. The first one was commenting on the data collection methods which were practised in the weekly assignments. Practising interviewing and observing interactions and then reflecting on these assignments in the class gave students a new analytic stance on the work that people do in circulating knowledge and maintaining social relations in everyday life. The second student quoted here focused on the class environment. He described some of the teaching and learning processes which were designed to bring an ethnographic dimension into the classroom. The openness and reflexivity which these processes aimed to produce involved students in being more explicit about their assumptions and attitudes. This, in turn, encouraged feelings to be openly discussed.

The hidden aspects of emotional life, together with imagination and fantasy, are often ignored in educational programmes. Despite the influence of psychoanalysis on popular culture and aspects of informal learning, it is rare to find courses in modern languages and intercultural learning or indeed, most humanities, which view the individual learner as anyone other than a rational knowing subject. The power of the unconscious, the assumption that subjectivity always intrudes and that emotions are always intertwined with the structures of human life are not ideas that sit comfortably in the modern languages curriculum or in most other parts of university education. Yet the experience of intercultural communication is an emotional one. For this reason, the introductory course attempts, albeit in small and often indirect ways, to raise to the surface some of the feelings about difference and otherness which students will experience while abroad.

As well as epistemological and subjective awareness, the practical skills of participant observation (PO) and ethnographic interviewing are central to the ethnographic method (Hammersley & Atkinson, 1983; Spradley, 1979, 1980). Students need to learn how to 'lurk and soak' (Werner & Schoepfle, 1987). As one student said about her PO:

Well I think the conclusions you come up with, you can't just come up with them if you have seen it once. So you need to be culturally aware, you have to spend a hell of a long time actually looking at it. And every time you look at a certain situation you observe different things and then they lead you on to other things.

But they also need to learn how to find out what sense informants make of their own lives, through ethnographic interviewing:

> I think the greatest thing was that I really did get to know the people I was writing about ... I think I got to know a lot more German people that way than I would have done doing another project – because you're more involved. I mean you have to speak and you have to listen. I mean it's not a matter of going to the library – you know get some books out and just sit in the library, you know you have to meet people and talk to people and that's what I liked about it really ... you get more enjoyment, more satisfaction yourself in doing it because you know it's your own work, you know you've done it yourself and you really do know what you're talking about ... I had to listen a lot because I couldn't record so I was really relying on my notes, which at the beginning I found quite difficult but later I sort of was able to take notes and if I wrote them up quickly afterwards I usually got most of the information.

This growing sense of responsibility for a project which students feel they own can also seep into other aspects of the intercultural experience. For example, students begin to take more responsibility for making any intercultural encounter work. Instead of concentrating only on whether they can produce a competent account for their listener, they begin to orientate towards the intersubjectivity of the encounter. Data collection requires so much interacting with individuals and groups that the embarrassment and awkwardness of doing foreign language talk is replaced by conversational involvement.

During

While abroad, students can make both conscious and unconscious choices about the extent of their participation and hence the extent of their learning. In one way, participation is learning. Just being there in the new environment is a kind of learning. But with ethnographic preparation, students are not simply strangers, as we have said, they can participate and learn in much more conscious and systematic ways. For them, learning is participation in Lave and Wenger's (1991) sense of situated learning. Learning in this sense is a continual shifting from legitimate peripheral participation to full participation in a community of practice. The student ethnographer may not negotiate full participation but as they become more familiar with the practices of a particular group so they move beyond the periphery. Toni, a British student in Seville who was herself a catholic, found herself participating in Sevillano catholic practices and comparing them with her own experiences:

Toni's project in Seville

Decidí que quizás existiera una fuerte conexión entre la religión y la comida después de una conversación con Maribel en la cual me explicó varios aspectos de las fiestas religiosas en las que participa la familia y mencionó varias veces la comida. Me comentó por ejemplo que una parte integral de la peregrinación al Rocío es la comida y el hecho de que todos beben y comen juntos. Dijo que'en Sevilla lo celebramos todo con las copas y la comida, cualquier acto social, desde las bodas, los bautizos, ir a misa el domingo, después lo normal es tomarse una cerveza, reunirse, hablar, contarse cosas'. Pero curiosamente, y lo que me llevó a escribir esta sección del proyecto, cuando quise indagar más en esta cuestión, ella insistió en que 'no había ninguna relación entre la comida y la religión en sí: eso no tiene que ver con la Iglesia, ni con la religión ni con nada'.

[*Translation.* I decided that there could be a strong link between religious practices and eating following a conversation with Maribel when she explained how her family participates in religious celebrations and mentioned food several times in this context. She explained that an integral part of the pilgrimage to Rocio is the food and the fact that everybody eats and drinks together. She said several times that 'in Seville we celebrate everything with food, any social event, from weddings and christenings, to going to mass on Sundays, you normally go for a beer afterwards, to meet friends, chat etc.'. But what led me to this section of the project was her insistence that there was no relation whatsoever between religion and eating: 'it has nothing to do with the Church, or religion or anything]. (Roberts *et al.*, 2001: 19–20)

As a catholic herself and working as an au pair, looking after a five-year-old, she participated in the family's religious and eating practices. As such, she undertook the kind of ethnographic study which Agar (2000) would call a 'new' ethnography. He contrasts new ethnographies, which focus more on participation and on bringing the self into the process of learning, and 'old' ones. In the old ethnography, the ethnographer stood outside the group, participated to get access but then observed and looked for patterns. The new ethnographies are also more sensitive to the complexities and contradictions which do not fit into neat patterns. For the novice ethnographer, this focus on the relationship between self and other and this acknowledgement of the untidy and contradictory is something of a relief. They are not professional ethnographers nor are they attempting a polished account. Rather they are using the ethnographic process to develop a reflexive intercultural understanding which may be transferable to many different settings in the future. The habit of reflexivity is apparent in these student quotes:

When you are doing ethnography it's you and the place it's you and the people. You can't not write yourself into it. You are part of it.

And you've already had an upbringing somewhere else that's played a part in creating the person that you are, you can't lose that, there's nobody who's a neutral person. So, I suppose that's one thing that really did become apparent you know, you felt that they let you into their group or they let you become involved but only up to a point.

The habit of reflexivity is also part of the post-modern thinking which includes de-centring and constuctivism. Reflexivity involves a critical reflection on the social processes and practices in which we are involved. The old confidence in reason and progress and in the natural order of things is in a continuous process of revision in what Giddens (1990) calls the 'super-reflexivity' of our age. Part of the process of learning to do ethnography is to learn about and how to use reflexivity, which, paradoxically, relies on reason! Students are encouraged to reflect on the processes of data collection and analysis in order to see that they themselves are part of the social world that they are writing about. As the student in the example says 'You can't not write yourself into it'; and this reflexivity can have a wider influence on the experience of intercultural education. Just as the ethnographic researcher has to see her/himself as helping to construct the reality of the 'other' so they also can begin to see how they themselves are constructed in and through interaction with others.

Another central theme of ethnography is the idea that a study should be holistic: whatever you study, however the small the unit of analysis (Erickson, 1977: 59), you should study it as completely as possible:

[An ethnography can still be holistic] . . . not because of the size of the social unit but because the units of analysis are considered analytically as wholes, whether the whole be a community, a school system . . . or the beginning of one lesson in a school classroom.

Whatever size unit is chosen, the ethnographer's job is to understand it from every angle. Often, the best course of action is to focus right down on something small and examine it in detail. This 'smallness and slowness' (Silverman, 1999) can reveal just as much as and perhaps more than a superficial study of a large theme. For example, one student studied a network of four people who were all from Seville in order to investigate the notion of Sevillano identity. Another focused on the life in one kitchen area in a student hostel in Marburg University.

As well as trying to do a holistic study, the experience itself can be called holistic. It involves the whole social being struggling to make sense of him or herself as she or he tries to make sense of others. Participant observation and ethnographic interviewing are not simply matters of accumulating data but are also personal encounters which can disturb taken for granted assumptions:

> You learn a lot through experiences in life and this ethnography is a very big experience for me anyway. And it's good because you don't just take things cut and dried, you start looking at a situation. But then when you look at a situation you might not like the conclusion that you come out with. You know they might be negative conclusions. And then you think 'O God' and then you start asking questions about yourself, questions about people that you know.

Just as students are taught to see reality as socially constructed, as they gather data for their project and start the process of analysis, they become increasingly aware of their culturally constructed selves:

> the study of consciousness becomes central because people always act (however imperfectly) relative to their desires, plans, whims, strategies, moods, goals, fantasies, intentions, impulses, purposes, visions, or gut feelings. No analysis of human action is complete unless it attends to people's own notions of what they are doing. Even when they appear most subjective, thought and feeling are always culturally shaped and influenced by one's biography, social situation and historical context. (Rosaldo, 1989: 129)

Involving the ethnographer's own cultural self in the process of analysis is part of the 'new' ethnography which Agar (2000) also describes as 'narrative' ethnography as opposed to the older style more objective 'encyclopaedic' ethnography. One way that student ethnographers can come to an understanding of themselves as cultural beings is through narrative. Initially, as they start the process of ethnographic interviewing, they hear the personal narratives of their informants. As the stories are told, people present themselves as having particular identities. As Georgakopoulou (1997: 13) says, narrative is the point of entry into the presentation of 'self':

> this involves the construction of personal and sociocultural identities, such as gender ... age ... and peer group membership. In particular the personal narratives or life histories lend themselves to such an enquiry, as the prime discourse mode for identity constructions.

For example, Sophie studied some aspects of the Carnival in Nice with her key informant, Annie Sidero, whose narratives about organising carnivals provided a way into understanding her own identity as a forceful and successful woman excluded from being a 'carnavalière' because of her gender. Such narratives provide material which offer a contrast to the novice analyst's own narratives and own experiences of inclusion and exclusion: How did Annie's experiences compare with similar situations in England? How did they compare with Sophie's own experiences of inclusion and/or exclusion?

After

The 'before' and 'during' phases of the period abroad, I have suggested, focus on issues of identity concerning the 'self' and the 'other' and on ways of learning. Once the students have returned to the home institution, a period of intense reflection and writing begins. This does not mean that issues of identity, learning and participation are no longer important – far from it. But in this phase, students have to commit themselves to *knowing* something of the group they have studied. The whole ethnographic process has warned them against generalisations and stereotyping of societies and groups and yet they have to draw together the complexities and differences into some kind of coherent whole to represent the experience they have been through.

There is now an extensive anthropological literature on writing and representing 'the other' (Clifford, 1988; Clifford & Marcus, 1986; Hallam & Street, 2000). Ways of knowing about a particular group are always connected with ways of writing about them. As soon as the student ethnographer starts to write they are faced with difficult decisions: What evidence do I have for making this claim? How far can I make a general statement based on what only a few people have said to me? Was I told these things only because I'm a 'stranger' and if so what value do they have? These questions are not easily answered. But they can be partially answered if students are encouraged to see their writing in less traditional ways. Ethnographic writing is not a set of facts but is something constructed, made by them. Their ethnographies are rather what Clifford and Marcus (1986: 6) call 'true fictions'. The writer has included some things and excluded others and this has been based as much on who they are as who their informants were:

> Ethnographic writing can properly be called fictions in the sense of 'something made or fashioned', the principal burden of the word's Latin root *fingere*.

So their writing, just like their data collection and analysis, is a social construction of reality in which both the 'other' and the writing self are social and cultural beings. In representing the other, they are also representing the self:

> Representing 'otherness' is about complex processes and channels through which representations flow in different directions: the representation of 'other' is integrally related to the representation of 'self'. (Hallam & Street, 2000: 6)

One element of writing the ethnographic project is, therefore, a reflexive one. The aim is for the reflexivity developed before and during the period abroad to be extended to this crucial phase of writing. Students are expected to write explicitly about themselves as their own research instrument (Hammersley & Atkinson, 1983). This includes being reflexive about how their data and analysis are produced and interpreted through their own consciousness which itself is a product of their social and cultural history. They are also expected to be reflexive about their own writing, acknowledging both the issues of claims and evidence and the choices they make in the rhetoric of their project.

The problem of generalisations is one that students frequently voice. Ethnographic projects are geared to the small, the local and the detailed. Often, only a few people have been informants, and events and activities observed may have been one-off occurrences. Students may have worked out certain patterns but are also aware of discrepancies and complexities which do not easily fall into patterned behaviour. Here, Mitchell's (1984: 239) argument for 'telling' rather than 'typical' cases is important:

> the search for a 'typical' case for analytic exposition is likely to be less fruitful than the search for a 'telling' case in which the particular circumstances surrounding a case serve to make previously obscure theoretical relationships suddenly apparent.

With small-scale ethnography, it is fruitless to write about typical activities or behaviour. But the smallness of the project allows even the novice ethnographer to research in some depth and to find richness in the small detail of everyday life. A 'holistic' ethnographic project should describe not only the narratives and activities of a group but the circumstances and conditions under which these were produced. So an ethnography can draw out concepts from a particular set of circumstances and can argue that if similar circumstances were to prevail, then similar behaviours and narratives might occur. For example, the discourses of exclusion that prevent Annie Sidero from becoming a 'carnavalière' in Nice are the result of a particular social and historical moment. They told Sophie something about gender relations at that time and place and might tell of similar gender relations elsewhere if similar conditions were to prevail.

This particular example raises one final set of issues: issues of power and politics. Annie's absence from the carnavaliers is not simply a fact of Niçois cultural life. It is the product of power relations. As Clifford (1988:14) says:

> Cultural difference is no longer a stable, exotic 'otherness'; self-other relations are matters of power and rhetoric rather than of essence.

It is not natural for women to be excluded, although the male carnavaliers may see it as such. It is part of the gender politics of that particular community, based on assumptions about male power derived over centuries. So the student ethnographer in the 21st century has to reflect on culture and their own cultural learning within the context of relations of power:

> Ethnography always deals with context and meaning . . . But the last fifteen years have taught us to ask another question – what systems of power hold those contexts and meanings in place? . . . You look at local context and meaning just like we always have, but then you ask *why* are things this way? What power, what interests wrap this local world so tight that it feels like the natural order of things to its inhabitants? (Agar, 2000: 26)

Conclusion

In this chapter I have drawn both on recent theories in anthropology and on studies of ethnographic method to consider the processes of change that students might go through if they take on an ethnographic perspective for and in a period of residence abroad. 'Intercultural learning' is a commonplace of language learning discourse these days. It means many different things to different people. I have deliberately tried to contrast what it might mean to the language learner as ethnographer with widespread assumptions about intercultural learning as acquisition of cultural knowledge from texts. In doing so, I have focused on the integration of conceptual, analytical and personal development which 'living an ethnographic life' can offer.

Although, this case study has concerned students who are specialist language learners, there is nothing in the process described which is not also relevant to any student, whatever their discipline, who goes abroad for a period as part of their course. Most of them will be expected to communicate in a foreign language and all of them will be living in a new cultural environment. To this extent they are like the traditional anthropologists who went out to some distant village not because they were language learners but because they wanted to research a cultural and social world very different from their own. Whether these students have to operate in a foreign language or in English as a *lingua franca*, the ethnographic experience provides an intellectual framework, a set of methods and a new orientation to learning from the everyday things of life which should enhance their period of residence abroad and develop a new consciousness for their future work and learning.

Notes

1. The idea of *learning ethnographically* developed out of an ESRC project directed by Mike Byram and Celia Roberts at Thames Valley University in Ealing. Details of this and subsequent developments have been written up as part of the LARA (Language and Residence Abroad) project at Oxford Brookes by Shirley Jordan and Celia Roberts.

References

Agar, M, (2000) *The Professional Stranger: An Informal Introduction to Ethnography*. (2nd edn). London: Academic Press.

Berger, P. and Luckmann, T. (1966) *The Social Construction of Reality*. Harmondsworth: Penguin.

Clifford, J. (1988) *The Predicament of Culture: Twentieth Century Ethnography, Literature and Art*. Cambridge, MA: Harvard University Press.

Clifford, J. (1992) Traveling cultures. In L. Grossberg, C. Nelson and P. Treichler (eds) *Cultural Studies* (pp. 96–112). New York: Routledge.

Clifford, J. and Marcus, G. (eds) (1986) *Writing Culture: The Poetics and Politics of Ethnography*. Berkeley, CA: University of California Press.

Egan-Robertson, A. and Bloome, D. (eds) (1998) *Students as Researchers of Culture and Language in Their Own Communities*. New Jersey: Hampton Press.

Erickson, F. (1977) Some approaches to inquiry in school/community ethnography. *Anthropology and Education Quarterly* 8(3), 58–69.

Georgakopoulou, A. (1997) Narrative. In J. Verschueren, J. Östman, J. Blommaert and C. Bulcaen (eds) *Handbook of Pragmatics* (pp. 1–19). Amsterdam: John Benjamins.

Giddens, A. (1990) *The Consequences of Modernity*. Cambridge: Polity Press

Hallam, E. and Street, B. (2000) Introduction: Cultural encounters – representing 'otherness'. In E. Hallam and B. Street (eds) *Cultural Encounters* (pp.1–12). London: Routledge.

Hammersley, M. and Atkinson, P. (1983) *Ethnography: Principles in Practice*. London: Tavistock.

Heath, S.B. (1983) *Ways with Words*. Cambridge: Cambridge University Press.

Heller, M. (1994) *Crosswords: Language Education and Ethnicity in French Ontario*. Berlin: Mouton de Gruyter.

Hymes, D. (1980) *Language in Education: Ethnolinguistic Essays*. Washington: Centre for Applied Linguistics.

Jordan, S. and Roberts, C. (2000) *Introduction to Ethnography*. (Language and Residence Abroad (LARA) Project). Oxford: Oxford Brookes University.

Lave, J. and Wenger, E. (1991) *Situated Learning: Legitimate Peripheral Participation*. Cambridge: Cambridge University Press.

Mitchell, C. (1984) Case studies. In R. Ellen (ed.) *Ethnographic Research: A Guide to General Conduct* (pp. 237–39). London: Academic Press.

Roberts, C., Byram, M., Barro, A., Jordan, S. and Street, B. (2001) *Language Learners as Ethnographers*. Clevedon: Multilingual Matters.

Rosaldo, R. (1989) *Culture and Truth: The Remaking of Social Analysis*. Routledge: London.

Silverman, D. (1999) Warriors or collaborators: Reworking methodological controversies in the study of institutional interaction. In S. Sarangi and C. Roberts (eds) *Talk, Work and Institutional Order* (pp. 401–26). Berlin: Mouton.

Spradley, J. (1979) *The Ethnographic Interview*. New York: Holt, Rinehart and
    Winston.
Spradley, J. (1980) *Participant Observation*. New York: Holt, Rinehart and Winston.
Werner, O. and Schoepfle, G. (1987) *Systematic Fieldwork: Vols 1 and 2*. Thousand
    Oaks, CA: Sage.

Chapter 9

Searching for the Intercultural Person

PHYLLIS M. RYAN

In Turkish the phrase *örümcek beyin* characterises the closed-minded person. It stereotypes this person as someone who has a 'spider web' covering his or her brain inhibiting interaction with others. The metaphor can also mean someone who is controlled by this invisible web, often unable to break away from it. Carlos Fuentes (1990: 13), in referring to group cultures, discusses the frailty of cultures that are closed to outside influences, aiming to protect themselves and maintain their 'pure' state. In an interview in a Mexican newspaper, he commented that

> *Una cultura que se quiere 'pura', y cierre sus fronteras a la invasión de otras culturas, es una cultura destinada a perecer. No se encuentra a si misma, no se encuentra su identidad sino en el contacto con el otro. No somos lo que somos sino el conocimiento de lo que no somos.*
>
> [*Translated by author*: A culture that wants to be 'pure' and closes its borders to the invasion of other cultures is a culture destined to die. It doesn't find itself, it doesn't find its identity except in contact with the other. We are not that which we are without the knowledge of what we are not.]

The search for understanding of what we are, as well as what we are not, takes us through paths of experience involving languages being learned, cultural identities being formed, the range of attitudes we hold toward contact with other cultures, and our receptiveness to engaging with 'otherness'. Curiosity about people and open-mindedness toward cultural differences lead the way to being receptive to intercultural experiences and gradually becoming intercultural. We can reflect on the role experiences play in someone's life in becoming intercultural as we read autobiographies, memoirs, biographies, life histories, oral histories, ethnographic interviews (Creswell, 1998; Josselson & Lieblich, 1993), all of which are rich in narrative detail, thick description and reflection. Here are the stories of individuals, some of whom have been prompted to write after learning that they have life-threatening diseases (Said, 1999), some who want to talk about their lives in diverse cultural settings and the multiple language contacts they have had during periods of historical events (Hoffman, 1989). They have experienced directly living in different social settings when political and historical changes affected their lives and the lives of those they were around (also note Kristeva, 1997; Todorov, 1989).

When we accept that learning a foreign language lies partly in the domain of language and culture and their interplay, we find people learning foreign languages involved in a process that may lead through new linguistic and cultural contacts to increased curiosity about intercultural topics, ultimately challenging *örümcek beyin*. How can we describe this person who is intercultural? In what way are personal experiences involved in becoming intercultural? The concept of intercultural is complex and raises deep issues related to types of experiences, direct contact between groups of people, openness to learning about others, attitudes, purpose, interests and needs for learning a foreign language. Let us begin by considering the foreign language learner and the intercultural speaker.

Introduction to the Foreign Language Learner and Interculturality

The term intercultural is used to refer to those whose life experiences have brought them into contact with people of cultures other than their own. It implies that the person has lived in more than one country for short or long periods of time during his/her life. It does not specify why these experiences took place, that is whether they were prompted by work, tourism, political asylum, economic advancement or adventure. However, residence in another country does not automatically produce interculturality.

In foreign language learning settings, the person who is involved in the process of acquiring an intercultural perspective is drawn into contact with the interactive nature of language and culture, often going beyond structuralist views of learning connected with the mastery of grammatical rules and linguistic conventions and the restrictive goals of instrumental learning. The learner is called upon to rely on existing knowledge of the cultures of speakers of the language s/he is learning to unravel meaning of language and to discover inner resources that lead to refining as well as extending one's knowledge. In the context of student study abroad, where the learner is challenged by the newness of phenomena, Byram (1997: 37) writes that 'the skill of discovery as an ability calls for recognizing significant phenomena in a foreign environment and eliciting their meanings and connotations and their relationship to other phenomena'. In this new context the existing knowledge of the person is called upon when one is involved with documents in the classroom setting or with social interactions with speakers of the language being studied:

It is through social interaction that the individual draws on existing knowledge, has attitudes which sustain sensitivity to others, and operates skills of discourse and interpretation while managing dysfunctions that arise in interaction with others. They may be called upon to act as a mediator betwccn people of different origins and identities. It is this function of establishing relationships, managing dysfunctions and mediating that distinguishes an 'intercultural speaker' from other speakers and makes him/her different from a native speaker. (Byram, 1997: 37).

Attention has been drawn to developing goals for intercultural communicative competence of learners in contact with learners of other countries and interacting with foreign cultural phenomena (Byram, 1997; Byram & Zarate, 1997; Buttjes & Byram, 1991; Kramsch, 1998). Byram (1997) outlines goals for assessing intercultural communicative competence of the foreign language learner in the areas of attitudes, knowledge, skills and education. This model, written for teachers and participants in curriculum development, describes features that leads one to becoming an intercultural speaker. For example, curiosity about people and open-mindedness toward cultural differences and engagement with otherness are essential to reaching this intercultural state. Therefore, when students' strong negative attitudes toward certain cultures challenge being open-minded toward other cultures, this affective factor may initially prevent the learner from desiring to gain knowledge about certain cultural groups and in interacting with them (see the later discussion of negative attitudes in the section on Guadalupe).

The four areas in Byram's model are deeply involved in the narrative of the two women in this article, Mary and Guadalupe. Their narratives provide perspectives on interculturality, including their vision of the intercultural person, how interculturality functions, as well as its limits, and allow us to outline possible conclusions that will speak to whether interculturality is too ambitious a concept for foreign language learners and to whether it can be appropriately applied to such learners and their language goals.

These two women were selected on the basis of the contact they have had with other cultures as they learned or acquired languages. They live in Mexico and speak a variety of foreign languages. The first woman, Mary, has had experiences with multiple languages, various direct contacts with cultural groups in Eastern Europe and the Middle East as well as Americans and Latin Americans. Her life began in Russia and was affected by events of the Second World War in the European setting. Eventually she emigrated to the United States and ultimately to Mexico. She speaks fluent Russian, Turkish, German, English and Spanish. I would like to propose her for consideration as an intercultural speaker. She was interviewed as a person with a command of languages and strong beliefs about the effect of interculturality on a person. The other woman, Guadalupe, is an advanced student of English as a foreign language in an urban university in Mexico. Her major is political science but at the same time she is interested in learning French, Russian, Arabic and English at her university's centre for foreign language study. She has not had any experience living in or visiting countries outside of Mexico, her country of origin; she too is an intercultural person.

Both women represent distinct differences in age, nationality, type of culture contact, purpose for learning a foreign language and linguistic and cultural interests. Their perceptions of what interculturality means vary as they touch upon the areas involved in how a person develops an intercultural persona, including its essential features.

The purpose of the article is to allow Mary and Guadalupe to tell their own stories, allowing us to participate in the thinking of two people who might be described as being intercultural. Their narratives show us that a more formal ethnographic study of participants with varying degrees of interculturality would provide a wealth of data about the inner thoughts of the intercultural person as well as those who may be described as being on the way to becoming intercultural and those who, for various reasons, are not, or have no wish to be, intercultural. This article will discuss the two women and their perceptions of what it means to be intercultural, of interculturality as a state and of processes involved in becoming intercultural.

Mary

Let us start with the perceptions of the woman whose early life was shaped by the historical contexts of various countries at the time of the Second World War. Her adult years included professional work, marriage and children. She defines interculturality as follows:

> a person that lived, studied or worked in certain countries and learned the language. After living in a country you start to think, act and understand better these people and how they think, so that when you go back to that country after many years you still feel like you are right there at home . . . like the other cultures you learned after that, when you lived in other countries, don't exist. They go away from you. You start to act and think again the way of people in that country do.

Was she giving up her culture base to do that? She answered, 'Absolutely not!'

> I think your origin stays the way it is. It is just that you become part of that society. You become accepted and in a way you start to think the way they think there. For example, when I am in Russia, when I hear people talking about their problems, about their lives, it feels like I understand them very well. Like I never lived in the United States. I just drifted away from that way of living in the United States. The tempo of the life and thinking . . . I just go back to Russia again. I kind of become a part of them. I understand them very well. I don't try to rationalize that they are doing this wrong, that they are thinking wrong because in other countries it is considered a different way of thinking. I don't mix it up at all.

Her examples about understanding a 'different of way of thinking' start with Russia. Although she was born there and lived there until she was 10 years old, she is a Crimean Tartar and Turkish is her mother tongue. Russian was her school language. She explained how her family lived as a minority group:

> I think that certain minorities in many countries survived only through their families that kept a tight hold on their traditions that they practised at home. Their children carry on these traditions. So usually this type of minorities survived stronger, they kept on their traditions stronger, than maybe for example the old country. From my experience when I went to Turkey I found myself much stronger traditionally than Turkish people.

Her life is filled with events of a Turgenev nature in each cultural setting that need to be maintained separately and not compared. An example she pointed out a way of buying food in Russia that stands out as an illustration of this difference:

> When they tell me they have to leave their work and they have to go to run to stand in a line to get a certain product to me it seems to be normal. Because if you think in the American way, to leave your work and run and stand in a line to buy yourself meat would be absolutely unheard of. But in Russia that is very normal to do. In fact, you will go and ask your friends if anybody wants meat too. And then you buy meat for the two or three people that work in your office. And they would do the same way for you. If they have to run and buy some bread, they would ask you, 'Do you need bread? I am running to get some bread.' In the meantime, your friends will cover up your work and they will do your

work in the office while you are standing in line. The boss will know but he will close his eyes, because when it is necessary for him to go and buy something he will do the same and you will cover it up for the boss.

I feel that I understand them very well when they do this. For example, if you take an American person, for him it would be absolutely unheard to leave his job and do this kind of thing, and have everyone in the office cover up for him.

Why do I find it [this Russian way] so normal? Why do I go back straight into this type of life? I think understanding the problems of the country and living with the people many times becomes a part of your nature and it looks to you absolutely normal. Now, when you go to another country and you start to live another type of life in another country you put this behind you; you have to put it behind you otherwise you would be very unhappy. You should never compare, just accept.

She stressed the importance of adjusting to a new country:

What is done normally and accepted in one country definitely is not accepted in another country. If you start to say, 'Over there it is done like this', you will not be able to live there. Because it will be awfully hard to fight it. You should just learn the way these people live.

I think that living in a foreign environment, as for example we did as a minority living in Russia, made us naturally have to survive. For this reason, the parents had to be stricter with each of their children, teaching them at home traditions, language, religion, customs, values ... the way of living in the house. That is the way I felt in Turkey. We were much more aware of these things than Turkish people that lived in Turkey.

Her opinion was that an intercultural person has to have lived for a period of time in different countries, while at the same time this person needs to be open-minded toward other countries and have curiosity about people there:

Of course, there is a way of learning a language that people have to learn in school. They learn a foreign language but that is because they need it for work or school. In that way you learn only the grammar and vocabulary of the language unless a person is very open-minded and wants to learn all about the history and the character of the people of the language they are learning. It is kind of hard. Many people that learn Japanese never have a chance to go to Japan and see how they live. They have to then be very, very open-minded to learn and very hard-working people to learn their literature, their way of living, to try to picture what is their character, what makes them tick.

I asked her what she meant by 'character'. She explained that it is what you are born with as well as the way you are brought up. There are many ways to understand the character of people of different cultures. One way she points out is through reading the literature of a country:

> Well, I know many people who did read Russian literature, for example, and they did know very much about Russian character that is kind of sentimental, romantic, kind of pessimistic type of personality that sometimes you meet in Tolstoy's books and Turgenev's. So it is really an old Russia type of character.
>
> So how would you learn a Japanese person's character? You might get an idea reading the books about the way they live, what they think, what their values are. I really don't know if you can really get the feeling of it if you don't live there or if you don't visit. Do you?

Stages of life

Mary recounted many of her life experiences concluding that they fell into five stages or chapters:

> Definitely, I think I became a more interesting person. When I was young, I lived in only one or two countries. All this living in different countries moulded me to what I am now. If I had stayed in the same country I would have been completely different.

I asked more precisely about these stages she found her life falling into. She said:

> Well, I take culture from each country. I think of where I was born, Russia. I have a very fond, very romanticized memories. A warm feeling of constantly helping each other to survive. I remember living in a village sitting by the candle light reading books and no other entertainment. It left me with this warm feeling . . . all children were sitting around the table and reading our books in one room with a stove that was burning, warm, and no radio, no televison. It left me with the warm feeling. The feeling of the closeness of the family, of sharing, of loving.

'Discipline' characterized her second stage:

> And then of course after the war started, trying to survive, also sharing the bread with your mother or your brother. Then, moving to Germany. It taught me that working hard was a type of discipline. That you had to put away other feelings, you had to finish your work, you

had to be on time all the time. You had to do things in a certain way. So it was a disciplined type of life. Although in Germany you had the feeling of warmth, like music, getting together, enjoying little things . . . picnicking with just boiled potato and a piece of bread was the best memories I had . . . somewhere in the mountains. Germany gave me the feeling of discipline which I don't think I had much of in Russia. I was there until I was 15, so it was a time when you couldn't do anything until you did your homework.

Her the third stage might be called 'sybaritic', a love of enjoyment, enjoying things, liking to be pampered:

Then I went to Turkey, the middle east, and what I learned in Turkey was the beauty of the people's expressions. The love of beautiful things, enjoying things. You could go to the Bosporus, sit there for hours seeing the water run. You would have a cup of coffee. In Turkish there is one word. It is '*kaif*'. *Kaif* means to enjoy something thoroughly. Now that is something I can't really describe or translate because you can sit and have coffee and look out of the window and having the feeling of enjoying the cup of coffee so thoroughly . . . having the feeling of *kaif*.

During her fourth stage, her professional or productive years, she lived in the United States. She calls this her 'working or productive' stage:

So then I went to the United States. It was a place of discipline, hard work, good friendship . . . you also enjoyed your life. Your hard work earned money you could spend well. You were able to get things you wanted. I think the US is very productive, that you are doing something. You feel that you are fulfilled. The US culture is something that gives a person something of fulfillment. Maybe also it was my age that I already understood and appreciated many things. Maybe I had to go through all those stages of my life to get to this, to enjoy it to appreciate it. The US was a country where I appreciated everything. The other cultures prepared me for it.

The past 30 years in Mexico she calls her fifth stage or that of 'reflection':

I think that in Mexico I ripped off all the wonderful things I learned everywhere else and I finally started to enjoy my life. I definitely did. Here I was not working. I could do things I wanted to do. I was at home I was raising my child, talking about my past. It was becoming more reflective, sorting through all this. Actually having time for myself. I think here finally I had time to think. Before I never had time to think. You have responsibilities.

Mary added one additional comment about her reflections. She asked if I had seen the sun series of paintings by Diego Rivero at a museum in Xochimilco (a section in the south of Mexico City). I said no. The tones, ranging from yellow to dark amber, in the series capture the stages that she is describing here.

Through Mary's account we find her relating her concept of interculturality to specific times and events when she lived in different countries. She closely ties understanding a culture to understanding the character of the people of the culture. Her beliefs about interculturality are so closely tied to her life experiences that she basically finds it impossible for foreign language students to reach these goals except, of course, at a superficial level. Her concept of culture places is as separate from her concept of learning a foreign language.

Language learning

During these five stages of her life, Mary learned each new language she came into contact with by relating it to the one she already knew and devising her own way to remember new words. Russian was her first foreign language, followed by German. In Germany the children in her family were not permitted to attend school as they were considered '*Ausländer*' or foreigners. Even so, she learned to speak German while playing with the German children. One method she used for remembering new words was through word association, comparing the sounds of similar words, phrases and sentences. Her system enabled her to acquire German very quickly and speak it fluently to the extent that later when she was able to go to school after the war, one of her German teachers commented: 'You must be a German child. Don't be afraid to tell me if your father was in the SS or something that you are hiding. Don't be afraid to tell me.' Mary said that he was convinced that she was hiding this information and could not believe that she came from another country and was not German. She explained that the fact that she loved to read may have helped her with the language.

When Mary entered nursing school in Turkey she was 18 years old. Her classes were in English with a translator provided. The technique she now used for learning a language developed more fully into 'word association'. It was much easier now to associate words in English with words in German: 'It was unbelievable how fast I went from knowing German to speaking English. It was like a wave. I just went into it.'. Basically, however, she spoke German in Turkey:

> Turkey was very Germanic from being an ally during the First World War. Turkey always had this admiration for German militarism since Turks are very militaristic themselves. They had lots of German high schools, admired many things and copied many of their characteristics

such as being punctual and hard working. In the intelligensia you could find many people that spoke very perfect German. Since my cousin was in medical school and I always went to their parties, you could find people who spoke constantly German. When they saw that we were not so well in Turkish, they were willing to talk to us . . . our dialect was very different . . . in German not in Turkish. At home we talked all the time in German, not with our mothers however. Although German represented the war for us, we still had a soft spot for Germany. I cried my heart out when we left Germany . . . we didn't have anything to eat and we were going to Turkey which had everything. We missed very much Germany.

Mary had less schooling than she wished, especially with respect to studying literature in her classes. She said:

I didn't speak Turkish very well. It was a dialect that I was speaking, so when I went to school I mostly had to concentrate on mathematics and science. I was very much behind because of the literature. They said to me that you have to read lots of books at home. We can't give you all the literature that you missed all these years so you have to read up yourself at home, concentrating on literature at home and mathematics in school.

She explained further:

In Turkey they had two types of literature which were taught. One was the folk literature and the other was the divan literature which means high class, aristocratic literature used in the courts of the Sultans. The folk literature was of the people who live in the country written in plain Turkish language. This was much nearer to our dialect of Central Asia. They had words that we used in the Crimea, so that it must have come from Central Asia. Then, there was the divan which was full of words of Arabic and Persian which, of course, I didn't know.

She did not like it that the Turkish language was quickly losing Arabic and Persian words. She said, 'I hated it. They threw out all those beautiful Arabic words. They were simplifying the language to such as degree.' What she was referring to was the linguistic changes that took place during the time of Ataturk, the 1920s when the language was simplified by removing the Arabic and Persian words, replacing them with words from the Anatolic language originating in the languages of Central Asia (see the discussion of Turkish in Comrie, 1992).

Mary found it hard in her courses to orient herself toward both divan and folk literature: ('I found some of my notebooks. They have some of the most beautiful poems written in divan.' The divan literature, or 'classical literature', she talks about refers to the remains of the literary activity of the Ottoman period during the 16th century when the Ottoman State experienced a golden age. The proportion of Arabic and Persian words and forms increased in the 14th and 15th centuries when Istanbul became the centre for nurturing great masters of literature and turning Turkish into the Ottoman language with many foreign elements. During the same period literary works were created by the less educated in their own Anatolian Turkish which was influenced very little by Arabic and Persian. The folk literature remained deeply rooted in the Central Asian traditions. Divan literature addressed the court and the higher classes with its complicated and flowery language and the folk literature told about the feelings and thoughts of the people (see University of California at Los Angeles Materials Turkish Language Profile, 2001). The folk literature variety of Anatolian is very similar to standard Turkish today (Comrie, 1992).

Mary's adjusting to the US involved learning a new language as well as the history and literature of the US. She wanted to be certified as a nurse, but was unable to get transcripts of her high school years in Germany during the war. Since it was impossible to get transcripts of these years, she had to take an equivalence exam to qualify for a high school diploma that would enable her to become registered as a nurse. She recalled:

> I remember I went to Detroit and it was a two day exam. It was like a nightmare. I had to write an essay on Shakespeare. So when I walked out from there – it was a rainy, slushy day there in downtown Detroit – I thought then to myself I better commit suicide. It was the only time in my life I wanted to commit suicide. I will throw myself under this car coming because I will never make this and I will never be able to work in the United States. I had a baby to take care of and my mother. Anyway, they said in three days you come back to get your results. I went home and slept 24 hours. When I returned they said, 'You passed'. I said, 'Are you sure? Will you check it again?' They said, 'Yeah, you passed!'

During her years in the United States she worked by herself to develop strategies for improving her English. One exception was when she was working as a nurse in a large hospital in Santa Barbara, California. She took a course in contemporary literature to increase her knowledge of the language and literature. In short, if asked how she would summarise her method of learning a language, she would say that she is a self-made and self-educated woman.

Guadalupe

Guadalupe presents an entirely different perspective on interculturality. Unlike Mary she depended on her institutional foreign language learning experiences as she relates to her concept of interculturality. To understand her perspective on interculturality calls for a pause in this discussion first to look at the role of English as a foreign language in Mexico and second to consider strong negative attitudes toward studying English.

First of all, English stands out in the national setting of Mexico as an international *lingua franca* used by Mexican speakers of different language backgrounds (both Spanish and indigenous). In professional, academic and social contexts, both urban and rural, there is a tendency for Mexicans to find the forces due to the globalisation of English intrusive, penetrating their daily lives, a problem that is not unique to Mexico. Kachru and Nelson (1996), as well as Charaudeau *et al.* (1992), recognise this danger (especially in Third World countries) and tie it to forces of power and dominance. Contrasts appear in this *lingua franca* setting between the pedagogical positions taken in foreign language learning, whether instrumental or cultural or a combination of both. (See research findings that report on the impact of English as a foreign language on Mexican students: Chasan & Ryan, 1995; Gómez de Mas & Ryan, 1999; Ryan, 1994; 1998; Ryan *et al.* 1999.)

Interest obviously creates a strong force toward rapid acquisition of a foreign language if other factors are positive, but pressure of the sort that a *lingua franca* creates can take away the free selection of the language one wants to study, creating an impression for some that it is being imposed by outside sources (Gómez de Mas & Ryan, 1999). From the standpoint of foreign language teachers of English in large urban universities in Mexico, a large number of students want to learn English without learning about cultural aspects attached to the language (Ryan, 1994). English is seen by some students as a vehicle for political penetration in their daily lives. One of the teachers points out:

> Many of the students I've had here would like to learn English without learning the culture. I think most of the students who come with that idea are ones who drop out after one or two semesters because they have an idea they can learn English just for instrumental use. (Ryan, 1994: 258)

Other teachers talk about imperialism associated with Americans (*norteamericanos*):

> I have my own opinions of why they are taking English. I tell them there's a lot of cultural imperialism: US and UK. Most come to (name of institution) because of cultural imperialism. *La llave del éxito* (Key to

success). What keeps them here is that it's so ingrained, no matter how much I tell them, they will still stay here. I tell them that there is a conflict: 'I need to study English and I dislike Americans'.

When asked to learn other things that can be more identified with the culture of the people, they usually react against that. I heard some student say, 'I don't want to know that. I don't want to know whether in the US you have to be punctual or not. I don't care. I just want to speak English and that's all'. (Ryan, 1994: 259)

In effect, in a number of research studies the idea that English is imposed creates a major conflict for urban *universitarios* (university students) and one that needs to be given considerable attention (Chasan & Ryan, 1995; Chasan *et al.*, 1998; Francis & Ryan, 1998; Ryan, 1994). Some *universitarios* talk about a 'tension' that is created over the value of having their culture in contact with other cultures through foreign language study. They are proud of having a flag, a past, a nation, a language and traditions. Others feel good when watching a group of foreigners enjoying a ride, while listening to Mariachi bands, on a *trajinera* (a boat) through the channels of Xochimilco (a section of Mexico City with floating gardens, remnants of the Pre-Columbian period). While they appear to be open to other cultures through language study, they acknowledge that a protective shield develops if their home culture is threatened by the new ways of seeing the world other cultures bring. They express concern about losing one's national pride while learning a new language and about new cultures ('Why do people want me to change what I have now, what I am proud of?' 'Do I have to change?' 'If I am seeing the world through a different set of eyes, where does my original point of view go?') (Ryan *et al.*, 1999).

For many *universitarios* they say that their own culture base should not be invaded by learning a foreign language ('Don't touch my culture!' 'Don't teach culture!' 'Learning not losing!'). Their words capture the desire to protect one's culture from outside threats that learning a foreign language might impose. Their attitudes can be represented graphically along a continuum (see Table 9.1).

Universitarios also recognise existing political, historical and economic relationships between Mexico and the United States and the attitudes these relationships provoke. Surveys reveal students react most negatively to the intervention of the United States in foreign countries and in the daily life of Mexicans, to attitudes of the United States toward Mexicans, and to attitudes toward Mexicans working in the United States (see student responses in Chasan & Ryan, 1995; Ryan, 1998). Interviews reveal both ambivalent as well as strong negative attitudes towards Americans as speakers of English (Gómez de Mas & Ryan, 1999: Ryan, 1994, 1998). These

Table 9.1 Defensiveness reflected in student discourse (adapted from Ryan *et al.*, 1999)

Defensive	*Neutral*	*Non-defensive*
Don't touch my culture.	Learning about culture.	I would be interested in studying cultural aspects.
Learning not losing.	Is a help but not necessary.	
Don't teach culture.	Culture is not indispensable but useful.	I would like a little more about the US in my English classes.
We don't allow culture to be imposed.		

attitudes appear as stereotypes in such phrases as 'cultural imperialists' and 'cultural penetrators', observed in studies with Mexican and Canadian foreign language students (Gómez de Mas & Ryan, 1999). Mexican students of French and German and Canadian students of Spanish provide an example of how attitudes toward Americans appeared spontaneously as secondary to the main purpose of the study. It was observed that Québecois talked about Mexicans as being 'warm, cheerful, hospitable, empathetic, poor people'. Mexican students described Canadians (Québecois) as being 'friendly, cultured, calm people, hard workers.' The two groups differed, however, in the way they talked about images they held of each other. When the Mexicans talked about Canadians, they contrasted them with Americans, saying that Americans are 'not friendly, not cultured, racists, imperialists, people with few values'. It is interesting to note that Canadians, however, did not mention Americans in their descriptions of Mexicans. Figure 9.1 represents this phenomenon:

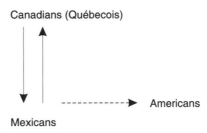

Figure 9.1 Mexican and Canadian stereotypes observed in studies (Gomez de Mas & Ryan, 1999; Ryan, 1994)

Tajfel (1981; see also Tajfel & Turner, 1986) suggests that oversimplified mental images such as these create 'in-groups' and 'out-groups' out of a need to maintain or enhance the positively valued distinctiveness of the 'in-groups' compared to the 'out-groups'.

Now let us return to Guadalupe, keeping in mind the special case of Mexican students learning English, and follow her views expressed about interculturality and the foreign language learner as part of a process that is beginning for this learner, *una visión más amplia* (a more extensive vision). She defines interculturality as *'un intercambio entre las dos culturas, entre la cultura de la persona que aprende el lenguaje, y la de la lengua extranjera'* (an exchange between the two cultures, between the culture of the person who is learning the language and that of the foreign language). She adds:

> *La persona conoce la cultura extanjera a traves del lenguaje. Hay un intercambio de estas dos culturas y un enriquecimiento. Es como una presentación que se da de la cultura extranjera a través de la lengua. Yo pienso que es un enriquecimiento de la cultura de esta persona que amplia su vision. Entonces tiene una vision 'más amplia' de lo que pasa en su país. En su misma cultura lo puede ver desde otro punto de vista, al conocer la otra cultura. Es más amplia la visión de la cultura misma, de la tuya, y de la otra también. Enriquece ambas culturas.*
>
> [*Translation*: The person knows a foreign culture by means of the language. There is an exchange of these two cultures and an enrichment. It is like an introduction to the foreign culture by means of the language. I think that it is an enrichment of the culture of this person that extends his vision. Then, he has a more extensive vision of what happens in his country. He can see his own culture from another point of view by knowing the culture of others. The vision of culture itself is more extensive, of yours and of the other also. It enriches both cultures.]

When asked how accurate this vision is, she explained:

> *Al principio yo me imagino que es muy general la visión porque no se tiene un conocimiento de cada uno de los puntos que se requieren para conocer bien la otra cultura. Entonces, el estudio de la lengua extranjera nos da una visión más bien general que se puede ir haciendo más precisa en algunos puntos si se sigue estudiando tanto la lengua como otros aspectos de la cultura de ese otro país que pudieran ser la historia, y las manifestaciones culturales, como el día de muertos y costumbres que guarden de otros paises.*
>
> [*Translation*: At the beginning I imagine it is very general because he does not have the knowledge of each of the points that are required to know the other culture well. Then, studying a foreign language gives us a more general vision that can continue being made more precise in

some areas if one continues studying both the language and other aspects of culture which could be in the history and cultural manifestations such as the 'day of the dead' and customs of other countries.]

Una vision más amplia

I asked Guadalupe in what way a student's vision of a culture changes and becomes as she had mentioned, '*más amplia*' when the student has the opportunity to live in another country:

> *Es otra manera de entrar en contacto con otro país. Enriquece más la visión. Algunas personas cuando van al país extranjero se quedan en comunidades de la misma cultura de la que ellos vienen. Lo que pasa es que depende mucho de que la persona quiera conocer más allá, no? de la otra cultura. Porque cuando se va al extranjero es un contacto que quizás no enriquezca mucho, no? Porque son cosas que uno ya conoce. La cuestión sería ampliarlo al convivir con otras personas para comprender la otra cultura desde otro punto de vista.*
>
> [*Translation*: It is another way of entering into contact with another country. It enriches the vision. Some people, when they go to a foreign country, stay in communities of the same culture they themselves came from. What happens depends heavily on the person wanting to know more there, no? of the other culture. Because when you go abroad it is a contact that perhaps does not enrich much. Because they are things one already knows. The question would be to increase them by living with people in order to understand the other culture from their point of view].

Ser tolerante

What about the learner in the classroom situation? She points out that negative attitudes, such as those previously mentioned, exist toward certain cultures of native speakers of English. Even so she adds that one, nevertheless, needs to understand and be tolerant (*ser tolerante*) of these cultures. She refers to Americans in particular:

> *Muchas veces la gente está cerrada a ciertas culuras. Entonces, es cuando yo pienso que se debe ser tolerante con esas culturas. Quizás si no le interésa a uno no tienes que estudiarlas si no le parecen interesantes. Tampoco, está en contra de eso. Hay que ser tolerante para entender estas otras culturas.*
>
> [Many times people are closed to certain cultures. Then when I think that one must be tolerant of these cultures. Perhaps if someone is not interested then he doesn't have to study them, if they don't seem interesting. I am also against this. You have to be tolerant to understand other cultures.]

By avoiding the aspects of culture tied to contexts where English is spoken and focusing on the language instead, instrumental goals may be viable to an extent (such as in the case of reading comprehension in an academic area). Guadalupe accepts this fact but also suggests that everyone should develop an interest in studying English:

> *Inglés es como un instrumento para avanzar su carrera. Por ejemplo, como un químico quién querría leer artículos en inglés y presentarlo en un congreso, pero no importa la cultura de los nativohablantes del idioma. El objetivo de esta persona es muy instrumental cuando no tiene mucha interés en la cultura.*
> [English is like an instrument for advancing your career. For example, when a chemist would like to read articles in English and present one at a conference, the culture of the native speaker of English is not important. The objective of this person is very instrumental when he obviously does not have much interest in the culture.]

> *Este es lo que pasa con muchas personas que estudian inglés actualmente en la universidad. En la mayoría de las carreras lo que les piden es como un requisito. Es decir, 'tengo que estudiar inglés para obtener el título.' En ese sentido, quizás o si estén de acuerdo con sus objetivos, quizás no haga falta ser más tolerante, no en el sentido de que están aprendiendo la lengua extranjera, no hace falta ser más tolerante porque no les interesa ir más allá en el aspecto de la cultura. Los alumnos dicen que los maestros 'nos dan la gramática y ya!' Quizás falta que a la hora que ellos estudiaran el idioma se les dieran más aspectos de esa cultura extranjera para empezar a despertar el interés, sino que se puede trascender un poco más el nivel académico y ellos por si solos pudieran decir, 'Ah, mira! la cultura también es interesante!'*
> [This is what happens with many people who are studying English at the university. In the majority of the majors that they take it is a requirement, that is to say: 'I have to study English in order to obtain my degree.' In this sense, perhaps if they agree with its objectives, it is not necessary to be more tolerant, not in the way that they are learning a foreign language, it is not necessary to be more tolerant because it does not interest them to go into the aspect of culture. Students say to teachers, 'Give us grammar and that's all!' Perhaps what is lacking when they study the language is that they be given more cultural aspects in order to awaken their interest, that is they can transcend a little the purely academic level and they themselves could say, 'Ah, look! Culture is also interesting!']

> *En el caso de la persona que estudia química, puede decir, 'Ahora que sé inglés, puedo leer artículos en inglés, entender conferencias acerca de mi carrera, y escribir artículos en inglés pero también puedo leer libros en inglés, periódicos*

en inglés y tener conversaciones con personas de allá que no necesariamente tienen que ver con la química'. Sino que es otro contacto que ya va más por el interés, que por el gusto.

[In the case of the person that studies chemistry, he can say 'Now that I know English, I can read articles in English, understand talks in my major and write articles in English, but I also can read books in English, newspapers in English, and carry on conversations with people from abroad that don't necesarily have to do with chemistry.' This is another type of contact that comes more through interest, through pleasure.]

Gaining interculturality: The process

The process Guadalupe sees as possible is that of teaching a little culture in a foreign language course in order to overcome the feeling of being forced to study English ('*Tengo que estudiar inglés para obtener el título*') and change negative attitudes toward certain speakers of English such as Americans ('*norteamericanos*') by awakening student interest ('*Ah, mira! la cultura también es interesante!*') and encouraging the desire to learn more. In this way, the vision of culture becomes '*más amplia*'.

I wanted to know more about student interest in becoming intercultural. One topic that was very popular was Australia. Guadalupe pointed out that the Olympics had just taken place during the summer:

Quizás el profesor no conozca mucho de Australia. Habla inglés pero no ha estado jamás en Australia. Por ejemplo, puede conseguirse libros, periódicos, revistas, noticiarios grabados, programas de televisión, de radio, y transmitirlos aquí y ver cual es la idiosincracia de la gente que habla en aquellos lugares. Ambos, el maestro y los alumnos, están en un proceso de aprendizaje también.

[Perhaps the teacher does not know much about Australia. He speaks English but has never been to Australia. For example, he can get books, newspapers, journals, recorded news, television programmes, radio programmes, and transmit them here and see what idiosyncracies of speech exist in those places. Both the teacher and the students, are in the process of learning.]

Si uno vea un documental de Australia, dice que Australia es un lugar bellísimo y cuando uno habla después con un nativo de Australia dice que pues sí. Entonces, es un enriquecimiento muy diferente porque se entera de las cosas oficiales y las experiencias personales que son las que dan a uno más o menos el parámetro de como es que se vive allá. Por ejemplo, muchas amigas comentan que la gente piensa que francia es un lugar muy bello. No es, porque también hay dificultades, no? Estos tipos de experiencias con contacto directo con per sonas nativas de aquellos lugares que nos imparten estas experiencias puede hacer más amplia la interculturalidad.

[If one sees a documentary about Australia, it says that Australia is a beautiful place and when one speaks later with a native of Australia and that person says, 'Well, yes.' Then, it is a very different enrichment because one finds out about official things and personal experiences that give one more or less the parameter of how it is that one lives there. For example, many friends comment that the people think France is a beautiful place. It isn't, because there are also difficulties. This type of experiences with direct contact with native people of those places who tell us about their experiences that can make us more intercultural.]

Her advice for teachers was to provide students with opportunities to have contact with nationals from English speaking countries:

Se puede establecer contacto directo con personas, con hablantes de los otros paises y las otras culturas. El profesor trae personas de California o Inglaterra o habla personalmente con nativohablantes. Ya establece un cambio diferente de los que se ven en los libros o en las revistas, o en programas de televisión. Ellos hablan sobre sus experiencias. Hablan de sus percepciones a nivel de personas.

[They can establish direct contact with people, with speakers of the other countries and other cultures. The professor can bring people from California or England or have the students speak personally with native speakers. This will establish a different way than what is seen in books or magazines on in television programs. They are speaking of their experiences. They speak of their perceptions at the human level.]

Guadalupe commented on the way other foreign language teachers (Russian, French and Arabic) handle their classes. She compares them to English and its role as a *lingua franca*:

El punto es que necesitan conocer inglés y ya. Esto es lo que se hace aquí en el Centro en otros idiomas. Los profesores captan que la gente entra por gusto. Una persona quiere estudiar arabe. En arabe obviamente no tienen solo reglas gramaticales siempre dan aspectos culturales.

[The point is that it is necessary to know English and that's it. This is what is done here at the Centre in other languages. The teachers think that people take the course because of interest. A person wants to study Arabic. In Arabic obviously one does not have only grammatical rules, there are always cultural aspects.]

Inglés es un idioma universal que muchas personas aprenden, por ejemplo, en el campo de la química, economía, las finanzas, pero ellos lo ven como un caso separado de la cultura.

[English is a universal language that many people learn, for example, in the fields of chemistry, economics, finance, but they see it as something separate from culture.]

Guadalupe noticed differences in foreign languages other than English that she had studied:

Tomé otros idiomas aquí en el Centro, como francés, ruso, e inglés. Una cosa que fue importante, por ejemplo, mis maestras de inglés siempre han sido mexicanos, de francés, mexicanos, pero mi maestra de ruso es rusa. Entonces, es muy diferente porque la maestra de ruso nos platica de las formas de vida en Rusia y de las costumbres de Rusia. Tiene una pronunciación muy diferente porque ella es de allá. Ella toda su vida ha vivido allá. Aquí solo lleva cinco años.

[I took other languages here at the Centre, such as French, Russian and English. One thing that was important for example was that my English teachers have always been Mexicans, French teachers, Mexicans, but my Russian teacher is Russian. It is very different because the Russian teacher talks to us about the Russian way of life and the customs in Russia. Her pronunciation is very different because she is from there. She lived there all her life. She has lived here only five years.]

El nivel o grado de contacto al aprender una lengua extranjera depende de quién lo enseñe, porque nuestro maestro de cuarto nivel de inglés, nos presentó algunos amigos inglesas, incluso manejamos un libro inglés. Ella vivió en inglaterra y nos platicaba sobre las costumbres de inglaterra. Se aprende por medio de estos contactos.

[The level of contact on learning a foreign language depends on who is teaching it, because our Fourth Level English teacher introduced us to some British friends. She had lived in England and talked to us about English customs. One learns through these contacts.]

Nuestra maestra nos trajo algunos compañeros de California, estudiantes también. Obviamente el nivel es muy diferente. Se conoce bastante la cultura a través de las lecturas, peliculas, y de todas maneras de expresión cultural que podrían ser la literatura, la danza, la música, la pintura, todas son formas de expresión cultural a través de las cuales también se aprende bastante de la ideología.

[Our teacher brought us some friends of hers from California, also students. Obviously the level is very different. One knows a lot about the culture through reading, films, and all types of cultural expression that could be literature, dance, music, painting, all are forms of cultural expression by means of which one learns a lot about the ideology.]

Guadalupe's vision of *más amplia* required that the student be tolerant of people of other cultures (even though it does not necessarily imply knowledge of a cultural group; perhaps 'respect' would be more appropriate here). Could this vision, *más amplia*, and a tolerant attitude be the means of initiating the process of interculturality in the learner? She said, 'Yes, it can.' She admitted that some distortions are inevitable when one doesn't know the other culture:

Cuando se llega con personas de este pais les plantea sus ideas. Es una distorción porque no conocen aquello.. Si tiene conocimiento, puede decir, sí es la verdad.

[When you meet people of this country they tell you their ideas. They are distorted because they don't really know that country. If you have knowledge, you can say, 'Yes, it's true.']

Discussion

This article began with the intention of entering, in a limited context, into the world of the intercultural speaker and their identity. It immediately revealed the role experience, both direct and indirect, plays in creating an intercultural person. The two participants, Mary and Guadalupe, who varied considerably in their contact with foreign languages and cultures, described what it means to be intercultural. Mary is strongly convinced that one can only be intercultural if one lives for a period of time in another country. She believes that an intercultural person must have experienced this direct culture contact and learned how to react to that experience. The same was not true of Guadalupe, who has not experienced living in a country outside of Mexico. When asked if direct culture contact is necessary, Guadaupe admitted that it is ideal, but in practical terms the foreign language learner may not have that possibility and may have to rely heavily on indirect experiences in the classroom. For her, the intercultural person is someone who is experiencing the contact of two or more cultures, the learner's culture and the cultures represented by the language being learned. She believes that a foreign language learner is enriched by knowledge of foreign cultures acquired through the language being studied. Direct culture contact was beneficial but not essential to this enrichment.

We have seen the role experience plays for Mary and for Guadalupe in their oral histories. They defined the intercultural speaker through the lens of these experiences. Mary's discussion of her life experiences revealed understandings about people of other cultures that she believed could not have been acquired otherwise. Moreover, attitudes of willingness to discover and interact with speakers of the new language, skills described by Byram (1997) as part of intercultural communicative competence, are seen in Mary's openness to whatever language or culture she comes into contact with. She believes that her contact with other languages and cultures enriches her, especially her knowledge of others. Guadalupe, on the other hand, given her lack of direct culture contact through experience living abroad, viewed the intercultural person in terms of pedagogy. She focuses on the cognitive aspect of interculturality. For her, interculturality is a state of mind one gradually attains by developing attitudes of tolerance of or respect toward speakers of other languages. As she talked about experiences, she related them to how teachers and students search for both direct and indirect cultural contact and how they deal with contrasts between the students' culture and others. Indirect experiences with languages were enriched by the ability of the teacher to create situations where students' visions of culture become broadened or '*mas amplia*'.

Returning to the objectives mentioned previously in Byram's model of intercultural communicative competence (that is, attitudes, knowledge, skills of discovery and interaction, skills of interpreting and relating, and critical cultural analysis), we find throughout the oral histories an emphasis on attitudes interacting with both knowledge and these skills. For Mary, attitude and the ability to adapt are central to a person's cultural knowledge and skills necessary for interacting interculturally. Guadalupe, on the other hand, has general ideas about attitudes and interculturality that lead to increasing one's cultural knowledge. Intercultural skills have been initiated for the learner during the process of learning a new language, but are in an early stage.

The issues raised in the beginning of this article of *örümcek beyin* and open-mindedness, receptivity to new ideas, beliefs, behaviours, actions, values and world views are present in both Mary's and Guadalupe's oral histories. Both women envision ways of defusing negative attitudes toward learning about the cultures of English speakers. We have seen interculturality functioning in the lives and perceptions of these two women.

A question was raised early in this discussion about how relevant intercultural communicative competence is for the foreign language learner. We may tentatively conclude that experiences strongly aid the development of the intercultural person. Mary's position has been that the learner is greatly limited if he or she has not lived in various countries and Guadalupe's that indirect classroom experience initiated the beginning of intercultural attitudes, knowledge and skills that with time may mature. However, the two participants, and their narratives, one who has lived in a variety of countries and speaks multiple languages, and the other who has lived only in Mexico and has studied different languages, demonstrate the need for additional research involving formal ethnographic techniques and additional subjects with varying degrees of multicultural / linguistic backgrounds.

Taking into account Carlos Fuentes' words of caution about closed cultures mentioned in the introduction, it is hoped that further long-term studies will lead to a concern in foreign language study with including intercultural communicative competence. One hopes that a pedagogy will emerge that will stimulate students to remark: *'Ah! la cultura también es interesante!'*.

References

Buttjes, D. and Byram, M. (eds) (1991) *Mediating Languages and Cultures: Towards an Intercultural Theory of Foreign Language Education.* Clevedon: Multilingual Matters.

Byram, M. (1997) *Teaching and Assessing Intercultural Communicative Competence.* Clevedon: Multilingual Matters.

Byram, M. and Zarate, G. (1997) *Sociocultural Competence in Language Learning and Teaching.* Strasbourg: Council of Europe.

Charaudeau, C., Gómez de Mas, M.E., Zaslavsky, D. and Chabrol, C. (1992) *Miradas córzadas, Percepciones interculturales entre Mexico y Francia.* Mexico: Universidad Nacional Autónoma de México, Coordinación de Humanidades, CELE, and Instituto Frances de American Latina.

Chasan, M. and Ryan, P. (1995) Actitudes de alumnos de inglés hacia la cultura de nativo-hablantes del inglés. *Estudios de Lingüística Aplicada* 21/22, 11–26.

Chasan, M., Mallén, M. and Ryan, P. (1998) Students' perceptions of culture and language: open spaces. In A. Ortiz Provenzal (ed.) *Antología*, IX Encuentro Nacional de Profesores de Lenguas Extranjeras. México: Universidad Nacional Autónoma de México.

Comrie, B. (1992) Turkish languages. In W. Bright (ed) *International Encyclopedia of Linguistics*, Vol. II (pp. 305–10). New York: Oxford University Press.

Creswell, J.W. (1998) *Qualitative Inquiry and Research Design, Choosing Among Five Traditions.* Thousand Oaks, CA: Sage.

Francis, N. and Ryan, P. (1998) English as an international language of prestige: Conflicting perspectives and shifting ethnolinguistic loyalties. *Anthropology and Education Quarterly* 29 (1), 25–43.

Fuentes, C. (1990) Entrevista a Carlos Fuentes por G. Scarpetta: El barroco contra la ortodoxia. *El nacional*, México, D. F., 21 August (pp. 13–20).

Gómez de Mas, M. and Ryan, P. (1999) Emergencia de estereotipos sobre EUA en la enseñanza de lenguas extranjeras: Un acercamiento psicosocial. In A. Ortiz Provenzal (ed.) *Antología, 10o Encuentro Nacional de Profesores de Lenguas.* Mexico: Centro de Enseñanza de Lenguas Extranjeras, Universidad Nacional Autónoma de México.

Hoffman, E. (1989) *Lost in Translation. A Life in a New Language.* New York. Penguin Books.

Josselson, R. and Lieblich, A. (eds) (1993) *The Narrative Study of Lives*, Vol. 1. Newbury Park, CA: Sage.

Kachru, B. and Nelson, C.L. (1996) World Englishes. In S.L McKay and N.H. Hornberger (eds) *Sociolinguistics and Language Teaching*. Cambridge: Cambridge University Press.

Kristeva, J. (1997) *Etrangers à nous-mêmes*. France: Librairie Artheme Fayard.

Kramsch, C. (1998) The privilege of the intercultural speaker. In M. Byram and M. Fleming (eds) *Language Learning in Intercultural Perspective*. Cambridge: Cambridge University Press.

Ryan, P. (1995) Foreign language teachers' perceptions of culture and the classroom. PhD dissertation, University of Utah. ERIC Clearinghouse on Languages and Linguistics, ED 385 135 (pp. 1–25).

Ryan, P. (1998) Investigaciones sobre el papel de percepciones socioculturales y lingüística en la enseñanza de idiomas. *Estudios en Lingüística Aplicada* 16 (28), 101–12.

Ryan, P., Byer, B. and Mestre, R. (1999) Reconocimiento de información cultural en la experiencia de aprendizaje del inglés. *Antología, 10o Encuentro Nacional de Profesores de Lenguas*. Mexico: Centro de Enseñanza de Lenguas Extranjeras, Universidad Nacional Autónoma de México.

Said, E.W. (1999) *Out of Place. A Memoir*. New York: Vantage Press.

Tajfel, H. (1981) *Human Groups and Social Categories*. Cambridge: Cambridge University Press.

Tajfel, H. and Turner, J.C. (1986) An integrative theory of intergroup relations. In S. Worchel and W.G. Austin (eds.) *Psychology of Intergroup Relations* (pp. 7–24). Chicago, IL: Nelson.

Todorov, T. (1989) *Nous et les autres*. Paris: Editions du seuil.

UCLA Language Materials Project (2001) (http://www.lmp.ucla.edu/profiles/proft04.htm)

Chapter 10

Changing the Focus: A Discussion of the Dynamics of the Intercultural Experience

AMITA SEN GUPTA

Introduction

> Having an Egyptian father and a Russian mother I believe I have managed to retain the essential cultural values of both my Egyptian and Russian heritages. I have lived In Russia, Egypt, Libya and the UK. I consider myself to be literate in English, Russian and Arabic. Whether this is a blessing or a curse is not a serious concern, but that it is a growing feature of most inhabitants of developing communities proves that the world has definitely become a smaller place or as some would say, a Global Village.

The impact of globalisation on the educational sector can be seen in the increasing numbers of people either having to, or choosing to, study in more than one country. In addition the phenomenon of time–space compression, the information super-highway and all associated technologies means that the young people entering our classrooms are emerging from a sociocultural context vastly different to the ones with which we are familiar. Both students and teachers are faced with a set of challenges both pedagogic and academic that in some cases are fundamentally different to those which may have been previously encountered. In working with these students there are a range of issues which present themselves: for example, studying in a second or even third language, educational values and requirements, teacher expectations and modes of instruction. Although these variables may be experienced to a greater or lesser extent the one variable which is common to all situations is the individual's contact with the 'other'. It seems as if our students are more likely to encounter difference and diversity within their classrooms rather than sameness and homogeneity. However, in the face of the rapidly increasing heterogeneity of our

155

environments there is a steadily growing desire for people to establish and maintain their attachment to their own cultural systems (Hall, 1981; Bredella, this volume). Through continuous interaction with difference and diversity individuals and groups are becoming more aware of their own cultural uniqueness and identity. Therefore, in the first instance, it would seem that any type of intercultural pedagogy would need to strike a balance between learning about the cultural systems of others and developing an enhanced awareness of one's own cultural systems.

'Culture is the thousand people sitting in your seat' (Pederson, 1997). This statement seems to me to exemplify two of the key characteristics of working with culture. First, that culture is always with us and each of us is a product of, and transmitter of, potentially huge amounts of cultural information. Second, rather like the infamous iceberg metaphor, the largest amount of culture is invisible to us. The groundedness of our experience in cultural systems forms the basis of this chapter which will be exploring three different approaches to understanding the dynamics of the intercultural experience within the classroom. In the first instance I will be looking at *enculturation* as the product of our primary socialising experiences and the starting point for any individuals' entry into the intercultural space. Second I will be looking at *acculturation* as a process of encountering other cultural systems and incorporating them within an existing operational framework. In addition I will look at some of the consequences of the acculturation process. Third, I will be looking at culture as providing the basis for a sense of self in terms of collective identity and its associations with inter-group relations. Finally I will be looking at the impact on pedagogy of these different viewpoints.

The purpose of this chapter is threefold: to extend the domain of analysis to areas beyond traditional ones of competence and training (Byram, this volume); to explore the notion of educational value within the context of the intercultural experience; and to examine some of the challenges of delivering an intercultural programme. I will be using examples derived from teaching within an international, multicultural milieu to illustrate and elucidate the points raised. In moving away from the traditional domains of analysis which include training methods and programs for cultural immersion I would like to explore the dynamics of the intercultural classroom. By doing so I would like to extend our view of the intercultural experience and pedagogy to account for the way in which material is experienced and processed within this particular type of educational encounter. To facilitate the discussion I will be making reference to the famous figure–ground distinction of Gestalt psychology where the viewer constantly moves between two different perceptions dependent entirely on what is chosen as the figure and what is chosen as the background. The attributes of this perceptual phenomenon are ones that I find particularly helpful when working with cultural systems. In fact, my first use of the analogy would be to highlight the shift in focus that I associate with contemporary attitudes to intercultural work. Historically, this material has always been in the background and has been overshadowed by more conventional systems and canons of knowledge. I feel our goal as educators working in the field of intercultural studies is to bring cultural systems into the foreground so that it becomes central to our disciplinary discourse and our pedagogy when we are working with students who are part of the Global Village.

> Throughout my life I have met and dealt with individuals from all parts of the world, instilling in me a false air of experience as far as my social skills were concerned, which came under severe scrutiny after I took this course. I realised I wasn't paying attention to the differences I was observing.

Culture

Academia and education are two of the many environments in which 'culture' is becomingly increasingly popular as a basis for analysis. Given the variety of contexts of use of the term 'culture' I feel it would be useful to review some of the uses and clarify how the term will be used in this chapter. Definitions of culture include:

- *Descriptive*   definitions are comprehensive lists of all aspects of human life and activity thought to be examples of 'culture'.
- *Historical*   definitions emphasis the importance of tradition and heritage.
- *Normative*   definitions emphasise the shared rules governing the activity of a group of people.
- *Psychological* definitions focus on specific features such as learning, problem-solving assimilation etc.
- *Structural*   definitions are concerned with the pattern or organisation of culture.
- *Genetic*   definitions look at the origins or genesis of culture.

Kroeber and Kluckhohn (1952) have proposed the following definition:

> Culture consists of patterns, explicit and implicit, of and for behaviours acquired and transmitted by symbols, constituting the distinctive achievements of human groups, including their embodiments in artifacts; the essential core of culture consists of traditional (i.e. historically derived and selected) ideas and especially their attached values; cul-

tural systems may on the one hand be considered as products of actions, on the other as conditioning elements of further action. (cited in Berry *et al.*, 1992: 166)

However, despite the range of definitions of culture that exist and the abstract nature of many of the definitions of culture, there are some aspects of culture, which are common to all these definitions. First of all 'culture' is something shared and transmitted both within and between generations. Cultural phenomena are superorganic, i.e. they are collective phenomena that exist above and beyond individual people. Related to this is the idea that although culture depends on individuals for its existence, no single individual 'possesses' all of the culture of a particular group. Culture is also to be regarded as a system that in its totality allows individuals to make sense of their living environments. Finally one of the most important facets of culture is that it exists both at the explicit and implicit level. Although some cultural phenomena are overt and easily observable there are also the organising principles that lie behind patterns of behaviour and these are not readily observable and may only be inferred.

In addition to the many definitions of culture there is an added layer of complexity which comes from the different uses of the term 'culture', and which can be misleading. Often when people refer to culture they use the term as a noun – this is problematic because of course culture is not a thing to be possessed. As previously discussed above it is a descriptive term that encompasses a fundamental aspect of the human condition. Like it or not we all have culture! Another problem with the word culture is that it is often confused with nationality, ethnicity or race. This is extremely problematic as all of these concepts are very different to culture. Culture is a much wider concept that embraces all aspects of our lives. In view of this I think it might be useful to refer to 'cultural systems' in which people participate and to which individuals may be exposed within the intercultural encounter, for example, referring to the 'Hindu cultural system' as opposed to 'Hindu culture'. One of the advantages of focusing our analysis on 'cultural systems' means that we can avoid problems such as assuming that individuals represent whole 'cultures'. It also allows us to focus the discussion on specific aspects of culture that can be identified as a cultural system, such as patterns of child-rearing. This means that we can avoid the trap of talking about and comparing whole 'cultures' in essentialist terms and instead create culture as a background with specific cultural systems as the foreground.

The Intercultural Experience

Reviewing some of the classic texts in the area of intercultural training it becomes clear that the term 'intercultural' is used loosely to describe any encounter between people of different cultures. Much of the time the term is used interchangeably with 'cross-cultural' (e.g. Berry *et al.*, 1992). Understandably this can lead to some confusion when it comes to analysing and discussing the intercultural experience. In view of this, it is useful to elabo rate on some of the terms that are most commonly used with a view to distinguishing between them such that they may each provide a different domain of analysis.

The term *multicultural*, although often applied to methodology and techniques, may be more clearly understood as being descriptive of a group of people or a body of knowledge; for example, the multicultural classroom, where the students are seen as representatives of a variety of cultural systems (Leuner & Sen Gupta, 1999). The term *cross-cultural* may be used analytically to indicate a specifically comparative methodology where two or more cultures are compared on one or more variables with a view to identifying similarities and differences; for example, the comparison of children's play in Africa and the USA. The term *intercultural* may be regarded as defining a cultural encounter that goes beyond the passive and the observational. Intercultural may be used to refer to encounters where individuals are immersed, either temporarily or permanently, in cultures other than their own (Asante & Gudykunst, 1989). The immersion may take different forms: it may involve living in a new culture: and it may involve intense exposure to cultural products and materials. In describing intercultural in this way, the implications are that the individual is actively engaged with cultural material and systems, and that the consequences of the encounter are that, for all individuals concerned, something will have changed, some part of the process will have been internalised within the individuals concerned.

Intercultural education then may take place with individuals who are, to a large extent, culturally homogeneous, in that they may be exposed to information about other cultural systems for extended periods of time. It is also possible that a multicultural classroom is not necessarily an intercultural classroom if cultural material does not form a central part of the pedagogy. Given these distinctions it is clear that intercultural does not mean simply being in the presence of more than one cultural system; it does require that culture be the central discourse and that individuals are required to actively engage with cultural material.

Paige (1993) has argued that intercultural education is both psychologically and pedagogically challenging and, in this section, I present briefly the challenges that are encountered in the intercultural classroom. In discussing the challenges and characteristics of the intercultural environment I hope to bring into focus aspects of the intercultural encounter which have hitherto remained in the background of the prevailing discussions about intercultural training and teaching.

> The realisation of the pervasiveness of ethnocentrism became clearer through reading specifically cross-cultural material, conversations with people from different cultural backgrounds and self-reflection.[1]

The inevitability of ethnocentrism, or viewing the world through a particular set of cultural lenses, has been well documented and provides a suitable starting place for examining the intercultural encounter (Wurzel, 1988). Although it is not necessarily challenging to encounter different ways of doing things, such as modes of dress or types of food, it is challenging when the encounter forces us to evaluate our own fundamental beliefs and value systems. This experience affects our cognitions of everyday issues such as child-rearing, as well as affecting social cognitions.

> I was confused because I wasn't sure if I had the right to feel such animosity towards him when he was just reflecting the ways of his society.

Accompanying the cognitive aspects of this encounter are the affective components. The range of feelings experienced varies from anger and anxiety to excitement and relief. The emotions come from many sources: fear of encountering something new, excitement at the discovery of new and different ways of thinking, relief through self-expression, anger that a deeply held belief may have been challenged. Sometimes the affective component is intense and in some few cases can be overwhelming, leading to a denial of material – in fact I have had a student say to me that she thought the reading material had simply been fabricated!

> Throughout this course I have been able to reflect on myself and my culture in terms of how and why I do the things that I do. Why do I eat my meals using a knife and fork in a specific way rather than eating with my hands?

Cushner and Brislin (1997) have pointed out that self-awareness is a necessary part of the intercultural experience, without which individuals rarely become aware of their own world view. The role and importance of self-reflection is crucial to the intercultural encounter as it provides a method for participants to move beyond the superficial exchange of information about the 'other'. It requires that individuals use the intercultural encounter specifically to learn something about themselves as well as learning about others.

The class was a unique environment in itself because it allowed different people from different places and backgrounds to openly discuss their experiences.

Given the characteristics described here it is obvious that the intercultural encounter is a challenging encounter for all involved. These challenges and risks apply both to teachers and students in the intercultural classroom. As such, the experience may seem risky to those who are taking part. In order for the experience to be a valuable and positive one, it is imperative that the educational environment should be supportive of such an endeavour. This support needs to be institutional as well as being located in the classroom. At an institutional level the intercultural experience should be part of the general discourse and should not be marginalised and placed at the edges of disciplines; rather it should be made central to the way in which all disciplines are taught. In the classroom the teacher has the responsibility of delivering the material and managing the encounter such that a safe environment is created. In the absence of this support it is very possible that the students concerned become jaded and disillusioned with the experience and therefore emerge from the intercultural encounter with the minimum of positive outcomes.

Enculturation

I have the cultural up-bringing that has come from my family, especially the older generations in my family, and I have the culture that has come from the people around me, such as my peers, and the places that that I have lived in. When I was a child the culture that affected me the most was the culture passed down to me from my family . . . Throughout the time I spent with them their values attitudes and beliefs were the ones that shaped me the most.

The transmission of cultural material and the immersion in cultural systems brings about 'enculturation'. When cultural material is acquired within one's 'own' culture the process is deemed enculturation (Herskovits, 1948). As the previous quote implies, enculturation is the product of the process of primary socialisation (Kagitçibasi, 1996). It is through the process of enculturation that the individual acquires the rules, values and behaviour that allow us to become effective and competent members of our sociocultural environments. Initially, enculturation occurs primarily within the home and, later, this extends to other important individuals and social institutions such as schools. Enculturation involves both the horizontal and vertical transmission of cultural material.

> It was not until I started this course that . . . I started to question things that I had never really actively thought about before.

This process of transmission and acquisition is rarely deliberate and / or didactic in nature. Enculturation takes place as individuals are born into, and raised within, sociocultural environments. The acquisition of cultural information begins from birth when infants are reared by individuals with specific attitudes to child care, nutrition, appropriate behaviour etc. As a consequence effective enculturation produces ways of being, doing and thinking that are so deeply entrenched that they are automatic and we are simply unaware that our behaviour is determined by these unconscious mechanisms. These are the invisible and implicit aspects of culture. This is the starting point for those entering the intercultural classroom, they are not just cultural beings, they are also enculturated and part of the process of being involved in the intercultural encounter is to unwrap some of the unconscious layers and bring them to the surface, make the invisible and automatic, visible and conscious.

> I was not aware of my filter until coming to school here. I had always been in an environment where everyone basically had the same experiences and no-one had experienced anything new and totally different to what they were used to.

Enculturation also lays the foundation for our own ethnocentrism and the acquisition of our cultural lenses through which we view the world. The intercultural classroom is an environment where the encounter with different cultural systems is one which allows for these implicit aspects of culture to become explicit. The encounter with difference shifts the focus from aspects of ourselves with which we are familiar to aspects of ourselves with which we are unfamiliar, and moreover, that we were not even aware existed.

> Looking at myself and judging myself was very difficult and uncomfortable. It was an unpleasant experience.

Given that enculturation incorporates all our attitudes, beliefs, values and behaviour it follows that the examination of this may well be an uncomfortable process. Although some may find it a useful starting place to understand why they do what they do, others may not find the experience pleasant, for example, if a student realises that his / her parents' attitudes to people are intolerant and that his / her own intolerance is related to his / her familial experience. Many students may also feel that in assessing the effects of enculturation, they are being asked to evaluate or judge their own experiences in terms of right and wrong.

> I had not realised how non-religious I am until speaking with people in class. Religion is the last thing that affects my life and for some it is everything.

Enculturation also includes our attachments, albeit unconscious, to aspects of our environment. For example, we are not aware how much we value 'fish and chips' until it becomes unavailable to us. The intercultural classroom brings to the forefront things we have taken for granted about our ways of life and this may be both positive and negative. There are those who respond to their discoveries with pleasure and appreciation and others who may respond with envy or embarrassment. The common factor in this dynamic is the element of surprise, which is the cornerstone of the intercultural experience.

Acculturation

> the class has indeed changed me in some ways . . . The progress that I made can be seen indirectly, through my understanding of myself as a person, through my interaction with others and through a changed understanding of cultural issues.

Acculturation is the outcome of an individual's experience of a changing cultural context. The culture change that occurs is specifically due to a contact, direct or indirect, with other cultures. The term 'psychological acculturation' (Graves, 1967) is used to refer to the changes experienced by an individual as a direct result of their contact with other cultural groups or systems. The three criteria for acculturation are continuous and first-hand contact or interaction with another cultural system, some permanent or semi-permanennt change in the individual; and third, two more stages – dynamic activity during and after contact which is followed by a period of stability which is the result of the process (Berry *et al.*, 1992). The intercultural experience may be regarded as a specific cultural system with its own values, systems, beliefs and behaviours and, when combined with the criteria mentioned earlier it is possible to regard participation in an intercultural environment as an acculturative experience. The individual is consciously required to learn new and different ways of being and thinking by virtue of being in a different environment and because of their explicit contact, whether direct or indirect, with other cultural systems.

> I do not feel that comfortable in my culture any more. I have come to adopt many aspects that I have encountered here.

The effects of acculturation processes at the individual level include changes in identity, attitudes, beliefs and values (Berry *et al.*, 1992) One of the consequences of the acculturating experience is that aspects of the acculturated group become different from their original group before the cultural contact. This in itself can clearly give rise to problems and would easily explain the anxiety and possible feelings of alienation that participants may feel about moving away from their original groups. The intercultural classroom involves a transient but relatively intense exposure to cultural material. The participants may be unwilling to change as they are aware that they will be returning to a situation where cultural homogeneity is the norm. They may not want to risk becoming outsiders in their culture of origin. One of the consequences of this is that individuals may retrench themselves in their pre-exposure beliefs and resist attempts to look at their own cultural systems from the point of view of the 'other' (Friederichs & Sen Gupta, 1995).

> I must admit that it is overwhelming, I have reached confusion several times, because so much of the material and concepts were taken apart during the course.

A well-documented outcome of acculturation is acculturative stress (Sen Gupta, 1999). The transformation of ways of thinking and behaving may be an uncomfortable process that may leave individuals disturbed by the experience. Some of the common features of this kind of stress are feelings of marginality and alienation, identity confusion and heightened psychosomatic symptom levels, high levels of anxiety and depression (Sanua, 1970).

> In my teenage years I grew up in England, I kept to myself and became very reclusive, and one of the reasons for this is that people at school used to make fun of my accent.

By viewing the intercultural experience as a process of acculturation it is possible to see that there are many variables that will affect both the experience itself and the outcome of the experience. In view of this students are more likely to be resistant to the material if they feel isolated and/or marginalised in the classroom, if this is their first intercultural experience, if previous experiences have negative associations, if they feel they lack legitimacy or status or if they feel undermined.

Personal Identity and Self

> I've always seen culture in terms of 'where I come from' or in terms of 'my country'. As children we were taught what culture was about. This rudimentary perception of culture seemed consistent, stable and unchangeable or that it could resist change.

Individuals arrive in the intercultural environment not only with a sense of their own particular characteristics but also with a collective identification. As Hall (1996: 2–3) puts it:

> In common sense language, identification is constructed on the back of a recognition of some common origin or shared characteristics with another person or group, or an ideal, and with the natural closure of solidarity and allegiance established on this foundation'.

Social identity theory (Tajfel, 1978, 1982; Tajfel &Turner, 1986) proposes that group membership forms an integral part of our self-concept, but individuals do not typically distinguish between group and individual components of their personal identity. At the individual level identities are seen and experienced as being consistent and stable both at the personal and the collective level. It follows that encounters with a variety of cultural groupings other than one's own are going to have an impact on the individual's awareness of self and identity (Hall, 1990).

> Before the class I found I would automatically assume things about other people. However, I attribute some of this to the way certain people are perceived in the US. This is especially seen when referring to Middle Eastern cultures. The way that the media describes them is often negative.

The existence and formation of any collective identity, including cultural identity, presupposes the existence of the 'other' (Elliott, 1986). The demarcation of a cultural self requires that a distinction be made, either implicitly or explicitly, from the values, characteristics and ways of life of others. However, it is not just the construction of the other that is relevant, but the nature of that particular construction. Very often the 'other' is construed with negative attributes relative to one's own group membership, for example the dominant ideologies of the western world have emphasised the triumph of reason and empiricism and materialism. This is sharply contrasted with the rest of the world that is frequently portrayed as irrational, chaotic and unhappy. The distinctions between 'us' and 'them' are reinforced through the processes of enculturation and socialisation and so becomes part of our automatic thinking.

> Most students tend to 'stick with their own kind'. We associate with other people who are from the same cultural background and speak the same language.

Group membership which forms the basis of our collective identity is known to be associated with certain characteristics (Tajfel & Fraser, 1978). Assessment of out-groups is often more superficial and more subject to stereotypes than assessment of the in-group. Typically, in-groups are viewed as being more heterogeneous, because of increased knowledge and out-groups are viewed as being more homogeneous due to a lack of detailed information. The mere presence of other groups can make members more aware of their own group identity. Perdue *et al*. (1990) demonstrated the spontaneous nature of this activation of the 'us' and 'them' cognition. Being reminded of one's own group identity can lead to a positivity bias which favourably distinguishes between one's own and other groups. Group membership forms an integral part of our self-concept. Thus discrimination between groups enhances self-esteem as well as maintaining adherence to the group. In addition, where group members encounter a perceived failure in the group, they reclaim a positivity bias by enhancing group status by virtue of comparison with another group.

> The matter does not wholly lie in the fact that his [African] cultural beliefs are wholly different to those of western cultures. It's simply that western cultures as a whole have changed their attitudes towards homosexuality and wouldn't enforce some of the rules that non-western cultures would.

Ethnocentrism is a by-product of group membership where the views of the in-group serve as a reference point for assessing the out-group. Cross-cultural studies have shown that there is a widespread tendency to regard one's own group as being superior to other groups with respect to morality and trustworthiness (Brewer, 1986). Interestingly where an in-group recognises some aspect of group behaviour which is unfavourable in comparison with others they do not deny the distinction, rather they respond by either minimising the difference between the groups or by devaluing the dimension on which the out-group is superior (van Knippenberg & Ellmers, 1990).

> There was a major struggle within me trying to balance out the two different cultures [Indian and American] that had such an impact on my life. It was like I used to switch from one culture's values to the other depending on the situation I was in.

Hall (1996) has pointed out that the disturbance of the relatively settled character of populations in relation to the forces of globalisation has created an environment in which identities are increasingly fragmented and fractured. Individuals are constantly re-defining themselves according to the context in which they find themselves. This is particularly true of the intercultural classroom where individuals are constantly being asked to examine the nature and consequences of their group membership. Larrain (1994) proposes that identity becomes an issue in periods of instability, where there are real or perceived threats to well-established ways of thinking and doing, particularly when these threats take place in the presence of other cultural frameworks. In other words identity becomes an issue when something assumed to be stable, fixed and coherent is replaced by feelings of doubt and uncertainty.

Implications for Pedagogy

The issues described here are all part of the intercultural experience. The challenge for educators is to be able to integrate the responsibility of delivering a sound academic programme as well as pursuing the goals of a productive intercultural encounter. In discussing pedagogical issues I have found it helpful to remind myself of the purpose of this chapter which has been to explore the educational value of the intercultural experience. The intercultural experience described in this chapter takes place within a formal educational setting and institutional requirements affect the content and structure of any programme; these, in turn, affect the scope of the material covered and methods of evaluation and assessment. In terms of value, we are looking for the delivery of a sound academic programme and the creation of an optimal learning environment. The perspective of intercultural competence offers an additional set of guidelines which incorporate the following abilities: the ability to move easily between different cultural systems, tolerance of ambiguity, empathy, respect, the ability to respond to others in a non-judgemental and evaluative ways, the ability to give and receive information about cultural systems. The educational value of this type of competence would reflect the individual's increased ability to understand difference and to experience a transformation in their self-perception, such that their awareness of their own cultural identity is 'un-frozen' and extended in parallel with the increasing awareness of other cultural systems (Lustig & Koester, 1999). In terms of teaching and assessment these outcomes are not only unfamiliar but also difficult. Therefore in addition to traditional methods of delivery and assessment, the intercultural teacher needs to use less traditional methods in order to evaluate the more subjective outcomes of intercultural competence as previously described. The following discussion looks at three aspects of teaching method and finally the overall assessment of intercultural competence.

> It was purely the interaction between teacher and student and student with student that opened my eyes and made me as the saying goes 'wake up and smell the coffee'.

The intercultural classroom needs to have a dynamic and interactive atmosphere where, in addition, to traditional questions regarding the material, students are actively encouraged to share their personal experiences. It is important that students learn how to relate and discuss their experiences in such a way that all concerned benefit from the interaction. In order for personal experience to be an effective teaching device, students need guidance and monitoring. As mentioned earlier, students may be alarmed at the notion they are expected to talk about themselves, whereas other students may see this as an opportunity to side-track discussion or, in the case of some, to enter into a diatribe about their personal feelings. For example, difficulties can be experienced when students make broad generalisations about a cultural practice or about a group of people, another common experience is when students express a personal opinion as though it is a generally held belief. The rules of the intercultural classroom can be constructed such that these kinds of experiences are minimised as they are potentially damaging to the creation of a positive learning environment. The ability to show respect and communicate effectively is clearly a positive learning outcome, that is best assessed informally through the encouragement of discussion rather than through more conventional methods of testing and assessment. As this particular quotation implies the role of interaction in the intercultural classroom has another valuable component in terms of pedagogy. Students often remark how the opportunity to engage with material immediately and through dialogue is a valuable aid to understanding and comprehension. Interactive discussion is a useful way to help students when they are making the transition from the hypothetical and the abstract to the real and the practical. Interactions with their peers allows them to explore cultural experiences first hand; they have the opportunity to question and reflect on the experiences of individuals within a cultural system as well as also having to find a way to describe their own cultural experiences. Interactions with the tutor, who is also able to draw on his/her own personal experiences, provides a valuable model to students as to the importance of relating theory to practice (Shade *et al.*, 1997).

> Through the discussion we had in class and from the openness of those that were willing to share their personal experiences I learnt so much about different cultures and the attitudes, values and beliefs of those cultures that were represented in the class.

One of the key aspects of the intercultural classroom is the scheduling of discussion groups as part of the curriculum. In the course being described in this chapter there were two types of discussion groups: small group discussion which took place in groups of three students, where each student took it in turns to lead the discussion; and large group discussion which was facilitated by the course tutor. The value of group discussion in the intercultural experience is also related to the fact that the intercultural experience does require immersion in other cultural systems.

Group discussion is a non-prescriptive way for individuals to encounter and explore information about other cultural systems as well as being put in the position of having to describe and explain their own cultural systems. In other words, the role of being the 'other' constantly shifts between individuals. Group discussion is a relatively non-threatening environment in which students can encounter difference; and can learn that acceptance and understanding do not necessarily go hand in hand. Finally, group discussion, particularly in small groups, helps students who normally find it difficult to express themselves. Participation in these groups allows students to realise that they are not alone in feeling uncomfortable and that others also experience difficulty in expressing themselves.

> The journal discussion made it easy for me to learn about other people's customs and traditions and 'washed away' the images and interpretations I had before, of what they were like, how they would behave and talk.

The importance of requiring students to keep an ongoing record of their learning, as well as giving them the opportunity to reflect on their experiences both within and outside the classroom, cannot be overstated. It is an essential part of the pedagogy of an intercultural classroom, as one of the stated objectives of intercultural competence is that students should learn to use information about cultural systems to reflect on themselves and how they function as cultural beings. In addition the journal provides a good basis for discussion, rather than students simply reacting on the spot. Students have the opportunity to reflect on their reactions, and this forms the basis of a useful dialogue or discussion. Journals put students in a position where they need to focus on the material that has been presented to them, providing an opportunity for them to give some time to the course material that is reflective as well as any other work they might do to fill course requirements. As teachers we strive to encourage our students to extend their learning process outside the classroom and keeping a journal is one way of accomplishing this objective. Students have many different responses to the task of being asked to keep journals. Although some students may be familiar with the process, others do find it difficult to keep such a record of their thoughts and feelings. They are often unsure as to what needs to be discussed and how much of themselves needs to be revealed. One of the important aspects of using journals in this environment is that students are requested to keep their journals private. They may then be as personal as they wish. Even though they bring their journals to class and present material for discussion, they choose what they want to present to the rest of the group.

Before I came here I used to judge people for their physical appearance, or from their nationality or cultural background. Even after spending a few months here I realised that my ethnocentric way of thinking did not change at all. However, after taking this class I am able to understand and adapt to other people's ways of thinking, even to accept that my culture, like all cultures, has negative aspects that I was not able to see before I had experienced another culture.

As Lustig and Koester (1999) have proposed, intercultural competence may be assessed by the individual's ability to 'unfreeze' their awareness of their own cultural limitations. As this student describes, simply being in a different cultural environment is not sufficient. The intercultural classroom requires much more of students than simply learning what happens elsewhere in other cultural systems. Students learn to reflect on themselves and their own cultural systems and gradually come to realise the extent of their own ethnocentrism and how this influences their ways of thinking and communicating. The awareness of self and other can be evaluated not only through their improved ability to communicate in class discussion, but also through their performance in a self-reflective essay. In their essays students are able to discuss how their perceptions of culture have changed and the key elements of their experience which have contributed to this change. This is the single most important activity which allows students and teachers alike to evaluate enculturation, acculturation and the impact on identity. This activity locates the intercultural experience squarely in the realm of education and learning, rather than some more hypothetical and abstract activity (Gochenour, 1993). As educators we are looking for some aspect of personal growth and this is facilitated by the interactive nature of the intercultural classroom, and evidenced in individuals records of their personal journey through the course itself. The self-reflective essay allows students the opportunity to find different ways of approaching themselves and their discipline and I have found students inspired to express themselves in variety of ways, such as writing poetry, doing drawings or calligraphy or re-reading a favourite text. In terms of the figure–ground illusion described earlier, the emphasis moves from a focus on outcomes to a focus on the process of learning.

Conclusion

On the 8th of September I took a journey that I have never taken before. In this journey I learnt what it means to appreciate those things that I considered foreign, and most of all I gained knowledge about myself. It was both exciting and educational.

The overall value and positive outcomes, both educational and social, of the intercultural experience are obvious to the participants. Most students are exhilarated by the exposure to information that they never knew existed. They rise to the challenge of the questions and conflicts that may emerge as a result of becoming more aware of themselves as cultural beings. Their critical and analytical skills are extended because the domain of criticism and analysis is also extended. They also respond positively to a different type of educational experience that allows them to think about education itself and the role that it plays in cultural systems. The validation of personal experience and the training to use this effectively in an academic environment is also immensely beneficial for the students. For educators delivering intercultural programs there is an in-built mechanism for updating material and looking critically at existing canons of knowledge. As with students it is quite exhilarating and liberating to find completely different ways of understanding problems within the discipline areas. Participation in the intercultural experience is one way to prepare young people to function in the Global Village as responsible and thoughtful adults. The process of education is challenging as we, the educators, strive to deliver the requirements of a discipline while at the same time wishing that our students will be able to use the experience to move beyond the factual and the predictable. The intercultural experience offers a wealth of opportunity for educators and students alike to experience the unpredictable, to discover something new about themselves which would not have possible in any other situation. Teachers and students participate in a journey where the unpredictable becomes the cornerstone of achievement and success (Garcia, 1994).

The intercultural experience is not always a pleasant one nor is the journey necessarily a smooth one. Students and educators may find themselves experiencing discomfort, impatience and anxiety. According to van der Post, People and countries are mirrors to one another . . ., but they rarely recognise themselves, mostly they see what is hidden within themselves reflected in one another' (cited in Adams, 1996: 147). However, it seems as if the intercultural encounter is an inevitable part of the Global Village, and therefore our duty as educators is to strive towards developing a suitable pedagogy for this experience.

Notes

1. All the quotations used have been taken from student essays that form part of the course work for the course 'Introduction to Psychology and Culture'. The essays used for this paper were the Self-Reflection essays. The details of the course can be found in Appendix I.
2. Fowle, S.M. (1995) *Intercultural Sourcebook: Cross-cultural Training Methods*, Vol. 1. Yarmouth, ME: Intercultural Press.

Kohls, R.L. (1994) *Developing Intercultural Awareness: A Cross-cultural Training Handbook* (2nd edn). Yarmouth, ME: Intercultural Press.
3.   See Sanua (1970) for a review of this area.

References

Adams, M.V. (1996) *The Multi-cultural Imagination: Race, Colour and the Unconscious.* London & New York: Routledge.

Anderson, W.T. (1996) *The Fontana Post-modernism Reader.* London: Fontana Press.

Asante, M.K. and Gudykunst, W.B. (eds) (1989*) Handbook of International and Intercultural Communication.* Newbury Park, CA: Sage.

Berry, J.W., Poortinga, Y.H., Segall, M.H. and Dasen, P. (1992) *Cross-cultural Psychology: Research and Applications.* Cambridge: Cambridge University Press.

Brewer, M.B. (1986) The role of ethnocentrism in intergroup conflict. In S. Worchel and W.G. Austin (eds) *Psychology of Intergroup Relations* (2nd edn). Chicago: Nelson-Hall.

Byram, M.S. (1999) On being bi-cultural and intercultural. This volume.

Cushner, K. and Brislin, R.W. (1997) *Improving Intercultural Interactions: Modules for Cross-cultural Training Programs,* Vol. 2. Thousand Oaks, CA: Sage.

Deaux, K., Dane, F.C. and Wrightsman, L. (1993) *Social Psychology in the 90's* (6th edn). Los Angeles, CA: Brooks Cole.

Elliott, W.A. (1986) *Us and Them: A Study of Group Consciousness.* Aberdeen: Aberdeen University Press.

Friederichs, J. and Sen Gupta, A. (1995) International education in a multi-cultural environment: An analysis of the impact on individual identity and group relations and a discussion of the important agents. *European Journal of Intercultural Studies* 6 (1).

Garcia, E. (1994) *Understanding and Meeting the Challenge of Student Cultural Diversity.* New York: Houghton Mifflin.

Gochenour, T. (edn) (1993*) Beyond Experience: The Experiential Approach to Cross-cultural Education* (2nd edn). Maine: Intercultural Press.

Graves T.D. (1967) Psychological acculturaltion in a tri-ethnic community. *Southwestern Journal of Anthropology* 23, 337–50.

Hall, S. (1981) The local and the global: Globalisation and ethnicity. In A. King (ed.) *Globalisation and the World-system.* London: Macmillan.

Hall, S. (1990) Cultural identity and diaspora. In J. Rutherford (ed.) *Identity.* London: Lawrence & Wisharrt.

Hall, S. (1996) Who needs identity? In S. Hall, S. and P. du Gay (eds) *Questions of Cultural Identity.* London: Sage.

Herskovits M.J. (1948) *Man and His Works: The Science of Cultural Anthropology.* New York: Knopf.

Kagitçibasi, C. (1996) *Family and Human Development across Cultures: A View from the Other Side.* New Jersey: Laurence Erlbaum.

Larrain, J. (1994) *Ideology and Cultural Identity.* Oxford: Blackwell.

Leuner, P. and Sen Gupta, A. (1999) Going global: A case study in managing an institutional bi-cultural identity. *Journal of International Education* 10 (1), 14–21.

Lustig, M.W. and Koester, J. (eds) (1999) *Intercultural Competence: Interpersonal Communication Across Cultures* (3rd edn). New York: Longman.

Paige, R.M. (ed.) (1993) *Education for the Intercultural Experience* (2nd edn). Maine: Intercultural Press.

Perdue, C.W., Dovidio, J.F., Gurtman, M.B and Tyler, R.B. (1990) Us and them: Social categorisation and the process of intergroup bias. *Journal of Personality and Social Psychology* 59, 475–86.

Sen Gupta, A. (1999) A pedagogy of intercultural experience or the experience of an intercultural pedagogy? Paper presented at the Intercultural Studies in Education Symposium, School of Education, University of Durham.

Shade, B.J., Kelly, C. and Oberg, M. (1997) *Creating Culturally Responsive Classrooms*. Washington, DC: American Psychological Association.

Sanua, V. (1970) Immigration, migration and mental illness. In E. Brody (ed.) *Behaviour in New Environments*. Newbury Park, CA: Sage.

Tajfel, H. (ed.) (1978) *Differentiation between Social Groups*. London: Academic Press.

Tajfel, H. (1982) Social psychology of intergroup relations. *Annual Review of Psychology* 33, 1–39.

Tajfel, H. and Fraser, C. (eds) (1978) *Introducing Social Psychology*. Harmondsworth: Penguin Books.

Tajfel, H. and Turner, J.C. (1986) The social identity theory of intergroup behaviour. In S. Worchel and W.G. Austin (eds) *Psychology of Intergroup Relations* (2nd edn). Chicago: Nelson-Hall.

Van Knippenberg, A. and Ellmers, N. (1990) Social identity and intergroup differentiation processes. *European Review of Social Psychology* 1, 137–69.

Wurzel, J. (1988) *Toward Multiculturalism: A Reader in Multicultural Education*. Maine: Intercultural Press.

Appendix 1

Introduction to Psychology and Culture

Catalogue description

This course looks at the relationship between psychology and culture by investigating the philosophy and methodology of cultural comparisons. The course focuses on what we can learn from relating the study of culture to psychology; topics covered include: moral development, patterns of parenting, perception and memory, values, prejudice and stereotypes.

Course content

This course is designed to illustrate the limitations of a culture-bound approach to understanding human behaviour. Most academic psychology is concerned with understanding the behaviour of a very small group of people who are not necessarily representative of the population of the world. This course asks students of psychology to evaluate basic psychological concepts when applied to people who are not necessarily middle-class Europeans or North Americans. The course also investigates research methodology, particularly when applied in a cross-cultural context. The course aims to promote an understanding of cultural issues by encouraging students to be self-reflective and examine their own cultural selves as a starting point for discussion. Topics covered in the course include: language and communication, personality and emotion, attachment and parenting, social behaviour, gender and personal relationships.

Course aims and objectives

(1) General aims
(a) To provide students with an understanding of the relationship between psychology and culture, and the importance of cultural perspectives in psychology.
(b) To provide students with an understanding of the important issues in cross-cultural research such as: methodology, etics and emics and ecological validity.
(c) To provide students with an opportunity to reflect on their own cultural experiences and use them in the understanding of psychological processes.

(2) Learning outcomes
(a) By the first assignment students should be familiar with methodological issues and the relationships between culture and cognitive processes.

(b) By mid-way through the semester students should be familiar with the relationships between culture and language, communication and socialisation.
(c) By three-quarters of the way through the course students should be familiar with the areas of culture and social behaviour and identity.
(d) By the end of the course students should be able to discuss and understand the relationship between culture and psychology, major issues in this area, research methodologies, and should be able to articulate how their own process of reflecting on their own cultural experience has enhanced their understanding of psychological processes.

Teaching methods

Course material is presented in three ways:

(1) formal lectures with handouts.
(2) readings and group discussion
(3) journal presentations

In all cases material being covered and assigned reading is indicated on the course schedule and students are expected to come to class well-prepared. A student who comes to class unprepared may be asked to leave and this will count as an absence.

Attendance policy

Attendance at classes is compulsory. There is a strict attendance policy which will be enforced without exception. A student incurring more than 4 absences will be asked to withdraw themselves from the course and students are expected to process their own withdrawal. Students are also reminded that it is now the University's policy that students are responsible for withdrawing themselves from a course if they are dissatisfied with their performance. A student who does not process a Withdrawal by the publicized deadline will be expected to sit the final examination. Being asked to leave a class because the student is unprepared will count as an absence.

Course evaluation

(1) Assignments
There are five components being evaluated for grade in this course:

(1) Journal presentation – 10%
(2) Research paper – 20%
(3) Self-development paper – 20%
(4) Mid-term examination – 20%
(5) Final examination – 30%

All papers should be approximately 2000–2500 words in length, should be word-processed and should contain a full bibliography. All sources should be properly cited using the standard format. All papers should be presented with a cover sheet containing the following information:
Title of the essay, name of the course and the tutor, name of the student, and a word count.
Papers handed in late will be penalised 0.33 of a grade point for each day they are late.

(2) Criteria for assessment
Journal presentation:
> Initiative, clarity, reflection and thoughtfulness, reading.

Research paper:
> Presentation, argument, analysis, independent research, critical thinking, bibliography.

Self-development paper:
> Based on journal, reflection of questions, concerns and feedback received during the course, students must assess what they have learnt about themselves and be able to relate this knowledge to the topics and issues raised in the course.

Mid-term examination:
> A short answer paper including assessment of the factual information presented in the first half of the course.

Final examination:
> Assessment of factual information with respect to critical issues relating to the entire course.

(3) Grading policy
As a guide the following general criteria apply to all work:

- Grade 'F' – a fail, applies to non-submission of work, late work, work which is illegible or chaotic, work which does not address the requirements of the assignment, work which is submitted for another class, plagiarism. In exams. this would represent a grade of 40% or below.
- Grade 'D' – applies to unsatisfactory work (D–), very poor work (D), or work which is extremely weak (D+). This grade band is used for work that shows little or no awareness of subject material and/or work that is badly presented. In exams. these grades would be used for scores between 40% and 55%.
- Grade 'C' – is used for work that has achieved the passing standard in an exam., between 55% and 70%. It is used for work that is basically competent (C–), competent and containing the minimum amount of

required information (C), and work that indicates that the student has paid attention to the requirements of the assignment (C+).

- Grade 'B' – is used for good work that obtains a grade of between 70% and 85% in an exam. It applies to work that shows a good grasp of subject material and shows evidence of critical thinking and independent research. Work of good quality is usually awarded a grade of (B–), work which is of good quality and is thorough and well presented receives a grade of (B), and in addition if the student shows evidence of independent and analytical thinking a grade of (B+) is awarded.

- Grade 'A' – is awarded for exceptional work which achieves a mark of 85% or above in an exam. Students must demonstrate a comprehensive understanding of concepts and issues. Students whose work is of exceptionally high standard receive an (A–) and students who also show an advanced level of critical and analytical ability receive an (A).

Course Textbook (To be bought)
Matsumoto, D. (1996) *Culture and Psychology*. Brooks Cole Pub. Co.

Additional reading
Berry, J.W., Poortinga, Y.H., Segall, M.H. and Dasen, P.R. (1992) *Cross-Cultural Psychology: Research and Applications*. Cambridge: Cambridge University Press.
Bleichrodt, N. and Drenth, P.J.D. (1991) *Contemporary Issues in Cross-Cultural Psychology*. Lisse: Swets & Zeitlinger.
Cole, M. and Scribner, S. (1974) *Culture and Thought*. New York: John Wiley and Sons.
Iwawaki, S., Kashima, Y. and Leung, K. (eds) (1992) *Innovations in Cross-Cultural Psychology*. Lisse: Swets & Zeitlinger.
Kagitcibasi, C. (ed.) (1987) *Growth and Progress in Cross-Cultural Psychology*. Lisse: Swets & Zeitlinger.
Lonner, W.L. and Malpass, R.S. (1994) *Psychology and Culture*. MA: Allyn & Bacon Inc.
Rath, R., Asthana, H.S., Sinha, D. and Sinha, J.B.P. (eds) (1982) *Diversity and Unity in Cross-Cultural Psychology*. Lisse: Swets & Zeitlinger.
Warren, N. (ed.) (1980) *Studies in Cross-Cultural Psychology* (Vol. 2). London: Academic Press.

Course Schedule
The assigned readings are taken from:

(1) *Culture and Psychology* by D. Matsumoto (M).
(2) *Culture and Thought* by M. Cole and S. Scribner (C&S).
(3) *Psychology and Culture* by W.J. Lonner and R.S. Malpass (L&M).

With the exception of the first class all readings should be completed before the designated class.

Weeks		Topic	Reading
1	a)	Introduction and Rationale. Why cultural psychology? Ethnocentrism in psychology	Ch.1(M)
	b)	Methods and issues when comparing cultures	Chs. 2 & 4(M)
2	a)	Role play, Listening skills, working in groups, communication skills	
	b)	**Discussion:** journals	
		Discussion: 'When psychology & culture meet'	L&M p.1–12
3	a)	Language & Communication	Ch. 14 (M)
		Culture & Non-Verbal communication	Ch. 13 (M)
	b)	Culture & Language	Ch.13 (M)
			Ch.3 (C&S)
4	a)	Culture & Language	Ch.13 (M)
			Ch.3 (C&S)
		Discussion: Journals	
		Discussion: 'World without words'	L&M Ch. 25
5	a)	Self, personality and emotion	Ch.3 (M)
	b)	Culture and self	Ch.3 (M)
		Essay 1 due	
6	a)	Culture and emotion	Ch.12 (M)
	b)	Mid-term review	
		Discussion: Journals	
		Mid-term break	
7		**Mid-term examination**	
8	a)	Enculturation and socialisation	Ch.5 (M)
	b)	Culture and attachment'	Ch.5 (M)
9	a)	Culture, values and gender	Chs. 5&10 (M)
	b)	**Discussion:** Journals	
		Discussion: 'Patterns of parenting'	L&M Ch.16
10	a)	Groups and social behaviour	Chs. 7&8 (M)
	b)	Groups and intergroup behaviour	Chs. 7&8 (M)
11	a)	Attributions and stereotypes	L&M. Ch.12
	b)	**Discussion:** Journals	
		Discussion: 'A multicultural view of stereotyping'	
12		**Journal presentations** a) Culture and education b) Bilingualism c) Culture shock BREAK d) Intercultural relationships e) Stereotypes f) Culture and gender	
13		Discussion: Re-entry shock Summary and review **Essay 2 due (Self-reflection)**	L&M Ch.36

Chapter 11

English for the English:
An Intercultural Approach

DAVID STEVENS

> News from a forrein Country came,
> As if my Treasure and my Wealth lay there:
> So much it did my Heart Enflame!
> Twas wont to call my Soul into mine Ear.
>
> Thomas Traherne (1637–74) On News

Starting Points

In 1921 George Sampson's seminal book on English teaching in British schools *English for the English* was published. Sampson was primarily concerned to establish the subject English – native language teaching, in effect – as the mainstay of the English school curriculum, and to point the way forward for literature-based English teaching as a humanising force in that curriculum. In so doing, Sampson was very much part – indeed he was one of the main instigators – of what might be termed the 'cultural heritage' model of English teaching: a way of transmitting, reinforcing and renewing the national culture in a time of increasing secularity and spiritual uncertainty. Charges of national exclusivity and intellectual elitism have been frequently levelled against such a position and yet, in practice, this model remains a powerful influence. My purpose here is to re-evaluate cultural heritage, and its attendant notions of an arts-based curriculum and student-centred creative self-discovery, in the light of gathering concern for intercultural identities in education. In the sense that good art, and perhaps especially poetry, *notices* things, we have a significant model for the intercultural venture. As Isca Salzberger-Wittenberg (1983: 61) maintains, 'What is needed in the first place is the willingness to pay attention; to listen and look and use all our senses to apprehend what is being communicated'.

This chapter, then, will focus on the central position of literature teaching for intercultural awareness, based on a slightly ironic re-working, or amplification, of Sampson's 1921 title of *English for the English*. In the present context of a book drawing upon international practices and points of view, perhaps a further word of explanation, if not quite apology, is necessary. For me, there is a sense in which native language teaching (in this instance, English) ought to stress intercultural concerns precisely because it may seem likely to avoid it. The alternative is to have a narrowly conceived and ultimately ethnocentric native-language education as the cornerstone of each nation's school curriculum. This would be wholly inappropriate as we move into the information / communications obsessed world of the 21st century; there are already quite enough nationalistic and ethnocentric influences at work, and I feel we need to counter them in a coherent and principled way.

But whereas most intercultural writing in this context has focused on the empathetic possibilities of literature teaching – how it *feels* to be of another culture in terms of time, place or class, for instance – I intend here to explore ways in which literature may be taught as a more personally liberating force: a rediscovery of innocence; a sense of wonder; and of strangeness. Literature in this context may be seen to carry fundamentally aesthetic rather than social connotations and, as such, its study is more an arts-based than a humanities-based subject, insofar as this distinction is helpful. As the novelist Aidan Chambers (1985: 2–3) maintains,

> I would go as far as to say that it is this particular use of language – the literary use that some have called 'storying' – that defines humanity and makes us human. . . .this particular form of language and our skill in using it empower us in being what we are, and make it possible for us to conceive of being more than we are'.

It is the latter part of this quotation, 'being more than we are', which for me chimes harmoniously with the intercultural quest. Harold Bloom says very much the same in his seminal (and significantly titled) *Shakespeare: The Invention of the Human* (1999). It is the sense of openness to experience which seems to me fundamental to any real intercultural development, and I attempt to draw on research (in two British schools) and a wide range of both contemporary and classic writers and commentators to explore some possibilities. In the 1999 Durham Intercultural Symposium, Lothar Bredella (1990: 1) made what was for me a key observation that

> we need complex intercultural encounters which can make us aware of what is at stake in intercultural understanding and what we can learn from it . . . . Literary texts can provide us with these complex situations

and are able to arouse our curiosity for others. Thus they can enable students to 'benefit rather than suffer' from intercultural encounters. (Bredella 1999: 1).

This seems an excellent starting point, suggesting as it does, perhaps, a synthesis of the two views of literature-in-education to which I alluded earlier: the empathetic and that of personal imaginative growth.

There are several other starting points too. First among these must be my own personal experience – how else could it be? – both professional and otherwise. I have only relatively recently become involved in intercultural matters, largely by means of a project through which British and Bulgarian student teachers had the enlightening opportunity to teach in each other's nations' schools. I am acutely aware that the bulk of my professional experience has been in teaching English to English children and, latterly, preparing student teachers for that profession. I cannot even claim that any of the four comprehensive schools I taught in had more than a sprinkling of children from diverse ethnic backgrounds, and my only, rather token, concern was for ensuring that there were several 'multicultural' books in English departmental stock-cupboards. Attending intercultural conferences with much-travelled multilinguists, as well as writing about, editing and discussing intercultural issues, has forced me to re-think my own position. And not only professionally: leafing through *The Times Educational Supplement* recently, I was startled to come across a photograph, illustrating a book about the *Kindertransport* experience, of my mother as a 14-year-old girl arriving in England in 1938 as a half-Jewish Austrian refugee. Sometimes it takes something like this to act as a catalyst in developing and crystallising my own thoughts and feelings. On discussing this obviously painful experience with my mother, I realised why she had not brought me up bi-lingually despite habitually speaking German to her mother: she was too ashamed of her Austrian heritage. In fact it took many years before she could once again visit her home country and enjoy its positive attributes, and, as she has told me, consequently live more easily in her adoptive country and its culture. What does this suggest about notions of interculturality? Well, for me, two things: first, that one has to feel easy about one's own cultural (national?) identity if another culture is to be additionally understood; and second, that all cultural identities must have in them, at least for sensitive participants, elements of ambivalence.

This ambivalence certainly struck me during a recent holiday in Austria, which I used partly to discover this aspect of my own background. One example may suffice: we visited the birthplace of my favourite composer, Anton Bruckner, which I found a deeply moving experience. I then discovered that he was also much loved by Hitler, who intended to enshrine his memory in the city of Linz, and that nearby was a horrific reminder of that era – Mauthausen concentration camp. Later, exploring my mother's home city, Vienna, I began to piece my thoughts together. It was, of course, in this cosmopolitan city that Hitler developed his xenophobia, if that is not too kind a word. In the midst of cultural, intellectual and artistic diversity represented by such people as Freud, Wittgenstein, Mahler, Klimt and many others, it was and is clearly possible to narrow one's mind in hatred and exclusion. Which is a long way round to saying that, whatever else it might be and however else it might arrive, interculturality, like its opposite tendency, is ultimately a state of mind, an outlook towards the world. And as such it is the legitimate province of education – perhaps especially native language teaching through literature study and subsequent open discussion – for that, if anywhere in the school context, is where young people's fundamental outlook is likely to take shape.

Other starting points may also connect. My research into the teaching of the poetry of William Blake, and the relevance of his thought to today's educational world, was one such. It strikes me that Blake in some ways is a strange intercultural model: he travelled very little, living virtually all his life in London, was largely self-educated and believed strongly in the potential of 'Albion' or England. And yet he appears to me as the ideal model for the liberating possibilities of imaginative creativity through the fostering of an openness to all experience – which I am contending here is the essential pre-requisite of an intercultural outlook. In fact, I would go further: it is the intercultural outlook itself. My work with sixth-form (age 17–18) English students on Blake provides one of the practical illustrations of my thesis here, and his guiding, inspirational words I quote frequently. Another starting point, as mentioned earlier, was my experience with student teachers in Bulgarian schools from 1998 to 2000 (Stevens, 2000a). These teaching visits, and the reciprocal visits of Bulgarian student teachers to English secondary schools, have led me to ponder on what precisely (or somewhat imprecisely) an intercultural classroom might look like, especially in terms of native language (English) teaching. Too broad and inclusive a definition would be meaningless – clearly it is not just 'normal' English teaching, whatever that is – and yet the characteristics of such a classroom have to emerge from good existing pedagogical practice if they are to take root and gain nourishment. This perception has informed recent research I have conducted into the nature of English as an arts-based subject, with specific reference to the teaching of poetry to Year 7 (age 11–12) students, and provides the second of the illustrative examples in this chapter. To round off my previous Bulgarian paper (Stevens, 2000a: 53–4), I quoted from Friel's play *Translations*, in which 'the available words and the available grammar' are mentioned as the essence of any language teaching.

However the question arises: 'But will that help you to interpret between privacies?', to which there is no answer: 'I have no idea. But it's all we have'. I optimistically concluded that ' "All we have" may be great deal more than I . . . thought possible', the present chapter attempts to develop this starting point and perhaps begin to show why that is.

Blake and Vision

William Blake, in one of his 'Memorable Fancies' from *The Marriage of Heaven and Hell*, wrote that 'If the doors of perception were cleansed, everything would appear as it is, infinite'. This seems an apt guiding principle for the intercultural project incipient in all of us: an appreciation of the infinite possibilities in all things, and particularly human beings. And the method? Blake had something to say about this too, and much of his thought may be directly applied to the field of education (see Stevens [2000b] for a fuller consideration of this topic). For the moment, though, his advice, from the epic 'Jerusalem',

> I give you the end of a golden string,
> Only wind it into a ball,
> It will lead you in at Heaven's gate
> Built in Jerusalem's wall

may suffice. This verse, it seems to me, encapsulates the role of the intercultural teacher – even if we are not always sure what sort of culture Heaven, or even Jerusalem, belongs to. Essentially it alludes to the balance – or perhaps tension – between the teacher and the student. the teacher, like the teacher quoted previously from Friel's *Translations*, provides 'the available words and the available grammar'; the student winds the ball. It suggests also a balance between teacher involvement in the process of learning and the ability to stand back, to give space. And for this to happen, there is a need for a capacity to 'de-centre' from the teacher – a sense of knowing how it feels to discover anew without undue interference, yet with the security of guidance if and when required. All these are essential features of the intercultural classroom, concerning itself with the microcosmic interculturalities of the classroom population itself as well as the broader implications of global cultural meetings. As Blake had it, 'To see a world in a grain of sand': truth is to be found not in grand statements but in the 'minute particulars' of life. This may be an apt comment on the nature of poetry too, emphasising its synecdochal qualities, and suggesting its appropriateness as both means and end of intercultural teaching.

I shall return to Blake in the practical classroom context later, and move now to a more recent (and prosaic) commentary on creativity in education:

the committee-written, but nevertheless valuable, *All Our Futures: Creativity, Culture and Education* (National Advisory Committee on Creative and Cultural Education (NACCCE), 1999). According to this report, focused as it is on the nature of the arts in the English education system, the foremost purpose of cultural education (and by implication, intercultural education too) is to 'enable young people to recognise, explore and understand their own cultural assumptions and values'. The report goes on to elaborate:

> Most young people belong simultaneously to a range of different cultural groups and communities . . . . All young people, particularly during adolescence, are faced with a complex task of constructing a sense of personal identity from what is now an accelerating traffic of images, ideas, pressures and expectations that surround them from home, friends, street culture, the media and from commercial interests of every sort' (p. 49).

Arts education, specifically when focused on literature in the present context, has a powerful role to play in making sense of this welter of confusing impressions – and not just during adolescence. As well as forging an idea of self-identity, such an education should provide the opportunity to understand, tolerate and empathise with other possible identities, both for oneself (whether teacher or student, for the boundaries inevitably dissolve) and for the other. The experience of reading literature gives us cause to reflect on these areas, holding up a mirror to our own cultural identities in order that this reflection may occur. In a rather more complex way, too, it allows for multiple reflections in so far as each reader, in the collaborative conditions of the creative classroom, brings new meanings and interpretations. It is perhaps, as ever, best to leave it to a poet to say this more succinctly and suggestively: Bob Dylan in the Blakean song 'Every Grain of Sand', noting

> . . . the broken mirror of innocence
> On each forgotten face . . .
> Sometimes I turn there's someone there
> Other times it's only me'.

This, then, is the flash of insight, carefully nurtured as it should be through proper education, that may give rise to the intercultural perspective. If it does not happen, in some form or another, the most rigorously structured study of the nuances of other cultures may be doomed to failure or, at best, superficiality. Although what we are talking about here is an intensely personal experience, it is also intensely interpersonal – intercultural, in fact. As Imison puts it (quoted in NACCCE, 1999: 50): 'If you only understand one culture it is like seeing with one eye only, but if you add the dimension of other cultures, you become binocular and things can be seen in perspective. It allows you to appreciate much more.' And the added appreciation is in terms of appreciation of one's own value – like a precious artefact – as well as simply broadening one's outlook by adding to the number of different cultures of which one is aware. To return briefly to Thomas Traherne: his vision of the world is powerfully child-like, celebratory and profoundly personal; and yet it espouses the potential of others too, precisely because of its subjectivity:

> You never enjoy the world aright, till the sea itself floweth in your veins, till you are clothed with the heavens and crowned with the stars: and perceive yourself to be the sole heir of the whole world, and more than so, because men are in it *who are every one sole heirs as well as you*. [my italics] (Century 1, 29 see Traherne, 1960).

This state of mind Traherne called 'felicity', and it provides the basis of his joyful philosophy, expounded principally in the *Centuries*. I think it would be entirely wrong to dismiss Traherne as an unworldly mystic; he was, in fact, acutely aware of the impediments to visionary fulfilment, not least through the processes of institutional education. He wrote perceptively of his own days at Oxford, having initially paid tribute to the breadth of learning possible there,

> Nevertheless some things were defective too. There was never a tutor that did professly teach Felicity, though that be the mistress of all other sciences. Nor did any of us study those things but as aliena, which we ought to have studied as our enjoyments. We studied to inform our knowledge but knew not for what end we so studied. And for lack of aiming at a certain end we erred in the manner. (Century 3, 37)

So, for Traherne, mere knowledge is clearly insufficient: it leaves people unrealised, unsatisfied. And it may still be utterly relevant to proclaim this, for it is the essence of the intercultural adventure.

Martian Poetry in the Classroom

Kress (1995: 90) brings us sharply up to date in his reminder that subjectivity, as for Traherne, is a vital element in productive classroom encounters – in an expansive rather than reductive, narrowing sense:

> In a view of English as central in the making of a culture of innovation the production of subjectivity is at the centre, between social and cultural possibilities and forces on the one hand – available resources, structures of power – and the individual's action in the making of signs on the other . . . [the child's] interest in the making of signs may range

from dispositions called 'conformity' to those called 'resistance' . . .
Whether in solidarity or subversion, the child's own production of her
representational resources is intimately connected, in a relation of reci-
procity, with her production of her subjectivity.

But I have delayed answering the previously posed question 'what
would the intercultural classroom (in the literature-based context already
outlined) actually look like?' long enough, sketching in the background.
My first more detailed example centres on the teaching of Craig Raine's
poem 'A Martian Sends a Postcard Home' (Bazzini & Leenerts, 2001), – and
not because I wish to extend interculturality to Martians. Not yet, anyway.
As readers may not be familiar with the poem itself, I am including it here.

A Martian Sends a Postcard Home

Caxtons are mechanical birds with many wings
and some are treasured for their markings –

they cause the eyes to melt
or the body to shriek without pain.

I have never seen one fly, but
sometimes they perch on the hand.

Mist is when the sky is tired of flight
and rests its soft machine on ground:

then the world is dim and bookish
like engravings under tissue paper.

Rain is when the earth is television.
It has the property of making colours darker.

Model T is a room with the lock inside –
a key is turned to free the world

for movement, so quick there is a film
to watch for anything missed.

But time is tied to the wrist
or kept in a box, ticking with impatience.

In homes a haunted apparatus sleeps,
that snores when you pick it up.

If the ghost cries, they carry
it to their lips and soothe it to sleep

with sounds. And yet, they wake it up
deliberately, by tickling with a finger.

Only the young are allowed to suffer
openly. Adults go to a punishment room

with water but nothing to eat.
They lock the door and suffer the noises

alone. No one is exempt
and everyone's pain has a different smell.

at night, when all the colours die,
they hide in pairs

and read about themselves –
in colour, with their eyelids shut.

If, in the present context, the appeal of poetry is to engender a sense of wonder in our familiar surroundings through the stretching, exploratory use of language, then this poem performs that role admirably. I have been greatly impressed by the responses of Year 7 (age 11–12) students, in a mixed ability class, to a reading of this poem – responses which showed a depth of feeling for the strangeness and wonder of life which I and other adults present in this lesson found quite startling. Raine's poem, of course, belongs to the 'Martian' school, for whom the 'making strange' of the familiar is central. In this sense there may be a helpful echo of Brecht, for whom 'alienating an event or a character means first of all stripping the event of its self-evident, familiar, obvious quality and creating a sense of astonishment and curiosity about them' (quoted in Brooker, 1994: 191). Brecht's term *'Verfremdung'* is appropriate here: a potentially liberating, even celebratory, de-familiarisation. Warnock (1976: 197) elaborates usefully on this essentially imaginative process:

> the creative artist, then, constructs an external form which is to be interpreted as signifying something which does not, in the same sense, exist. Both artist and spectator have to detach themselves from the

world in order to think of certain objects in the world in a new way, as signifying something else.

The attendant tension between involved engagement and critical distance must surely be central to the notion of the intercultural classroom. Like so much else of value, too, this notion is essentially Romantic: Shelley in his *Defence of Poetry* (1821; quoted in Barry, 1995: 24) maintained that poetry, potentially, 'strips the veil of familiarity from the world . . . [and] . . . purges from our inward sight the film of familiarity . . . It compels us to feel that which we perceive, and to imagine that which we know'. This seems a good place to start our practical consideration of poetry in the secondary school English lesson.

The lesson itself comprised several stages:

- The teacher reading the poem aloud, with copies previously distributed to each student
- Subsequent discussion on the nature of the poem, with an explanation given that the poem deals with eight different everyday objects or experiences seen through the eyes of the 'Martian' visitor to earth
- Whole-class guessing as to what precisely these objects/experiences may be. Several are pretty self-explanatory, although couched in unusual terms, such as

> Mist is when the sky is tired of flight
> and rests its soft machine on the ground:
>
> then the world is dim and bookish
> like engravings under tissue paper.

Others take more discovery, which is where the fun lies. For example, the telephone:

> In homes, a haunted apparatus sleeps,
> that snores when you pick it up.
>
> If the ghost cries, they carry it
> To their lips and soothe it to sleep
>
> With sounds. And yet, they wake it up
> Deliberately, by tickling with a finger'.

And the penultimate object, the lavatory, can cause much amusement – and not a little bemusement before successful guessing of the 'answer'

- Small groups then discuss, note and report back to the whole class on possible subjects drawn from familiar everyday experience, with a view to eventual poetic expression
- A further variation here might be to include photographic or artistic representations of 'normal' objects seen from unusual angles or in a new light (both literally and metaphorically), again with the possibility of awakening from the unseeing contempt so often bred by familiarity. There is in this the opportunity to develop a media-based exploration of images.
- Students then fashion their ideas and observations into 'Martian' poems, using the given convention of the Martian visitor trying to make sense of Earthly objects, customs and ideas. Possibilities include school, money, items of furniture and articles of clothing. Illustrations might also be interesting. Volunteers go on to read poems aloud, with the class guessing the subject matter of each poem.

I include some examples of extracts from poems written by students following this scheme of work, to give a fuller flavour of the possibilities:

> It lives on the ceiling
> It never moves
> But when it grows dark
> It gets angry and explodes. (Kimberley, age 14)

> I lie there watching the world
> Through a television that's been switched off
> I feel so scared
> I daren't even cough. (Laura, age 12)

> It's a giant snake with many mouths
> Which travels very fast
> Swallowing all its victims whole
> But people wave as their friends get eaten. (Paul, age 12)

It is important in planning and teaching literature-based work that acknowledgement is made of the likely stages of learning. In case this seems rather deterministic and mechanical, ignoring the subtle nuances of classroom relationships, we need too to keep a realistic sense that what is *taught* does not necessarily correlate in any predictable way to what may be *learned*. This important rider notwithstanding, it is useful to envisage the stages of learning in terms of

- the descriptive – the initial reading of the poem, for example;
- the reflective – which may include general or specific textual discussion and questioning;
- the speculative – the kinds of activity arising from textual study, such as pupils' writing their own poems, stimulated by, but possibly wandering some way from, the initial reading.

Clearly, the implication of reflection is as some sort of mirroring process; in itself it is not sufficient to provide a sound basis for the speculative, active, creative stage. As well as the *reflective*, then, we need to cater for and stimulate the *illuminative*, whereby the active begins to develop from the passive. In terms of 'A Martian Sends a Postcard Home', the poem suggests it is possible to find in everyday experience exciting scope for observation, description, reflection and illumination, not least through empathetic consideration of the 'narrative voice'. Further, there is a sense that everyday language works through metaphor, and an opportunity arises for an exploration of the nature of figurative colloquial language in diverse cultural contexts: poetry, as language working hard, can provide a springboard into various aspects of study. Sometimes the forms of the poems themselves derive from different cultural sources, and this too can be helpful. Anglo-Saxon *Kennings*, for example, work by shocking the reader into seeing something through its function (my daughter used to call her shoes a 'toes house') – apart from anything else, what a fascinating way into studying different languages. And then there are *Haiku*, tightly formed Japanese poems suggestive of a flash of insight.

Blake in the Classroom

I return next to Blake. Much of what follows is based on research I undertook on the teaching of Blake's *Songs of Innocence and of Experience* to a group of 14 Year 12 (16–17 year old) students specialising in English literature. I was particularly focusing on notions of what types of literal and non-literal understanding may be achieved through study of Blake's writing, and how the poems might connect to the students' broader cultural experiences. The immediate teaching context was to spend a term on Blake, based on a weekly session of one hour and forty minutes, culminating in a written coursework assignment focusing on an understanding of the relationship between innocence and experience in his writing. Early in Year 12 as it was, in their second term of study, the students had little experience of close textual reading, and none of Blake. My initial brief exposition of Blake's life and times served to remind me of the sixth-form students' general lack of awareness of the historical and cultural context Blake worked in. This too is an intercultural concern, in the very basic sense that we are really speaking about building bridges between cultural vantage points. I attempted to make this session as interactive as possible by asking students, working in pairs, to jot down responses to such terms as 'romantic', 'imagination', 'innocence' and 'experience', and to historically relevant details like '1789', 'the French Revolution', 'the slave trade' and 'the American War of Independence'. Certain interesting ideas did emerge, which gave us useful starting points – linking 'imagination' with 'innocence', for example – but there were few accurate perceptions of the broadly historical phenomena. In the end I talked through some of the relevant areas from the Resource Notes of my edition of Blake, which we were using, including the time line, and recommended a more thorough individual study before our next session.

The following week, the group, working in different pairs, went on to study self-selected poems – one each from *Innocence* and *Experience* – in the light of questions focusing on what may be understood literally and what metaphorically from a first reading, and how the two relate to each other. The basic questions I posed in an attempt to elicit this distinction were:

(1) In your chosen poems, list the main images; what is your understanding of them in terms of their literal reality in your experience?
(2) Explore possible connotations of these images, in terms of your own ideas and Blake's use of them in the poems. Do they 'work' for you as pictures in your mind's eye?

As a whole group we discussed these and related questions briefly, as the distinction between literal and metaphorical is an elusive one, before moving on to the task itself. I deliberately chose the pairs, attempting to combine students whose approaches and sympathies I thought would contrast, even conflict. Indeed, monitoring these explorations, I became conscious of a split developing within the group between those receptive – often quite excitedly – to Blake's ideas on the power of the imagination, and those who, not to put too fine a point on it, were becoming bored. Attraction or otherwise to Blake seemed to depend on attitudes towards conventionality in terms of thought and behaviour. Several of the group aspired to more unconventional ways of thinking, and they tended to find Blake a sympathetic figure at least in terms of the ideas expressed in the poems we studied: the liberating quality of the imagination and, by the same token, the limited nature of 'normal' consciousness. Others in the group took what may be described as a more common sense approach, tending to dismiss Blake as 'weird' – in similar terms to those used by his contemporary detractors. Clearly, an appreciation of literature and its possible personal impact depends largely on attitudes already

formed: imaginary experience depends on the thoughts, feelings and relationships readers can actively bring to bear from their own personal
lives. Take, for example, this extracted exchange on *The Clod and the
Pebble*:

Student A: It's about a clod of clay being squashed . . . but why write a
poem about it?

Student B: And what about the pebble .. surely a pebble can't float . . .

Student A: Perhaps it doesn't really matter . . . maybe it's really about
two different types of people . . . one's a clod who gets
stamped on . . . maybe he's too kind and generous and then
gets walked over . . .

Student B: Squelch of mud oozing everywhere . . . it still seems silly to
me: a poem about mud . . .

And so the conversation continued. One train of thought led from the
poem to expand its possible implications and meanings, whilst returning
constantly for fresh insights. The other got bogged down – if the expression
may be forgiven in this context – in the idea that meaningful, sensitive poetry
just cannot be written about lumps of earth and small pebbles. Similar conversations took place on other poems and in the subsequent whole-group
discussions. As both teacher and researcher, I was anxious not to give interpretations of the poems, but to allow students to grapple with the
possibilities and complexities at this stage with little explicit guidance.

Emerging here are crucial questions concerning who reads Blake's work
and how it may be interpreted. The impossibility, and undesirability, of a
definitive reading of any text has to be continually underlined by the
nature of our teaching approaches and activities, and this was certainly my
aim in teaching, publishing and researching Blake. I can think of no better
author to illustrate this sense of the reader's interpretive power over the
text: his openness to the possibilities of multiple readings and levels of
understanding is a significant part of that robustness to which I alluded
earlier. However, this does leave an important role for the teacher, in the
sense that guidance may well be required before deeper, more satisfying
readings can be achieved. I was also acutely conscious of needing to dispel
the all too prevalent 'hidden meanings' conception of poetry, whereby the
text is seen as some sort of coded puzzle needing only a particular key to
uncover the 'real' meaning. Some of the difficulties experienced by several
of the group – and other students I have encountered subsequently –
stemmed, I think, from the non-literal nature of Blake's verse. For the
literal-minded, indeed, the work can appear strange: the *Songs of Innocence*
may come across as mere nursery rhymes about lambs and angels – which,

in one sense, they are: Blake himself delighted in children's enthusiasm for the songs. A literal reading is likely to be limited rather than faulty, lacking the potential to develop beyond a rather one-dimensional appraisal. For another of the Experience songs, 'The Sick Rose', the following brief extract from a discussion between four of the students, combining two of the pairs who had chosen the same poem, is indicative of the contrasting approaches:

Student A: What I can't see is: how does a worm *fly? I mean I've never seen a* flying worm, have you?

Student B: Maybe it's a special sort of worm . . .

Student A: (sarcastically) Yeah, it could be extinct by now . . .

Student C: But it doesn't make any difference: the worm's an evil force, isn't it? It's symbolic.

Student D: (resignedly) Oh, that again . . .

A familiar tangle? One of the difficulties here for the teacher is in avoiding a hierarchical view of different interpretations, with the symbolic lauding it over rather more literal receptions of the poetry: this would clearly militate against the openness of an interpretive approach which underlies imaginative literature teaching. In a sense, however, we are not talking here of a particular interpretation being correct, or better than another, but rather about modes of interpretation. If literature is to be explored and fruitful connections made with other experiences of life – other cultures in effect – we need to equip our students with the appropriate interpretive tools. What is especially interesting about the sort of exchange quoted briefly here is that the literal interpretation, glib as it is, does not actually lead anywhere: it is unable to transcend its own literalness. Paradoxically, the less literal the approach, the more vivid is the image: witness Student C's 'evil force' idea. Effective English teaching elicits and develops such responses, but the very openness of discussion begs the question: what is the role of the teacher here? In the end, surely, the role of the teacher must be to teach, and fundamental to that is the making available to students some of the possible modes of textual, intertextual and contextual understanding. Over-arching all of this, clearly, is the intercultural dimension – for all texts and contexts derive from, illustrate and creatively lead away from intercultural cross-fertilisation.

My term's work on Blake continued through a more detailed appraisal of Blake's poems, increasingly focusing on definitions of and the relationship between innocence and experience. What emerged, excitingly for me, was a gathering appreciation of the link between

Blake's concept of 'Innocence' and a non-literal understanding of the world; and, correspondingly, the close resemblance of Blake's 'Experience' to literalness. As Blake's terms 'Innocence' and 'Experience' suggest, our primary, infant understanding may well be of the non-literal type, later to be replaced by experienced literal approaches. In the broadly intercultural context, literalness gets you nowhere beyond stilted translation and stilted misapprehension, whereas the language of poetry may lead to a broader intercultural awareness. In Blake we have an important ally in this project, not only in providing texts to study, but, rather more profoundly, in offering an insight into the nature of intercultural education through his art. The preposition *through* is significant here: Blake himself calls for seeing as understanding as opposed to merely recognising, for

> We are led to believe a lie
> when we see not through the eye (from *Auguries of Innocence*)

There are other important allies too, and we need all we can get. Several we have met in the course of this chapter; I will introduce three more by way of conclusion. C.S. Lewis, whose magical – realist writing has certainly awakened many children's and adults' eyes to the possibilities of wonder, wrote that 'through literature I become a thousand people and yet remain myself' (quoted in Chambers, 1985: 5). A contemporary English poet, Simon Armitage, widely taught in English schools, reminds us of the magic to be found in each person's experience of life, even when apparently lacking in glamour:

> I have not toyed with a parachute cord
> while perched on the lip of a light aircraft;
> but I held the wobbly head of a boy
> at the day centre, and stroked his fat hands.
>
> And I guess that the tightness in the throat
> and the tiny cascading sensation
> somewhere inside us are both part of that
> sense of something else. That feeling, I mean.

And T.S. Eliot tells us in 'Little Gidding' how all journeys take us back to ourselves – the essential theme of this chapter:

> We shall not cease from exploration
> And the end of all our exploring
> Will be to arrive where we started
> And know the place for the first time.

References

Andere, M. (ed) (1974) *Thomas Traherne: The Image and Other Selections*. Hereford: Express Logic.

Durly, P. (1995) *Beginning Theory: An Introduction to Literary and Cultural Theory*. Manchester: Manchester University Press.

Bloom, H. 1999, *Shakespeare: The Invention of the Human*. London: Fourth Estate.

Bozzini, G. and Leenerts, C. (eds) (2001) *Literature without Borders*. New York: Prentice Hall.

Bredella, L. (1999) *The Educational Significance of Intercultural Encounters in Literary Texts*. Unpublished paper presented at the Symposium on Intercultural Education, University of Durham.

Chambers, A. (1985) *Booktalk: Occasional Writing on Literature and Children*. Stroud: Thimble Press.

Dylan, B. (1987) *Lyrics 1962–1985*. London: Cape.

Eliot, T.S. (1963) *Collected Poems 1909–1962*. London: Faber and Faber.

Friel, B. (1981) *Translations*. London: Faber and Faber.

Kress, G. (1995) *Writing the Future: English and the Making of a Culture of Innovation*. Sheffield: NATE.

National Advisory Committee on Creative and Cultural Education (1999) *All Our Futures: Creativity, Culture and Education*. Sudbury: DfEE.

Salzberger-Wittenberg, I., Henry, G. and Osborne, E. (1983) *The Emotional Experience of Teaching and Learning*. London: Routledge.

Sampson, G. (1921) *English for the English*. Cambridge: Cambridge University Press.

Stevens, D. (ed.) (1995) *William Blake: Selected Works*. Cambridge: Cambridge University Press.

Stevens, D. (2000a) A reflective account of a working fortnight in Bulgaria with 12 post-graduate student teachers of English and Geography. *Journal of Education for Teaching* 26 (1), 45–54.

Stevens, D. (2000b) William Blake in education: A poet for our times? *Changing English* 7 (1), 55–63.

Traherne, T. (1960) *Centuries*. London: Mowbray.

Warnock, M. (1976) *Imagination*. London: Faber and Faber.

Chapter 12

A Framework for Teaching and Learning 'Intercultural Competence'

SUSANNE WEBER

The worldwide interrelationship between economies and industry, the tendency towards globalisation as well as the introduction of the European Market mean that employees and citizens will, increasingly, be interacting and exchanging ideas and knowledge all over the globe. These developments lead to intercultural encounters which have to be managed and designed both in work and education, as well as in private life. Therefore, on the one hand, intercultural training courses will be necessary to cope with these complex and dynamic intercultural situations whereas, on the other hand, educators on all levels and from all branches claim that they have the means to prepare young people, employees and citizens to deal with the possible difficulties, uncertainties, prejudices and misunderstandings which will arise in such intercultural encounters (Weber, 1997).

The first part of this chapter describes and defines 'being intercultural' and presents a framework ingegrating the 'mindful identity negotiation' approach of Ting-Toomey (1999) and Engeström's approach of 'expansive learning' (Engeström, 1987, 1999). In the second part an application of this theoretical framework is demonstrated for the field of business negotiation in a study with students from vocational schools.

Limitations of Current Intercultural Training Within Business

Currently the many existing intercultural training modules in business studies can be categorised by Brislin's (1989: 445) well-known matrix, according to whether the training modules focus on 'cognition', 'affect' and 'behaviour' as the *targets of training* or whether they provoke a 'low', 'moderate' or 'high' *involvement from the learner*. Thus, modules either include lectures from 'old hands' who have lived in the particular culture and who have dealt with problems similar to those facing the trainees or they include group discussions about topics like prejudice, racism, sexism and discrimination. Within other training courses role play and simulation are used, such as the well-known games Bafá, Bafá or Barnga in which trainees are expected to realise that familiar patterns of behaviour, communication etc. do not work in alien cultural settings.

There is, however, a lot of evidence to suggest that such training courses are not satisfactory:

- more than 50% of businessmen working abroad do their job inadequately (e.g. Dowling & Schuler, 1990; Bird & Dunbar, 1991; Tung, 1987; Bhagat & Prien, 1996: 217);
- mistaken behaviour in foreign countries often leads to extended negative consequences (e.g. Bhagat & Prien, 1996: 218);
- misunderstandings and interruptions take place within mergers and acquisitions negotiations (e.g. Bolten, 1995: 24);
- tensions in the workplace between employees from different cultural backgrounds hinder effective working (e.g. Kartari, 1996; Birsl *et al.*, 1999); and
- training courses in large enterprises are felt to be unsatisfactory (e.g. Warthun, 1997: 164).

Most of these training courses fail for the following reasons:

(1) a holistic theory for describing and analysing the intercultural interaction process is missing (Landis & Bhagat, 1996: XIII);
(2) the goals of modules are often not embedded into broader intercultural training programmes;
(3) the chosen instructional design models are often very traditional and not established within the broader sequence of the whole intercultural training programme;
(4) the total time for intercultural training is often very short;
(5) existing intercultural training modules are generally used for nearly all purposes;
(6) a lot of them betray ethnocentric intentions; and
(7) from a theoretical perspective the training modules neglect the dynamic and development of culture, situations, persons and interactions (cf. Weber, 2000a).

A Proposal for Teaching and Learning an 'Intercultural Competence'

To overcome these problems we developed a framework integrating the 'mindful identity negotiation' approach of Ting-Toomey (1999) and

Engeström's approach of 'expansive learning' (Engeström, 1987; 1999) (see also Weber, 2000a; 2000b; 2001). The 'mindful identity negotiation' perspective is an integrative theory that draws inspiration from four major scholarly disciplines: the work of social identity theory (e.g. Abrams & Hogg, 1990; Brewer & Miller, 1996), symbolic interaction (e.g. McCall & Simmons, 1978; Stryker, 1981, 1991), identity negotiation (e.g. Ting-Toomey, 1988, 1989, 1993) and relational dialects (Baxter & Montgomery, 1996). Engeström's 'expansive learning' approach returns to the social-cultural and historical learning assumptions of Vygotsky (1978), Leontjew (1981), Luira (1981) and their western interpreters (e.g. Cole & Wertsch, 1996; Cole & Engeström, 1993). The intention is to describe and analyse the interaction situation holistically.

With the help of elements from the 'mindful identity negotiation' model, the relationships and interaction processes in intercultural encounters can be isolated, described and analysed. However, just becoming aware of these findings does not automatically lead to an 'intercultural competence'. There needs to be an explicit and conscious integration of the issues which have been raised into the teaching and learning processes. Effective teaching–learning processes should be organised to include an interplay between the following three processes:

(1) *Knowledge acquisition* – initiated via different learning approaches such as 'learn-acting' (e.g. Tramm, 1996), self-organised learning (e.g. Sembill, 1992; Wuttke, 1999), anchored instruction (cf. the Cognition and Technology Group at Vanderbilt, 1997), cognitive apprenticeship (see, e.g., Collins *et al.*, 1989);
(2) *Acculturation processes* – initiated, for example, by 'community of practice' approaches (e.g. Lave, 1988; Wenger, 1998; Collins *et al.*, 1989; Edelson *et al.*, 1996; Zimmermann, 1996; for a new learning culture see Dubs, 1995; Müller, 1996, and for a 'culture of faults' Oser & Spychiger, 2000), and
(3) *Negotiation processes* – initiated via collective 'social-cultural learning' approaches (e.g. Salomon & Perkins, 1998: 8; Engeström, 1999) for developing a common understanding and meaning.

These different forms of learning foster (1) individual knowledge, (2) individual and/or collective knowledge and (3) collective knowledge. Therefore, the analysis has to move from the concept of knowledge transmission to that of an active learner, enhanced by social interactions and common negotiation, theorised by Engeström as 'expansive learning' (1987, 1996, 1999).

Processes of Intercultural Learning According to This Framework

Within intercultural encounters individuals find that their familiar patterns of behaviour, value systems, beliefs, certain practices (e.g. in doing business), symbols and other artifacts no longer function. Their counterparts do not understand them, they themselves are no longer effective in reaching their goals and they feel uncertain, excluded, helpless, vulnerable etc. Some individuals do not relate such problems to cultural issues. They attribute these conflicts to personal 'failure' or 'wrong behaviour'. Other individuals judge their own behaviour as superior and neglect otherness or mark the unfamiliar behaviour as 'bad', 'unfair', 'not right' etc. These people are ethnocentric and they have not followed the learning processes described earlier. In this case other preparatory measures must be conducted to open up and sensitise their minds. However, this is a normative goal which has to be discussed and legitimised (see the discussion of what 'intercultural competence' means; ie. knowing about other cultures or the ability to interact effectively with people from other cultures etc. e.g., Byram [for example in 1997 as well as in this volume] and Bredella [this volume]).

However, individuals, who are interested in solving these problems of misunderstanding and want to be understood by their counterparts, can find themselves in such intercultural clashes in an *object-orientated activity system* which is *mediated* by instruments, rules, division of labour/joint practice, a *lingua franca*, non-verbal communication or other means, facilitators etc. (Engeström, 1987, 1996, 1999; Ting-Toomey, 1999):

The confrontation between the differing interpretations, practices and identities can lead to some kind of reflection and self-reflection. There is a recognition that there are alternative ways to handle a situation and the personal alternative is just one possibility out of several others. Each person within him- or herself has different layers of identities which become relevant within a particular intercultural situation. However, all individuals have the same basic human needs for self-affirmation: security, trust, inclusion, connection and stability. At the same time their existing practice can be checked and compared. Very often a discussion in which both partners/parties evoke their own desired identities and goals and challenge or support the others' identities is not conducted harmoniously. Even if the participants in the activity agree on the surface level they often find huge contradictions on a deeper level. Nevertheless, an interculturally competent individual will interact in such a way that all participants feel understood, respected and supported.

To get more insight into alien patterns of interpretation and thinking individuals can develop situationally adequate instruments for mindful observation, mindful listening, techniques to recognise the verbal and non-verbal cues in the interactions, to discover the roles the interaction partners take in that particular situation, interview techniques for recovering the personal and/or situational background etc. On the basis of this information they are able to work out the identity needs and attitudes of other individuals or groups (e.g. their cultural, ethnical, gender, role-oriented identities and their degree of identification with these orientations), and their own needs and attitudes in more detail. Interculturally competent individuals do these analyses and model the core contradictions mindfully (which means that they are tolerant of ambiguity and are open, flexible, respectful, adaptable, sensitive and creative as well as metacognitive).

On the basis of these perceived identity needs and their extended cultural knowledge (e.g. knowledge about cultural value orientations, verbal and non-verbal communication styles, development of relationships, group interactions, conflict management, adaptation processes) they develop, by integration and transformation, mindful intercultural skills (e.g. techniques for supporting identities, facework management, seating arrangements, moderating multicultural group discussions etc.) in the sense of an 'expansive' solution.

When this integration and transformation achieve the necessary degree of appropriateness and effectiveness and each partner or group involved in the interaction is satisfied – i.e. when all participants feel understood, respected and supported –a commonly shared meaning can be negotiated and goals attained. From this negotiation process a new culture will emerge with shared meanings, values and norms between the interacting individuals and/or groups: a so-called 'inter-culture' (cf. Bolten, 1995) or 'boundary object' (cf. Engeström, 1999). Using this new culture business can be run and solutions implemented.

In principle, this whole process has to be repeated in each new encounter. In reality, the individuals automatise this process: they act on the basis of their already negotiated results or shared meanings. But this must be checked from time to time to avoid misunderstandings and failures within the interacting respectively within the 'activity system' (cf. Tuomi-Gröhn & Engeström, 2001; Ting-Toomey, 1999). The outcome of an activity system has also to be questionned, analysed, discussed, modelled and re-negotiated when new individuals join it or when it is integrated into another existing or new activity system.

Following this idealised learning process individual growth as well as re-structuring of the social context occur. In reality many intercultural learning processes do not follow these phases exactly in a uni-directional vertical way. They appear in different shapes: interrupted, disintegrated, fractional, regressive or discontinuously (see also Engeström, 1996: 136). How 'mindful identity negotiation' processes are conducted within certain intercultural interactions is an empirical problem that has to be investigated.

The Role of the Teacher Within Such a Learning Framework

Within this learning framework the role of the teacher shifts from a knowledge transmitter to a facilitator and counsellor. His or her task is to construct and arrange complex, stimulating learning environments which (hopefully) initiate the learning processes described earlier and in which collaborative interactions and negotiations are possible. In addition, the teacher monitors and counsels the students and interacting groups according to their specific requirements.

An Application of This Learning Framework

Description of the first step of experimentation

An intercultural competence understood as 'mindful identity negotiation' is a long-term project – also in the sense of life-long learning (e.g. Weber, 2000c), which includes different categories of knowledge (individual and collective knowledge; knowledge of oneself, skills and cultural knowledge etc.), reached via different learning activities initiated by various teaching and learning approaches (acquiring facts, self-reflection, socialisation and negotiation processes etc.).

As a very first step we ran a developmental study as a preparatory course with students from several vocational schools (with an average age of about 18 years). Our aim was to construct a learning environment for initiating a mindful-identity-negotiation process as a process of intercultural learning. We, therefore, used the idea of the simulation ECOTONOS (cf. Nipporica Associates, 1993) which combines role-play with a business case study. Within this simulation the course was divided into three groups of five to eight students. Each group was given cultural role cards and the task to 'acculturate' to their new fictive culture. In addition, they received the first part of the business case study which was to be solved by members of the new fictive culture (mono-cultural group work). Then the groups' respective fictive cultures were mixed to simulate 'intercultural clashes'. Within these encounters they had to solve the second part of the business case study – now as 'intercultural' group work. They were asked not to adopt one opinion quickly or to agree on a bad compromise but to get into a dialogue and to negotiate a commonly shared understanding and solution with regard to the problem. The tasks and problems given to the students within the case study were related to their commercial school curricula.

Selected episodes demonstrating the effects of this first experimentation as well as the tools and instruments used for analysing the processes

The simulation functioned as a *mediating tool* or *'mirror'* (Engeström, 1996) through which typical intercultural misunderstandings, prejudices and other interaction problems in intercultural encounters (*'contradictions'*) were demonstrated and experienced:

Situation

When the negotiation process got stuck in a group (group 2 in course 5) and the participants got very angry and unsatisfied about the interaction development one member remarked:

> We are taking the whole time and concentrating only on our objectives and content-related logical arguments. I have the feeling that we are talking at cross-purposes, aren't we? We really do not know anything about your culture [pointing to one of the 'foreigners', SW]. What are the important aspects for your culture concerning this issue?

Interpretation

Here a participant of a very dominant 'culture' recognises that they were not paying attention to the other foreign culture, and this was then the way they tried to figure out the main problem and misunderstanding. This verbalisation shows that they developed a sensitivity to and awareness of the necessity of broadening the situation and, thus, acting adequately, effectively and satisfactorily; i.e. to open up and to acquire knowledge about the views of their counterparts including their backgrounds.

Within the subsequent reflection phases the teacher facilitates the process of making sense of their experiences. In the following some examples are briefly presented and discussed:

Tool 1: Flipcharts

The students were asked to reflect on (a) their observed behaviour which occurred within the negotiation process, (b) positive and negative emotions which arose and related reasons and (c) strategies which fostered and hindered the negotiation processes. To visualise their findings they had to fix them on a flipchart. Some student notes in response to these questions are presented in Figure 12.1:

(With respect to question a) Observed and experienced unfamiliar behavior:
– members of the foreign culture did not take our arguments on board
– they stuck very close together
– they manifested an attitude of rejection
– they always interrupted the discussion partners
– they reacted very energetically
– they were dull and narrow-minded

(With respect to question b) Emotions Experienced:
– uncertainty in facing the other, foreign members
– rage, because of permanent interruptions while talking
– pride, when one could realise own goals
– uncertainty, because of the lack of good arguments
– certainty, because of good, strong and convincing arguments

(With respect to question c) Strategies which fostered (+) and which hindered (–)
the negotiation process:
– strong and convincing arguments (+), (–)
– open to compromises (+)
– persistence (–)
–undercover strategies (–)
–interruptions when people are talking (–)
– limited only to the own opinion ( )
– openness (+)
– understanding (+)
– interviewing the others (+)
– listening to others (+)

Figure 12.1 Flipchart notes from course 3

Interpretation
The evidence from these flipcharts shows:

- that the flipchart questions helped the students to sharpen their views on some particular aspects and elements of the interaction;
- that the students experienced 'intercultural interactions' which evoked not only positive but also negative emotions: they were hurt by the behaviour and reactions of their counterparts although the latter were behaving in an adequate and 'proper' way from their foreign

point of view and did not have negative intentions; at the same time they realised that they themselves hurt members of the other culture although they tried to be very gentle towards them, i.e. they realised that their patterns of behaviour no longer worked anymore or worked in a different unpredictable way;

- they also figured out and became conscious of the behaviour and strategies which influenced the intercultural negotiation process in a positive or negative way when approaching a commonly shared meaning and a satisfactory result as a consequence of which they can feel respected and understood. The main and most important issue was to listen to what the others were saying, to let all members participate with their opinions and views.

Tool 2: Questionnaire

Another tool to enable reflection was a questionnaire on 17 important aspects of the mindful identity negotiation, e.g. 'Did you feel certain or vulnerable during the process?' 'How would you judge the behaviour of the members of the unfamiliar cultures: adequate or inadequate?' 'Did you interview your counterparts to get information about their cultural background?' etc. These responses were given whilst still in the role as a member of the fictive culture.

Situation

While answering this questionnaire the learners are already reflecting on the crucial issues influencing the intercultural interaction or mindful-identity-negotiation process:

> When I really think about our group discussion: I did actually not ask the people from the foreign culture about their views and background as it was mentioned in the questionnaire. (A student of group 2 in course 4)

After condensing the responses of the students to all 17 questions, the following patterns in the simulated intercultural interaction process appeared (see Figure 2). These visualised interaction patterns served as a base for discussion and reflection.

Pattern 1 in Figure 12.2

> The members of culture C had the feeling that they *were not understood by the others* (question 7) during the intercultural interaction, that they were *not treated equally and did not have the same chance to participate* within the discussion (question 8), that *neither* their *membership* nor

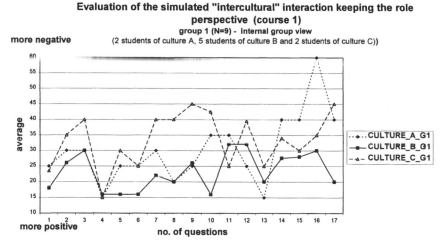

Figure 12.2 Evaluation of the simulated intercultural interaction according to the central dimensions of the mindful-identity-negotiation process

their *contributions were estimated very highly* (questions 9 and 10) by the members of the other cultures. The members of culture A felt in a similar way that their *contributions were not highly estimated* by the others (question 10). In contrast, the participants in culture B had the impression that their *contributions were highly recognised and estimated* (cf. the patterns of answers).

Interpretation of pattern 1. The students became aware of their own and others' basic human needs: e.g., of inclusion, respect and esteem. Members of culture C in particular were not supported in these identity needs. Instead they were excluded, not respected and their activities were not valued. This is a phenomenon which occurs very often in intercultural encounters. We discussed these findings with the students.

Pattern 2 in Figure 12.2

The majority culture B said that they *were able to explain their opinions adequately* at any time during the discussion (question 17) and that they *were confident with the result* of the negotiation process (question 6) contrary to the other cultures involved although they knew that they did *not come to a common understanding* across their cultures and that the minorities did not reach their desired goals (question 12).'

Interpretation of pattern 2. With regard to this intercultural group an additional aspect has to be taken into consideration: the structural dominance of culture B. Within the simulation we also composed explicitly 'minority–majority' groups so that they experienced the dimension of 'power'. The results in Figure 12.2 show that the simulation created this imbalance. The perceived dominance and ignorance of the majority culture B were discussed with the students.

Pattern 3 in Figure 12.2

Another very crucial phenomenon is shown by the behaviour of culture A:

> They *judged themselves as very open* within the interaction process according to the members of the foreign culture (question 13) but they actually *did not mindfully observe* (question 15) nor *interview* (question 16) the foreign people to gather background information on their behaviour, although they sometimes *evaluated the others' behaviour inadequately* and were therefore *surprised* (question 2).'

Interpretation of pattern 3. During the following discussion the students realised that just perceiving oneself as an 'open' person does not suffice. To interact in an adequate, effective and satisfactory way it is also important to 'observe', to 'listen', to 'interview' etc. mindfully. Only on the basis of extended and solid background or context information is it possible to model the interaction situation more holistically. This basis is necessary to interpret, evaluate and to judge unfamiliar behaviour in an adequate way, and is indispensable for an intercultural competent behaviour.

Tool 3: Fortune lines

In addition, the tool of drawing 'fortune lines' (White & Gunstone, 1992) was used. The students were asked to map out the whole intercultural interaction process on a graph. They thus had to judge ten events which occurred within the interaction process according to the dimensions of 'I liked it very much' and 'I did not like it very much' (see Figure 12.3).

Patterns appearing in the fortune lines

The graph shows that the students as members of a certain fictive culture enjoy *presenting their points of view* to the other cultures (event no. 2), *bringing their own arguments* into the discussion (event no. 3) and *representing the ideas and standpoints* within the negotiation (event no. 4) as well as *summarising the results* at the end of the discussion (event no. 9). Problems and dislikes arise very explicitly when they *have to show interest* in or to *deal with issues* airising from the foreign people (event no. 5).

Interpretation of these patterns. These phenomena very often appear in intercultural negotiation processes. On discussing these patterns with the

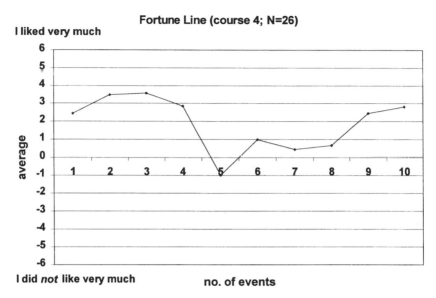

Figure 12.3 Fortune lines

students they recognised that empathy and flexibility are important capacities for coping with intercultural problems adequately, effectively and satisfactorily or as an interculturally competent person.

All these findings created by the simulation and visualised by the different tools were interpreted during the reflection phases in this way. on the one hand according to the theoretical dimensions of the mindful-identity-negotiation approach, e.g. *cultural knowledge* (different communication style, different ways of dealing with conflict, different time orientations), *communication skills* (mindful observing, listening, facework management), *identity needs* (connection, trust, security); and, on the other hand, related to certain research findings as well as to daily life interactions.

The main aims of this first step within a broader training programme are:

(1) to develop a general awareness of the complexity and misunderstandings of and within intercultural encounters;
(2) recognising the influence of culture on 'daily' behaviour and reactions;
(3) experiencing positive and negative emotions within intercultural encounters;
(4) learning to develop strategies for avoiding or reducing misunderstandings;

(5) experimenting with communication skills for achieving an adequate and effective interaction behaviour;
(6) experiencing negotiation processes and creating new expansive solutions
(7) developing fun and interest in interacting with people from other cultures.

In a second step within this first training module, which we cannot discuss here for lack of space, we tried to reconceptualise the concept of culture in the sense of a 'community of practice' (Lave, 1988; Wenger, 1998) by a discussion group with the students and encouraged them in their daily work and life practice, to isolate a 'misunderstanding' they have had with members of another culture (e.g., smokers versus non-smoker, vegetarian versus non-vegetarians, younger versus elder generation, school versus work etc.) and to negotiate this 'cultural clash' (within a so called 'practice activity').

Conclusions

Integrating Ting-Toomey's (1999) approach of mindful identity negotiation and Engeström's (1987; 1999) ideas of 'expansive learning' into one framework introduces a powerful theoretical basis for the field of intercultural learning for developing an 'intercultural competence' for the following reasons:

(1) As shown here the simulation was able to provoke typical misunderstandings and contradictions which have to be negotiated and solved in an innovative way (see also Kaiser & Kaminski, 1999; Fleming, this volume). The 'practice activity' as a shift into one's own real existing practice as well as a shift from perceiving cultures as nations to that of cultures as communities of practice seems to help the exploration of the living context in a different way. Furthermore, it also seems to help participants to experience their creative abilities, and themselves as change agents, in solving problems in work and daily life.
(2) The flipchart questions, the questionnaire and the fortune lines seem to be powerful tools for mapping out the central aspects of the interaction process, for helping people to become aware of the complexity of an intercultural encounter and for finding concrete points and capacities for achieving an intercultural competence.

The simulation and the practice activity as modes of implementing this theoretical framework represent only a starting point. Other tools and instruments need to be developed or selected from existing training programmes or from other disciplines like counselling, and anthropology in further realisations of this intercultural learning framework, for example:

- the 'Triad Model' from Pedersen (1994) to foster single communication skills such as 'mindful listening' and 'mindful interviewing';
- the 'cultural therapy' tool from Spindler & Spindler (1994; see also Alred, this volume) to help understand the background in order to model the intercultural encounter situation in more detail and more carefully as well as for developing and changing practice (cultural knowledge; identity needs etc.);
- conducting ethnographic studies for exploring the cultural contexts and diversity (Spindler, 1997; Roberts *et al.*, 2001);
- and of course, developing complex learning environments for solving actual complex problems via negotiation procedures and creation of expansive and innovative solutions e.g. by virtual classroom projects, with partner schools abroad, common projects between school and work.

References

Abrams, D. and Hogg, M. (eds) (1990) *Social Identity Theory: Constructive and Critical Advances.* New York: Springer.

Baxter, L. A. and Montgomery, B. M. (1996) *Relating: Dialogues and Dialectics.* New York: Guilford Press.

Bhagat, R.S. and Prien, K.O. (1996) Cross-cultural training in organizational contexts. In D. Landis and R.S. Bhagat (eds) *Handbook of Intercultural Training*, 2nd edn (pp. 216–230). Thousand Oaks: Sage.

Bird, A. and Dunbar, R. (1991) Getting the job done over there: Improving expatriate productivity. *National Productivity Review* 10(2), 145–56.

Birsl, U., Ottens, S. and Sturhan, K. (1999) *Männlich – Weiblich, Türkisch – Deutsch. Lebensverhältnisse und Orientierungen von Industriebeschäftigten.* Opladen: Leske und Budrich.

Bolten, J. (1995) Grenzen der Internationalisierungsfähigkeit. Interkulturelles Handeln aus interaktionstheoretischer Perspektive. In J. Bolten (eds) *Cross-Culture – Interkulturelles Handeln in der Wirtschaft* (pp. 24–42). Sternenfels, Berlin: Wissenschaft & Praxis.

Brislin, R.W. (1989) Intercultural communication training. In M. K. Asante and W. B. Gudykunst (eds) *Handbook of International and Intercultural Communication* (pp. 441–57). Newbury Park: Sage.

Brewer, M. and Miller, N. (1996) *Intergroup Relations.* Pacific Grove, CA: Brooks/ Cole.

Byram, M. (1997) *Teaching and Assessing Intercultural Communicative Competence.* Clevedon: Multilingual Matters

Cole, M. and Engeström, Y. (1993) A cultural-historical approach to distributed cognition. In G. Salomon (ed.) *Distributed Cognitions: Psychological and Educational Considerations* (pp. 1–46). New York: Cambridge University Press.

Cole, M. and Wertsch, J. V. (1996) Beyond the individual: Social antinomy in discussions of Piaget and Vygotsky. *Human Development* 39, 250–56.

Collins, A., Brown, J. S. and Newman, S. S. (1989) Cognitive apprenticeship: Teaching the crafts of reading, writing and mathematics. In L.B. Resnick (ed.) *Knowing, Learning, and Instruction – Essays in Honour of Robert Glaser* (pp. 453–94). Hillsdale, NJ: Erlbaum.

Cognition and Technology Group at Vanderbilt (1997) *The Jasper Project.* Mahwah, NJ: Erlbaum.

Dowling, P.J. and Schuler, R.S. (1990) *International Dimensions of Human Resource Management.* Boston: PWS-Kent.

Dubs, R. (1995) Die Suche nach einer neuen Lehr–Lern–Kultur. Ein weiteres Schlagwort oder ein sinnvolles Bemühen? *Schweizerische Zeitschrift für kaufmännisches Bildungswesen* 89, 174–80.

Edelson, D.C., Pea, R.D. and Gomez, L. (1996) Constructivism in the Collaboraty. In B.G. Wilson (ed.) *Constructivist Learning Environment* (pp. 151–64). New Jersey: Englewood Cliffs.

Engeström, Y. (1987) *Learning by Expanding: An Activity–Theoretical Approach to Developmental Research.* Helsinki: Orienta-Konsultit.

Engeström, Y. (1996) Developmental work research as educational research. Looking ten years back and into the zone of proximal development. *Nordisk Pedagogik* 16(3), 131–43.

Engeström, Y. (1999) Activity theory and individual and social transformation. In Y. Engeström, R. Miettinen and R.-L. Punamäki (eds) *Perspectives on Activity Theory* (pp. 19–38). Cambridge: Cambridge University Press.

Kaiser, F.-J. and Kaminski, H. (1999) *Methodik des Ökonomie-Unterrichts. Grundlagen eines handlungsorientierten Lernkonzepts mit Beispielen, 3. vollst. überarb. Auflage.* Bad Heibrunn/Obb.: Klinkhardt.

Kartari, A. (1996) *Deutsch-türkische Kommunikation am Arbeitsplatz. Zur interkulturellen Kommunikation zwischen türkischen Mitarbeitern und deutschen Vorgesetzten in einem deutschen Industriebetrieb.* Münster u.a.: Waxmann.

Landis, D. and Bhagat, R.S. (1996) A model of intercultural behavior and training. In D. Landis and R. S. Bhagat (eds) *Handbook of Intercultural Training,* 2nd edn (pp. 1–13). Thousand Oaks: Sage.

Lave, J. (1988) *Cognition in Practice: Mind, Mathematics and Culture in Everyday Life.* Cambridge: Cambridge University Press.

Leontjew, An. N. (1981) *Problems in the Development of Mind.* Moscow: Progress.

Luria, A.R. (1981) *Language and Cognition.* Washington, DC: Winston.

McCall, G. and Simmons, J. (1978) *Identities and Interaction.* New York: Free Press.

Müller, W. (1996) Betriebliche Restrukturierung und Reorganisation als betriebspädagogisches Problem. In K. Beck, W. Müller, T. Deißinger and M. Zimmermann (eds) *Berufserziehung im Umbruch* (pp. 209–24). Weinheim: Deutscher Studien.

Nipporica Associates (1993) *ECOTONOS: A Multicultural Problem-Solving Simulation.* Yarmouth, ME: Intercultural Press.

Oser, F. and Spychiger, M. (2000) Lernen aus Fehlern als Beitrag zum Lebenslangen Lernen. In W. Lempert and F. Achtenhagen (eds) *Lebenslanges Lernen im Beruf. Seine Grundlegung im Kindes- und Jugendalter,* Bd. IV (pp. 101–22). Opladen: Leske und Budrich.

Pedersen, P. (1994) Multicultural counseling. In R. W. Brislin and T. Yoshida (eds) *Improving Intercultural Interactions* (pp. 221–40). Thousand Oaks: Sage.

Roberts, C., Byram, M., Barro, A., Jordan, S. and Steet, B. (2001) *Language Learners as Ethnographers*. Clevedon: Multilingual Matters.

Salomon, G. and Perkins, D. N. (1998) Individual and social aspects of learning. In P.D. Pearson and A. Iran-Nejad (eds) *Review of Research in Education*, Vol. 23 (pp. 1–24) Washington: American Educational Research Association.

Sembill, D. (1992) *Problemlösefähigkeit, Handlungskompetenz und Emotionale Befindlichkeit*. Göttingen: Hogrefe.

Spindler, G. (1997) *Education and Cultural Process. Anthropological Approaches*. Prospect Heights: Waveland Press.

Spindler, G. and Spindler, L. (1994) *Pathways to Cultural Awareness*. Thousand Oaks: Corwin Press.

Stryker, S. (1981) Symbolic interactionism: Themes and variations. In M. Rosenberg and R.H. Turner (eds) *Social Psychology: Sociological Perspectives*. New York: Basic Books.

Stryker, S. (1991) Exploring the relevance of social cognition for the relationship of self and society: Linking the cognitive perspective and identity theory. In J. Howard and P. Callero (eds) *Self-society Dynamic: Emotion, Cognition and Action*. Cambridge, UK: Cambridge University Press.

Ting-Toomey, S. (1988) Intercultural conflict styles: A face-negotiation theory. In Y.Y. Kim and W. Gudykunst (eds) *Theories in Intercultural Communication*. Newbury Park, CA: Sage.

Ting-Toomey, S. (1989) Identity and interpersonal bonding. In M. Asante and W. Gudykunst (eds) *Handbook of International and Intercultural Communication*. Newbury Park, CA: Sage.

Ting-Toomey, S. (1993) Communicative resourcefulness: An identity negotiation perspective. In R. Wiseman and J. Koester (eds) *Intercultural Communication Competence*. Newbury Park, CA: Sage.

Ting-Toomey, S. (1999) *Communicating Across Cultures*. New York, London: Guilford.

Tramm, T. T. (1996) Lernprozesse in der Übungsfirma. Rekonstruktion und Weiterentwicklung schulischer Übungsfirmenarbeit als Anwendungsfall einer evaluativ-konstrukiven und handlungsorientierten Curriculumstrategie, Habilitationsschrift. Georg-August-Universität, Göttingen.

Tung, R. L. (1987) Expatriate assignments: Enhancing success and minimizing failure. *Academy of Management Executive* 1(2), 117–26.

Tuomi-Gröhn, T. and Engeström, Y. (2002) (eds) *New Perspectives on Transfer and Boundary Crossing*. Oxford: Pergamon Press.

Vygotsky, L.S. (1978) *Mind in Society*. Cambridge, MA: Harvard University Press.

Warthun, N. (1997) *Interkulturelle Kommunikation in der Wirtschaft*. Bochum: Universitätsverlag.

Weber, S. (1997) Zur Notwendigkeit des interkulturellen Lernens in der Wirtschaftspädagogik. *Zeitschrift für Berufs- und Wirtschaftspädagogik* 93, 30–47.

Weber, S. (2000a) „Kiss, Bow, or Shake Hands" – Zur Entwicklung einer interkulturellen Handlungskompetenz in der kaufmännischen Aus- und Weiterbildung. *Zeitschrift für Berufs- und Wirtschaftspädagogik* 96(3), 376–98.

Weber, S. (2000b) Zur Problematik der Vermittlung einer „interkulturellen Handlungskompetenz". *Schweizerische Zeitschrift für kaufmännisches Bildungswesen* 94, 79–101.

Weber, S. (2000c) Lebenslanges Lernen unter dem Aspekt interkultureller Bildung – Fokus: berufliche Erstausbildung. In F. Achtenhagen and W. Lempert (eds) *Lebenslanges Lernen im Beruf. Seine Grundlegung im Kindes- und Jugendalter*, Vol. IV (pp. 203–16). Opladen: Leske und Budrich.

Weber, S. (2002) Boundary crossing and transfer in the context of intercultural learning. In T. Tuomi-Gröhn and Y. Engeström (eds) *New Perspectives on Transfer and Boundary Crossing*. Oxford: Pergamon Press.

Wenger, E. (1998) *Communities of Practice. Learning, Meaning, and Identity*. Cambridge: Cambridge Press.

White, R. and Gunstone, R. (1992) *Probing Understanding*. London: Falmer.

Wuttke, E. (1999) *Motivation und Lernstrategien in einer selbstorganisationsoffenen Lernumgebung. Eine empirische Untersuchung bei Industriekaufleuten*. Frankfurt/ M. u.a.: Lang.

Zimmermann, M. (1996) Transferfördernde Berufserziehung in Schule und Betrieb. – Zum 'Expertenkulturansatz' in der Didaktik der kaufmännischen Berufserziehung. In K. Beck, W. Müller, T. Deißinger and M. Zimmermann (eds) *Berufserziehung im Umbruch* (pp. 45–60). Weinheim: Deutscher Studien.

Chapter 13

The Recognition of Intercultural Competences: From Individual Experience to Certification

GENEVIÈVE ZARATE

My purposes in this chapter are in part speculative: not only to discuss exist-ing ideas on teaching but also to attempt to consider the implications of structural changes created by a Europe which is already formed in the legal sense and by cross-frontier mobility which is becoming a common phenom-enon among new social strata in democratic societies on an international scale. This chapter thus takes its starting point in the European situation and uses this as a means of developing new concepts of intercultural compe-tences of a more general import.

In this new context of change, the intercultural dimension is acquiring a meaning which it did not have 30 years ago when the Council of Europe began its work on language teaching with the pupose of facilitating mobility and the mutual recognition of competences. If intercultural competences in the European marketplace and in international processes of certification are to be taken into account, there is a need for some prior reflection in order to define these competences and to define more precisely the nature of institu-tional certification in the course of these new changes.

What I shall do here is to describe the political and pedagogic back-ground which make possible the recognition of these competences and which are the conditions for establishing a cross-frontier recognition of intercultural competences independently of national contexts.

The Discrepancy Between Political Principles and Observable Reality

Because of the existence of competitive ideological relations between the great powers during the colonial and post-colonial periods, the ways in which European languages were spread outside their national frontiers were influenced by conflicting forces (universalism, capitalism, Marxism etc.) which aimed to promote politically orientated value systems. Yet the creation of a European identity, which is a political aim promoted not only by the member states of the European community but also by countries in east and central Europe, is founded on the principle of shared values with a common base in democratic values. For example, according to the action programme promoted by the Education Committee of the Council of Europe for 1997–2000, the establishment of a base of common values depends on the development of the individual described in terms of 'democratic security', 'social cohesion', increased 'personal mobility' and 'intensified exchanges' (CDCC, 1997: 11).

If these general objectives are to be achieved, I would argue, there is a prior need for the identification of the dissonances which weaken these principles. There is historical dissonance between countries which wish to become part of the European Union and those which already constitute an integrated Europe in legal and economic terms. There is economic and social dissonance between countries which already have or are willing to undertake a period of cross-frontier mobility and those where an experience of living outside their own national frontiers is unthinkable. And there are political and identity dissonances which are used to justify territorial conflicts and the creation of new identities using ethnic and religious categories to create peoples and states.

An example of this proliferation of identities is the case of Bosnia Herzegovina where after the Dayton Agreement there co-exist modes of identification with Bosniac, Serb or Bosnian communities and where all reference to Serbo-Croat is disappearing, to be replaced by a new codification of languages as either Croat, Serbian or Bosniac. As an example of the complexity of identity in this context, there is the use of the term 'Muslim' which before the Dayton Agreement referred to Islamic groups speaking Serbo-Croat and officially considered in the former Yugoslavia as a national group, whereas the Albanians and Turks who were Muslim were not considered to be part of this group.

Based on what was done in Franco-German relations during the 1960s, in order to reduce the effects of three wars (1870, 1914–18 and 1939–45), which led to the birth of the Office Franco-Allemand de la Jeunesse (the Franco-German Bureau for youth), we can hypothesise as a starting point for our discussion that there is more likelihood of overcoming a conflict if it is recognised because it is made explicit rather than repressed and inscribed in a negative national memory. The identification of the discrepancy between statements of political openness and actual social reality is therefore a preliminary to the arguments which follow here.

Intercultural Experience of Conflict

The analysis of international relations focuses on political and historical assumptions where relations between states are defined on the basis of their geo-political and ideological alliances or on assumptions of conflicting power relations between them. The analysis proposed here, on a different scale to that of individual experience, raises questions about the experience of a social actor who is involved in the relations between different national communities. Intercultural experience is defined here on the basis of an experience of otherness which is observable at the individual level and identifiable in terms of strategies, conscious or not, which the social actor uses to position him/herself in the different locations of identity with which he/she identifies. His/her intercultural experience is all the more complex because it is founded on diverse contexts, constructed in the relationships of conflict, latent or open, between communities, and based on a substantial experience of otherness.

What are the issues which can be taken from the individual lives of those people who have been obliged to relate to a sense of conflict between states? The examples given here are taken from a research project which was a response to a wave of anti-French feeling which went through public opinion in Australia when France re-started its nuclear trials in 1995 in the Pacific, putting in danger, in Australian eyes, the ecological system of the region (Maurer & Warren, 2000).[1] The people presented here were professionally involved in Franco-Australian relationships as symbols of France; they are a journalist, a restaurant owner and the president of the Alliance Française. They each used different strategies to confront the brutal contradictions between their private and public identities which unbalanced their identities at the time.

Jean, a well-known restaurant owner, of Belgian nationality, has a French restaurant in Canberra. The anti-French wave was for him a 'disastrous episode' for his business. He therefore adopted a strategy of re-positioning himself in terms of identity which he describes in terms of stages:

> At the time, it was necessary to make people forget that we were a French restaurant . . . So we did North-African food . . . People didn't know what that meant either . . . We had to say that it was Tunisian and Moroccan cuisine . . . For three months we tried to hold out and continue with French cooking because we had had awards . . . After three years all we could say was that we had got back to where we started.

Franck is a cook well known to the public from his television programmes on French cookery and he is also president of the Executive

Committee of the Alliance Française. On the basis of these two positions as a representative of France, he takes a critical view of those, who in his opinion, are not aware of their duties as representatives of France:

> If there is someone who represents a certain grandeur, a certain aura . . .
> I think you have to be flamboyant . . . The big problem with France is
> that they send people here in tourism who are not flamboyant who just
> do their job . . . But that's not really France.

During the period of anti-French feeling his public statements supported the official French position: 'I have to say that I am not someone who just keeps quiet. I was interviewed for example by the *Sydney Morning Herald* and they came to take my photo. I called everybody xenophobes on the front page of the SMH.'

Danielle and Florence, a journalist on the multicultural Australian television channel SBS, and a local correspondent for the French newspaper *Libération*, adopted strategies of different kinds vis-à-vis their editorial teams. Danielle referred to the code of professional ethics of her TV channel and said this: 'I realised that I had a role of a bridging agent and I saw it like that. A sort of link, intermediary. . . . You try to explain to both sides, you bring people together, you tend to plan exchanges.' But during the nuclear tests she became more determined:

> I am aggressive when I'm attacked and everybody here knows it.
> Nobody attacked me. There was one idiot who tried to ostracise me. He
> found that he had to explain himself. He was read the ethics code in
> detail. And from that moment nobody dared to try anything.

In contrast Florence adopted a strategy of de-dramatising the event vis-à-vis her Paris colleagues:

> Every time someone from Paris, from the newspaper, phoned me asking 'Are you all right?' as if I had barricaded myself in and was being
> attacked, I told them: 'I'm not saying there aren't any problems, I'm
> saying that I don't have any.' And I think they didn't really believe me
> in Paris. Because there were all those reports sent to Paris, and they
> were very excessive.

Intercultural Experience and Family Capital

How do these four different experiences of conflict demonstrate an acquired competence which is more than just an ability to observe? These people were selected for interview above all because they have influential positions in a bi-national context which is recognised professionally. Sometimes this comes from the Australian side, sometimes from the French, but in either case it is anchored in professional networks which are based on people's competences to interact with two national value systems.

However, the biographical dimension makes it clear that the positions of national representative and cultural intermediary are rooted in experience which precedes professional life. The interviews revealed just how much these professional positions are the continuation of aptitudes which are inherited from family traditions and, as will be evident from their life-stories, the interviews showed in detail how these aptitudes were formed.

Jean acquired, from childhood on and through the life-style of his parents who live in Belgium, an attitude of familiarity with travel, and the habit of relying on the hospitality of his family:

> My parents were big travellers for their time. In the 1950s it was a big adventure to get in the car and drive from Belgium to the South. We had friends everywhere in France. I remember that at Christmas we had some Parisians who came one year. Another year we would go there. We slept on the floor in sleeping bags.

So his decision to emigrate to Australia was a logical continuation of this family habit of travelling and he did not give up in face of the obstacles created by the need for an immigration visa in Australia, which was cost him much time and patience.

Franck did not have any family inheritance but his urge for cross-frontier mobility took shape at the age of 16 when, anticipating military service, he became a nurse in the Algerian War. This was just the beginning of an uninterrupted series of migrations, to New Caledonia, New Zealand, which led to him settling in Australia. Once there, he acquired a detached attitude to the complexity of languages:

> You never really speak languages . . . To speak languages you have to be born there . . . and even then you lose them! But I get by quite well in French, English, Arabic, Spanish, and Italian. I speak Provencal, I speak Arabic pretty well. I spoke a New Caledonian dialect but I've completely forgotten it . . ..

Danielle has inherited a dual religious tradition, catholic on her mother's side and Jewish on her father's side, and this has become a solid family policy 'ecumenical and tolerant'. Although her family consider briefly emigration to Palestine and then to Canada, it was in fact a move to Australia that actually took place. Danielle arrived there at the age of 14. She went to the French lycée, returned to France for university study and became an English teacher. But then she returned to settle in Australia.

Florence's professional mobility is a continuation of a familiar childhood mobility. Her mother is from Madagascar. Her father was born in

France and lived a long time in Vietnam, which was a source of imagination for the family: 'When we were in Cannes [on the Riviera, as a small child], the big occasion of Sunday lunch, ... My parents took us to the Vietnamese restaurant ... My sister and I loved that ... We looked forward to Sunday and going to the restaurant to eat nems'. Florence grew up in New Caledonia and did not return to France which was for her 'an exotic country', until the age of 18.

The skills of being a cultural intermediary who has a professional relationship to otherness have to be understood in the long term, over one or two generations, when cross-frontier mobility becomes commonplace from one generation to another and creates a source of imagination transforming geographical and / or cultural distance into proximity. Although these skills are sometimes seen as unusual in a given society, they comprise a capital of experience when they are seen independently of the societies in which they were formed and when the continuity of individual life-stories are acknowledged and accorded value.

Modelling Intercultural Experience: The Cultural Intermediary as Social Actor

In considering the strategies and the stories of cultural intermediaries, we see the properties which contribute to the positive evaluation of competences above and beyond individual experiences, which have hitherto been insufficiently recognised. Experience of mediation and of the various forms which it can take is realised, above all, in conflict situations, defined as a crisis situation resulting from the confrontation of points of view which are irreconcilable because equally based in law or social justice (Bourdieu, 1993: 9–11). The strategies of conciliation, of affirmation, of re-positioning of identity which were described earlier are just an outline of a field of study which needs to be systematised in order to be seen independently of conflict situations and thereby to gain in systematicity (Zarate, 2000).

Nonetheless there are certain properties which can already be identified as determining for the intercultural competences described. Early experience of mobility, before the age of choices made as an adult, can lead to the development of a capital of experience on the basis of which the individual can subsequently decide his/her major life choices. These choices may appear all the more 'natural' because they are part of a family tradition of mobility. They are thus the realisation of a family habitus.

A professional relation to otherness is often the result of varied experiences of cross-frontier mobility. Experience of tourism, taking place from time to time but nonetheless systematically, evolves through the time spent abroad into longer and longer periods of residence abroad and / or changes in purpose – study periods, periods of emigration – which can then produce professional change. Changes from one professional domain to another (for example, a language teacher may reverse what he / she teaches by becoming a teacher of the language he / she learnt in the family).

The notion of the social actor facilitates the recognition of these experiences as competences and of the concept of a social space based on exchange of social relationships beyond the context of schooling. This concept emphasises social engagement and efficiency and brings into play the identity of the individual. We therefore define the social actor as someone who occupies a specific position in social space. Having been socialised in one or more communities, he / she occupies an interface position of influence in the circulation of values between different social groups which create them (Byram & Zarate, 1996).

The notion of social actor can be compared with that of learner, a more classic concept in education. The latter has the advantage of placing the individual in a process of learning and links this learning to a systematised course of study. The social actor does not, however, necessarily follow a course which is determined by schooling. He / she constructs his / her path as a function of experience, of the discoveries made through cross-frontier mobility, of the continuities and breaks which he / she experiences between cultural communities. Whereas institutionalised pathways create a homogeneity in the competences acquired, lived experience has to be recognised for its diversity and its individuality and specificity. The exclusive systematisation of the concept of the learner leads to a reductive approach to the principle of interculturality which implies the recognition of identities based on experience among different cultural communities. Irrespective of any marker of nationality, the concept of the social actor situates the individual in a social environment defined in terms of cultural pluralism and promotes a dynamic vision of cross-frontier competences.

The Systematisation of Intercultural Competences

The recognition of intercultural competences, where the purpose is to valorise a maximum of diversity in the expression of identity, is dependent on the development of instruments which give value to the competences that every social actor wants to have valued in his/her presentation of intercultural competences. Yet there is a certain naiveté to be found in the area of certification as far as the instruments currently available are concerned. In the Common European Framework and the European Language Portfolio for example, it is assumed that the ways of operating in an educational context can be applied in a larger social context. On the one hand, schooling acts as if a learner should demonstrate his/her most advanced competences, whereas when we observe social behaviour, whether in school or out of school, we see that it is not necessarily in the interest of the individual to make explicit the origin of the whole of his/her intercultural competences. This dimension is often under-estimated: an individual may be socially marginalised by a language which he/she nonetheless speaks, or by his/her social origins if they are stigmatised. He/she may think it is not to his/her advantage to emphasise them in a country where they are not valued. On the other hand he/she may wish to bring them out in another form in another context where they will be valued more. The equalisation of all individual linguistic competences is based on an educational vision of learning where the learner is assumed to be best served by demonstrating as many competences as possible rather than on an approach concerned with identity, which itself is based on strategies using multiple facets of identity to avoid reductive stereotyping.

What is needed, therefore, in an approach which takes into account strategies of identity is a model based on success and on the production of diversity, inverting the traditional relationship to the foreigner which is one of risk and handicap. This approach necessitates giving up certain presuppositions which are all the stronger because they are taken for granted. These include the confusion between geographical proximity and distance and cultural proximity and distance. Distance can be simultaneously a source of exoticism and indifference; proximity can create the illusion of cultural continuity or on the other hand awaken a sense of threat to identity if neighbouring countries have a history of conflict. If proximity and distance between languages and cultures were not measured in terms of the national culture of the educational system where a language is taught, as the state would wish, especially in school textbooks, but rather on the basis of the personal experience of the learner, then those who develop assessment instruments begin to choose criteria which are independent of a national context. This means that the social actor comprehends the effects created by linguistic and cultural distance, that he/she is aware of the nature of the personal links, which he/she has woven between these languages and cultures, and that proximity does not mean facility because it is itself a source of false similarities.

The systemisation of the choices which have to be made in recognition of competences depends on the definition and description of categories of classification of the competences, such as the concepts of savoir-être (attitudes) and savoir-faire (skills). We have proposed four categories which make more explicit the intercultural dimension in the assessment of competences in language teaching (Byram & Zarate, 1996). These four categories are differentiated as follows: two of them, savoir-être (attitudes) and savoir-apprendre (skills of discovery) are defined as dependent on a given language whereas the two others, savoirs (knowledge) and savoir-faire (skills) are independent. Savoir-être and savoir-faire give value to competences acquired through the learning of a given language which are transferable into other cultural systems. What is meant by 'transferable' is that what is acquired as a consequence of learning a given language can be reinvested in the learning of another language whilst, nonetheless, requiring that the second language be taught.

There is, however, a difference in the way these two competences should be assessed: savoir-être should be assessed in the context of learning any foreign language, but this is not done in the same way for the first foreign language as for languages and cultures which are discovered later. Savoir-être can include, for example, the following competences: acquire a readiness for non-conflictual contact with the other; knowing the different phases of adaptation in a period of long residence abroad; ability to identify conflicting values; ability to act as a mediator between behaviours and convictions which are contradictory.

The assessment of savoir-apprendre is of a terminal kind, concluding the phase of learning a given language and measuring the skills which are transferable to a new language and culture. Savoir-apprendre values the ability to interpret a new aspect of a familiar language and culture and also in a context which is culturally distant. It can be assessed by confronting the learner with cultural practices which are unfamiliar and suggesting situations which he / she should be able to comprehend by using the strategies of interpretation acquired in contexts with which s / he is familiar.

This kind of competence is focused on cross-frontier interaction and, as such, is coherent with the fundamental nature of intercultural competences. They have nonetheless to be of sufficient significance and diversity to make it useful to recognise them in assessment systems which are different from the one in which they have been recognised for the first time. Cross-frontier recognition of this type of competence would promote the creation of a diversified, fluid and open market: diversified because all four types of competence would be recognised; fluid because it would be possible to pass from one language to another, from one culture to another, from a given culture to another language, using capital already acquired; open because the value accorded to an intercultural competence is not dependent on the value accorded to a linguistic competence at the same level. This flexibility ought to permit sufficient fluidity in a common space where intercultural competences can be exchanged.

The transfer of competences from one language and culture to another is based on a principle of economy: a beginner in a second foreign language can use the competences developed whilst experiencing a first foreign language and culture. The ways in which this transfer can take place depend on a positive attitude towards learning, on a concrete experience of a foreign country or a lived experience of otherness which does not necessarily pre-suppose actual geographic mobility. They should create a dynamic approach to pluralism: a language and culture with which a learner is familiar are a springboard for discovering another language and culture. From this point of view the separation of languages and cultures from each other begins to break down, and cultural pluralism is not reduced to an aggregation of cultures which the learner meets, but comprises experiences which de-dramatise the breaks inherent in the move from one linguistic and cultural system to another.

The Certification of Competences Related to a Third Place

A description which no longer focuses on a simplified and unequal model of communication, where the foreigner is expected to be subordinate to the native speaker, leads to a less radical model, based on the concept of a competent learner, which does not identify being a foreigner with being handicapped, and which makes a distinction between linguistic performance and social status. When the relationship to the other is envisaged in such a way that the foreigner is defined, first of all, in terms of being external to the society whose language he/she is learning, the point of reference is independent of national frameworks. It thus gives priority to intercomprehension situations, to interfaces, to experiences resulting from passing from one cultural system to another. It also links competences acquired in one's mother tongue(s) to competences acquired in other languages and cultures.

The social categorisation used in the 1970s and 1980s, for example in the Threshold Levels of the Council of Europe, made a distinction between tourists and travellers, on the one hand, and migrant workers and their families, on the other. This was based on a tacit opposition between voluntary mobility for pleasure and mobility imposed by economic necessity. Although this distinction is still relevant, it is inadequate in accounting for the current changes which are taking place with respect to mobility. In contemporary Europe and beyond there is a need for an understanding of the competences of all those who occupy positions at the interface between several value systems. The use of a generic category of mobility makes it possible to describe careers more objectively, even if they are differentiated in terms of the motives, objectives and the length of stay. It tends to neutralise the social marginalisation of the outsider and to give value to the capacities characteristic of being familiar with a third place.

There are several research avenues which would support the recognition of competences linked to the concept of a third place:

- Developing a conceptual instrument which is independent of national categories which are for the moment indirectly present in linguistic description. This would counter-act the distortions which result from inadequately acquired representations of other countries which, on a European scale, lead to a mish-mash of images.
- Develop a cultural description which focuses on cultural continuities and corrects the effects produced by the 'language barrier'; give priority to a de-dramatised vision of cultural difference and reject perceptions of the other as a threat, establish a graduated typology of conflicts and how to remedy them, and give examples of situations of cultural mediation.
- Introduce a symbolic dimension into descriptions of teaching which takes into account the complexity of identities which are sometimes hidden and sometimes revealed; use of an open range of identities (local, regional, national, ethnic, linguistic, European, international etc) which take into account the social actor's adjustments which take place as a consequence of transnational mobility; perceptions of the other which can be reversed when there is a change from non-contact situations to situations of lived proximity.
- Facilitate the recognition of transversal competences between different languages, such as those linked to savoir-être and savoir-faire, in such a way as to clarify and refine notions such as empathy, tolerance, openness to the other, skills of discovery etc.
- Create teaching instruments which can give meaning to cultural awareness, such as teaching approaches which function on the basis of bringing more than two languages and cultures together; recognition of the significance of intercultural expertise even if there is no corresponding linguistic equivalent; self-assessment of competences – the *European Language Portfolio* is the best approximation to this at the moment;
- Encourage the recognition of knowledge and skills which derive from out-of-school experience of otherness and the recognition of 'mobility capital'; this recognition should be related to educational or institutionalised analysis; recognition of this experience, simultaneously lived and put at a distance, ought to lead to the development of modes of assessment which are already outlined in the first prototypes of the *European Language Portfolio*, designed by the Council of Europe.

These approaches to analysis ought to support the spread and recognition of intercultural competences first of all by defining what is the object of transfer, then by increasing flexibility of transfer, and finally by guaranteeing the reliability and the transparency of what is exchanged. This can only happen if three epistemological obstacles are overcome. Hitherto it was the concept of difference, defined in national terms, which was the basis for educational definitions and national recognition of competences. Instead of this there needs to be a recognition of transnational individual experiences which are given value in a cross-frontier market of competences. Second, we need to partially uncouple the stages of linguistic progression from cultural progression. Finally, we need to begin to create a cross-disciplinary description of competences which is simultaneously required by the diversity of languages and necessitated by the conceptual vagueness which often dominates the descriptions of relations between cultures.

Notes

1. Entitled *Xénophilie/Xénophobie dans l'espace d'influence de la France et de l'Australie*, coordinated by P. Cryle (University of Queensland) and G. Zarate (ENS Foutenay/St Cloud). The extracts are from interviews conducted by Jane Warren (University of Melbourne) and Louise Maurer (Australian National University).

References

Bourdieu P. (1993) *La misère du monde*. Paris: Seuil.

Byram M. and Zarate G. (1996) Defining and assessing intercultural competence: some principles and proposals for the European context. *Language Teaching* (pp. 239–43). Cambridge: Cambridge University Press.

CDCC (1997) *Une stratégie pour l'action: les priorités du CDCC pour 1997–1999*. CDCC (97) 2. Strasbourg: Conseil de la Coopération Culturelle.

Maurer L. and Warren J. (2000) Représentations de soi et de l'autre dans des entretiens avec des intermédiaires culturels australiens et français. *Mots. Autour d'une crise franco-australienne. Stéréotypie xénophiles et xénophobes*. 64, pp. 77–96.

Zarate, G. (2000) *Certifications linguistiques en contexte européen et transfert des compétences interculturelles: conditions pour l'émergence d'un cadre didactique*. Unpublished manuscript for the Council of Europe, Strasbourg.

Afterword

What Does it Mean to be Intercultural?

LOTHAR BREDELLA

The symposiums in Durham in 1999 and 2000 directed our attention to two questions: (1) What makes an experience intercultural?; and (2) What is the educational significance of such an experience? The difference between these two questions is important. When we investigate what takes place in intercultural encounters, we will obtain desirable and undesirable results. Yet, what are the criteria for determining what is desirable and undesirable? And how can we bring about what is desirable?

The advantage of the two symposiums was that they were interdisciplinary and offered us the opportunity to examine the intercultural experience and its educational significance from the viewpoint of different disciplines. This was in itself a liberating intercultural experience which allowed us to discover new dimensions of being intercultural. Thus I would like to thank the organisers of the symposiums for bringing us together and creating an atmosphere in which intense dialogue was possible.

In the following pages I will refer to a few of the essays in this volume and indicate what I have learned from them and how I would integrate them in my conception of being intercultural.

An Enhanced Awareness of Oneself as a Cultural Being

In her contribution 'Changing the Focus: A Discussion of the Dynamics of the Intercultural Experience', Amita Sen Gupta, as a psychologist, explores what the intercultural experience means for the individual. For her, the intercultural experience is not necessarily a pleasant one, because it questions our beliefs and values so that we can no longer take them for granted and might feel insecure and uncertain. Such experiences could be accompanied by a variety of emotions: 'the emotions come from many sources: fear of encountering something new, excitement at the discovery of new and different ways of thinking, relief through self-expression, anger that a deeply held belief may have been challenged'. In some cases the emotions can be so intense that the intercultural encounter is broken off. If it is continued, however, it can lead to a self-awareness of one's cultural existence.

Why do we need the intercultural experience for a better self-understanding? Would it not be easier to reflect on our cultural existence without the detour of the intercultural experience? As Gupta points out, we 'acquire the rules, values and behaviour that allow us to become effective and competent members of our socio-cultural environment' in a 'process of transmission and acquisition [which] is rarely deliberate and/or didactic'. The consequence is that 'effective enculturation produces ways of being, doing and thinking that are so deeply entrenched that they are automatic and we are simply unaware that our behaviour is determined by these unconscious mechanisms'.

We grow up in our culture with the belief that our cultural system is 'natural' and 'rational' and superior to those of others. Intercultural understanding disappoints this narcissistic belief by making us realise that things which appear irrational and inhumane from our perspective are rational and humane from the others' perspective. Thus, being intercultural means acknowledging that we belong to a culture and exploring how we are shaped by our culture just as others are shaped by theirs. This narcissistic disappointment is an essential presupposition for tolerance. At the same time, Gupta's description of enculturation can illuminate the function of ethnocentrism: it protects us from the narcissistic disappointment by implanting in our mind the belief that our rules and values are superior to those of others. Ethnocentrism thus enhances the self-esteem of the individual. From the perspective of intercultural education, however, ethnocentrism has to be overcome because it leads to the misrecognition of others. Nevertheless, there are proponents of ethnocentrism who claim it is favourable since it strengthens the belief in one's group and culture. In his 1987 bestseller, *The Closing of the American Mind*, Allan Bloom justifies ethnocentrism by pointing out that we can only be loyal and preserve our culture if we believe that it is better than others:

> The reason for the non-Western closedness, or ethnocentrism, is clear. Men must love and be loyal to their families and their peoples in order to preserve them. Only if they think their own things are good can they be content with them. A father must prefer his child to other children, a citizen his country to others. That is why there are myths – to justify these attachments. (Bloom, 1987: 37f.)

In 1971, Claude Lévi-Strauss was asked by UNESCO to open 'the International Year to Combat Racism and Racial Discrimination'. In his speech, which caused a scandal, Lévi-Strauss justified ethnocentrism:

> Sometimes each culture calls itself the only genuine and worthwhile culture, it ignores the others and even denies that they are culture. Most of the people we term 'primitive' give themselves a name that signifies 'The True Ones', 'The Good Ones', 'The Excellent Ones', or even quite simply 'The Human Beings', and apply to other peoples a name that denies their humanity – for example, 'earth monkeys' or 'louse eggs'. (Lévi-Strauss, 1985: 7)

Those who want to preserve the diversity of cultures are suspicious of the intercultural experience because it might lead to new formations and third positions which transcend cultural boundaries. In my contribution to this volume I have pointed out that we live in an age in which identity politics demands loyalty to one's own group and accuses those who adapt to other cultures of betraying their own culture. Molefi Kete Asante justifies ethnocentrism emphatically: 'To lose one's terms is to become a victim of the other's attitudes, models, disciplines and culture; and the ultimate effect of such a massive loss is the destruction of self-confidence, the distortion of history, and psychological marginality' (Asante, 1995: 7). Asante does not see a problem in his justification of ethnocentrism as long as every group is allowed to be ethnocentric. Those who defend ethnocentrism want to save the members of their culture from the experience of insecurity and uncertainty which Sen Gupta described as being a result of intercultural encounters. In definitions of intercultural competence, however, insecurity and instability are rarely mentioned. Students are expected to be open and tolerant, but it is not mandatory that they question their own rules and values yet. Gupta's students experience alienation from their own culture. One of her students says: 'I do not feel that comfortable in my culture any more. I have come to adopt many aspects that I have encountered here'. Gupta is to be commended for pointing to aspects of the intercultural experience which are often ignored and for emphasising the fact that we live in a world in which many people are 'constantly re-defining themselves according to the context in which they find themselves'.

For Gupta, the intercultural experience is essential for an enhancement of our self-awareness as cultural beings; it helps us to understand how we are shaped by our culture and what the role of education is in this process. In certain situations this enhanced self-awareness might indeed be the most important thing, but in others it might be egocentric because our attention should not be directed towards ourselves but towards those others whom we have to understand in order to overcome discrimination and misrecognition.

The Reconstruction of the Foreign Frame of Reference

If we ask what the indispensable feature of the intercultural experience is, I would say that it is reconstructing others' frames of reference and seeing the world through their eyes. Applying our own categories and values often leads to degrading and humiliating images of them. Hence an indispensable feature of the intercultural experience is that we refrain from imposing our categories and values on others but instead learn to reconstruct their frame of reference and see them as they see themselves.

If we want to understand others who speak a different language, we must learn their language. In a similar way we must reconstruct the cultural rules, conventions and values which govern their behaviour if we want to understand them. Critics of intercultural understanding, however, contend that the reconstruction of a foreign frame of reference is impossible. Our categories, values and interests do not allow us to see others as they see themselves. In my contribution to this volume I have attempted to refute a few objections to intercultural understanding. (For a detailed discussion of these objections see Bredella, 2002.)

In her contribution 'Searching for the Intercultural Person', Phyllis M. Ryan gives an impressive example of a person who is able to reconstruct different frames of reference. Mary has lived in many countries – Russia, Germany, Turkey, the United States of America – and learned the languages spoken in these countries. When she is asked what an intercultural person is, she says, 'a person that lived, studied or worked in certain countries and learned the language. After living in a country you start to think, act and understand better these people and how they think, so that when you go back to that country after many years you still feel like you are right there at home'. According to Mary, the intercultural person is someone who becomes part of the culture she lives in and who thinks and behaves like the members of that culture without experiencing insecurity and uncertainty. She would not be an ideal intercultural person in Gupta's model because she does not look at a culture from the outside but only from the inside and willingly accepts its respective rules and values: 'I don't try to rationalize that they are doing this is wrong, . . . because in other countries it is considered a different way of thinking. I don't mix it up at all'. Mary, a radical relativist, accepts each culture on its own terms and refrains from comparing them. Her radical relativism allows her to be happy in every culture: 'Now, when you go to another country and you start to live another type of life in another country you put this behind you; you have to put it behind you otherwise you would be very unhappy. You should never compare, just accept'.

I said that an indispensable feature of being intercultural is reconstructing the frame of reference of others and seeing things through their eyes. This is often liberating and can prevent us from regarding others as inferior and from humiliating them. Yet there are situations in which it is not enough to reconstruct the others' frame of reference and refrain from evaluating it. In the following situation described by Zygmunt Bauman it would be cynical to merely reconstruct the others' frame of reference without evaluating it: 'I consider corporal punishment degrading and bodily mutilations inhuman', but I let others practise it because it is part of their culture and 'because I cannot believe any more in the universality of moral values' (Bauman, 1992: XXIII). The limits of intercultural understanding as the reconstruction of the others' frame of reference also becomes clear in the following example by David Hollinger: 'If the Massai women of east Africa are but breeding stock, and when barren of sons, are treated by their warrior masters as inferior to cattle, who are you to criticize? It's part of the Massai culture, after all' (Hollinger 1995, 113f.). In this context Mary's relativistic advice 'Never compare, just accept' is no longer liberating but inhumane. Refraining from evaluations might, in certain situations, be humane but in others it might be inhumane because it means that we close our eyes to exploitation and humiliation. Hence relativism cannot be the answer to the question of how to avoid ethnocentrism because we need a kind of rationality which allows us to evaluate cultural behaviour. Before I address this question, I will address another aspect, namely the significance of the classroom in the intercultural experience.

The Role of the Classroom in the Intercultural Experience

In 'Search for the Intercultural Person', the two women interviewed by Ryan answer differently the question concerning the role of the classroom for the intercultural experience. It is not surprising that Mary, who lived in a variety of cultures, 'is strongly convinced that one can only be intercultural if one lives for a period of time in another country'. Yet for Guadalupe, who has learned to speak several languages without living in a foreign culture, direct contact is not essential: 'She believes that a foreign language learner is enriched by knowledge of foreign cultures acquired through the language being studied. Direct culture contact was beneficial but not essential to this enrichment'. For Guadalupe, foreign language learning and understanding foreign cultures should be interdependent, although she admits that foreign language learning does not necessarily lead to an interest in the foreign culture and that one can learn a foreign language without being interested in its culture: 'For example, when a chemist would like to read articles in English and present one at a conference, the culture of the native speaker of English is not important'. Guadalupe makes suggestions on how foreign language teachers who have not been to the foreign culture can bring the foreign culture into the classroom:

> Perhaps the teacher does not know much about Australia. He speaks English but has never been to Australia. For example, he can get books, newspapers, journals, recorded news, television programmes, radio programmes, and transmit them here and see what idiosyncrasies of speech exist in those places.

For Guadalupe, the classroom can achieve what could best arrived at through direct contact. Gupta, however, develops a different perspective. The classroom is essential for the intercultural experience because it gives students the opportunity to reflect on their intercultural experiences and learn from each other: 'The intercultural classroom needs to have a dynamic and interactive atmosphere where, in addition to traditional questions regarding the material, students are actively encouraged to share their personal experiences'. In such discussions students can learn that they should not 'make broad generalisations about a cultural practice or about a group of people' and should not 'express a personal opinion as though it is a generally held belief'. Discussions in the classroom offer students the opportunity to explore what the intercultural experience means to them and how they might interpret it in the most appropriate way. What might have been an uncomfortable experience might, for example, be seen as an enrichment. Thus the classroom is not only a substitute for direct contact but a means of developing an awareness of what is at stake in the intercultural experience. Thus indirect experience can encourage reflections which are not possible in direct experience. From a different perspective this is also valid for Mike Fleming in his contribution 'Intercultural Experience and Drama'. He underscores how important drama is for intercultural education because it simplifies the complex direct experience and highlights certain aspects of reality in an invented scenario or story, and because it encourages involvement and reflection. I would like to add here that literary texts, in general, and drama, in particular, are well suited to involving students and allowing them to reflect on how they are involved. Being intercultural needs this dialectic which is part of the aesthetic experience (cf. Bredella, 2002).

The Contested Ability of Negotiation and Mediation in Intercultural Encounters

In his contribution 'Becoming a 'Better Stranger': A Therapeutic Perspective on Intercultural Experience and/as Education', Geof Alred looks at the intercultural experience from the therapeutic perspective and at therapy from an intercultural perspective. For Alred, the therapist's experience has to mediate between two frames of reference, that of the client and that of the therapist: 'A central activity in therapy is mediation between the therapist and client'. Mediation means 'living on the boundary physically and psychically', between two worlds. For the therapeutic as well as the intercultural experience it is essential that we be aware of the fact that there are different worlds and that we must talk 'relativistically and contextually about others'. Thus, looking at the intercultural experience through the therapeutic perspective can deepen our understanding of what it means to be intercultural. Yet there is also an objection: The therapist's frame of reference and that of the client are not of equal value. The client knows that he or she does not see things correctly and therefore looks to the therapist for help. Yet in intercultural encounters we face a different situation. Ethnocentric persons do not believe that they need the help of a therapist. On the contrary, they believe that it is 'natural' and 'rational' to believe that one's rules and values are superior.

Post-colonial critics will point out that the West has applied the therapeutic model and assumed that non-western cultures are the clients who must overcome their limited and distorted world-view. In addition, relativists will point out that cultures are closed systems which must be evaluated from their inner perspective. They see mediation between cultures as an act of violence. For Jean-François Lyotard any comparison between two incommensurable cultures will inflict injustice on one of them and will be experienced as an act of violence. We cannot mediate between cultures and genres, Lyotard writes, because 'a universal rule of judgment between heterogeneous genres is lacking in general' (Lyotard, 1988: XI). We shall see later that the therapeutic model can help to illuminate the intercultural experience. But first let us consider the arguments of those who regard mediations between cultures as impossible.

According to Stanley Fish, we can only claim to understand a foreign culture if we approve of what we understand. This implies, for example, that we have to approve of Khomeini's *fatwa* if we claim to understand the Islamic culture. If we refrain from approving it, we are only practising 'boutique multiculturalism', which he describes in the following terms:

> Boutique multiculturalists will always stop short of approving of other cultures at a point where some value at their center generates an act that offends against the canon of civilized decency as they have been either declared or assumed. The death sentence under which Salman Rushdie now lives is an obvious and perspicuous example. (Fish, 1997: 378)

Why does Fish level the distinction between understanding and approving of what we understand? Why should it not be possible to understand Khomeini's *fatwa* and criticise it? For Fish such criticism is ethnocentric and unjustified because each culture defines what is rational and humane. There is no common ground for an evaluation. Therefore we must accept strong multiculturalism and whole-heartedly approve of what we understand:

> It is strong because it values difference in and for itself, rather than as a manifestation of something more basically constitutive. Whereas the boutique multiculturalist will accord a superficial respect to cultures other than his own, a respect he will withdraw when he finds the practices of a culture irrational or inhumane, a strong multiculturalist will want to accord a *deep* respect to all cultures at their core, for he believes that each has the right to form its own identity and nourish its own sense of what is rational and humane. (Fish, 1997: 382)

Strong multiculturalism is, however, as Fish himself admits, self-contradictory. It is based on tolerance. We should accept each culture on its own terms, but this would imply that there is a universal value, namely tolerance. Yet for strong multiculturalism there are no universal values. Another reason which makes tolerance unacceptable for Fish is that we can only speak of tolerance if we do not approve of certain values and attitudes but do not want to see them suppressed. Fish, however, wants us to approve of every value and attitude of the other culture without reservations, because they are a sign of ethnocentrism for him.

From an emphatic concept of the intercultural experience, tolerance is insufficient because tolerant persons prefer their own beliefs and values to those of the other culture. Yet, the experience of intolerance makes clear how important tolerance is for the intercultural experience. The intolerant impose their beliefs on others because they are convinced that they are absolutely right and that the others must be redeemed from their wrong beliefs. Against this background it becomes possible to determine the limits of tolerance and to criticise the relativistic view that real tolerance must tolerate the intolerable because such a view would lead to the abolition of tolerance and a pluralistic society. Hence it is a weakness of strong multiculturalism that it asks us to commit a kind of intellectual suicide by prohibiting us to criticise intolerance. Of course, we must be aware of the danger that our evaluation of another culture as intolerant might be an expression of our own intolerance. Yet, we must also be aware of the danger that we close our eyes to exploitation and humiliations if we accept intolerant behaviour uncritically because it is part of a culture.

Another problematic assumption of strong multiculturalism or radical relativism is that it is based on a concept of culture as a closed homogeneous system which determines the individual's behaviour. This implies that we explain an action by pointing out that it is an expression of a certain cultural value. This kind of deterministic explanation is supported by the structuralist and deconstructivist belief that we not speak the language but are spoken by it (cf. a critique of this concept of language in Bredella [2002: 176 ff.]. Human beings are no longer seen as subjects but as objects of the cultural process. Andreas Wimmer (1997: 127) stresses that according to the relativistic concept of culture as a closed system, human beings are the clay out of which culture forms its creatures, or, to use another image, the culture prescribes the script of the roles the individuals have to play. Yet this concept of culture is not suitable for describing what is really going on in a culture. With reference to Zygmunt Bauman, Wimmer contends that the capability of questioning scripts and values is essential for being cultural. And this is not only valid for the realm of cognition but also for that of action. The relativistic concept of culture cannot acknowledge the insight that people frequently do not follow the culturally prescribed rules but act strategically (cf. Wimmer, 1997: 128f.). I would like to add that cultural beliefs and values are often contradictory. That is why we need to be creative and reflective individuals in order to mediate between them and to perform successfully in a complex world. Since strong multiculturalism believes in culture as a closed system, it cannot acknowledge that Khomeini's *fatwa* is criticized by members of Islamic cultures and defended by members of western cultures. The experience that decisions and actions in a culture often are contested indicates that culture is also a process of negotiation and mediation.

If strong multiculturalism leads to unacceptable consequences, how can we guard against them? Let me briefly discuss how Richard Rorty wants to avoid radical relativism. Like Stanley Fish, he stresses that there are no transcultural values. There is no Archimedean point from which one can determine what is right and what is wrong: 'We cannot find a skyhook which lifts us out of mere coherence – mere argument – to something like "correspondence with reality as it is itself"' (Rorty, 1991: 38). Yet Rorty rejects the radical relativism we find in Fish: 'We have become so open-minded that our brains have fallen out' (Rorty 1991, 203). He encourages us to maintain our belief in an anti-ethnocentric culture but adds that we must realise that our belief in an anti-ethnocentric culture is ethnocentric. Therefore he calls his position 'anti-anti-ethnocentrism':

> Anti-anti-ethnocentrism does not say that we are trapped within our monad or our language, but merely that the well-windowed monad we live in is no more closely linked to the nature of humanity or the de-

mands of rationality than the relatively windowless monads which surround us. (Rorty, 1991: 204)

Rorty wants to avoid relativism but ends in ethnocentrism. Our culture may be a monad with windows, but monads are closed systems with their own rules and values. If people tell us that they prefer ethnocentric cultures to anti-ethnocentric ones, according to Rorty, we cannot argue with them but only shrug our shoulders and point out 'that we have to work by our own lights, even as they do, for there is no supercultural observation platform to which we might repair' (Rorty, 1991: 213). If we were to tell Rorty that there is the possibility of 'unforced agreement', he would give us the following answer: 'Unforced agreement among whom? Us? The Nazis? Any arbitrary culture or group? The answer, of course, is us' (Rorty, 1991: 38). We are caught in our own culture, and therefore negotiations with the possibility of unforced agreement are impossible. Rorty is right in stressing that we cannot help understanding the foreign culture from our perspective, but this does not imply that we cannot acknowledge the others' beliefs and values and that the others will refuse to enter into a dialogue with us. It is indeed an ethnocentric attitude to believe that only we are interested in a dialogue. Before I describe the possibility of such a dialogue, let us briefly consider Wittgenstein's position. His concept of language games has often been used as a justification of the post-modern belief that mediations are impossible. In *On Certainty* Wittgenstein himself illustrates what might happen if we attempt to convince a member of a magic culture that ordeals by fire are wrong and this member regards our beliefs in physics as a form of superstition. Would he, Wittgenstein (1972), not be justified in defending his belief in physics with arguments?

> § 608: Is it wrong for me to be guided in my actions by the propositions of physics? Am I to say that I have no good ground for doing so? Isn't precisely this what we call a 'good ground'?

Yet Wittgenstein questions the expectation that the member of the magic culture will accept his arguments as a 'good ground' and is aware of the danger that he might regard him as 'primitive' if he does not accept his arguments:

> § 609: Suppose we met people who did not regard that as a telling reason. Now, how do we imagine this? Instead of the physicist, they consult an oracle. And for that we consider them primitive. Is it wrong for them to consult an oracle and be guided by it? – If we call this 'wrong', aren't we using our language game as a base from which to *combat* theirs?

If we follow Wittgenstein, the attempt to convince others of the rightness of our views is dangerous because it will lead to the depreciation and misrecognition of them and their cultures:

> § 611: Where two principles really do meet which cannot be reconciled with one another, then each man declares the other a fool and heretic.

It seems that we have to be relativists. Yet Wittgenstein cannot give up the belief in a common world so easily because this would imply that we have to accept an ordeal by fire which he regards as 'absurd' (§ 605). Therefore he takes up the question again whether the other could not be persuaded by arguments. But what happens if the arguments fail?

> § 612: I said I would 'combat' the other man – but wouldn't I give him *reasons*? Certainly, but how far do they go? At the end of reasons comes *persuasion*. (Think what happens when missionaries convert natives.)

If arguments fail, we might use force. Yet Wittgenstein acknowledges the distinction between arguments and force which is levelled by a variety of post-modern thinkers. For Lyotard, as we have seen, we must respect the incommensurability of cultures because it is an act of violence to apply strategies and norms from one culture in another one. Michel Foucault gives a devastating critique of knowledge in general:

> The historical analysis of this rancorous will to knowledge reveals that all knowledge rests upon injustice (that there is no right, not even in the act of knowing, to truth or a foundation of truth) and that the instinct for knowledge is malicious (something murderous, opposed to the happiness of mankind). (Foucault, 1977: 163).

The will to understand others is nothing but the disguised will to gain power.

The post-modern belief that arguments and words are not different from physical force is taken up by Stanley Fish in a surprising twist. He asserts that there is no difference between persuasions by speech and by physical force 'because everything we say impinges on the world in ways indistinguishable from the effects of physical action' (Fish, quoted in Gander, 1999, 124). Fish argues that we should welcome his belief because if speech were different from physical action and had no effect, it would be meaningless. Fish confronts us with the alternative: Either speech and physical action are identical or speech is meaningless. In his thorough analysis of Fish's arguments Eric Gander refutes this alternative:

> We can do so by seeing that meaningful speech, as distinguished from other forms of physical action, is associated with its 'consequences'

only in a *mediated* way. In other words, when I speak meaningfully, my words will have consequences (some intentioned, some not intentioned, some predictable, some not predictable, and so forth), precisely because these words are received and then 'processed' in the mind of another in myriad, complex, never *completely* explainable ways. (Gander, 1999: 125)

Speech can produce a counter-speech as arguments can produce counter-arguments. Therefore they do not force us as physical actions force us:

In sum, we need to insist . . . that, as inducements to action (or sometimes inaction) symbols (i.e. speech, writing, visual images, and so forth) can be resisted in a way that a bullet, for example, cannot. (Gander, 1999: 125f.)

As we have seen, relativists and ethnocentrists argue that cultures are incommensurable and incomparable. Each culture defines for itself what is rational and inhumane. Therefore, any attempt to mediate between them is an act of violence and injustice. Yet it is also true that we live in a world in which we could not survive if mediations between cultures were impossible. The events of 11 September, 2001 in New York and Washington underscore this insight. Consequently, we should have a closer look at the arguments of the critics of mediation. Tom McCarthy points out that the insight that there are no transcultural and absolute values does not justify the conclusion that we cannot negotiate and find solutions to our problems: 'To grant that every point of view is historically situated is not *ipso facto* to surrender all claims to validity, to drop any claim that one view is better than another' (McCarthy, 1989: 325). Hilary Putnam (1998: 58) argues in a similar way. The insight that we are culturally situated does not mean that we have to give up the notion of truth and falsity: 'What we say about the world reflects our conceptual choices and our interests, but its truth and falsity is not simply determined by our conceptual choices and our interests'. True, the concepts of rationality and humanity have been developped under different social and cultural circumstances, but this does not mean that they do not have certain features in common and that we cannot mediate between them. The relativists overestimate differences and underestimate commonalities.

We can transcend our culture and develop a third position which is the result of the interaction with other cultures: 'In short, while the open-ended 'conversation of humankind' rules out the assumption that our point of view is absolute, it does not require us simply to drop notions of cognitive advance or learning from experience' (McCarthy, 1989: 325).

If we perceive an action in the foreign culture as meaningful, McCarthy points out, our own concept of rationality comes into play because we do not have to convince the members of the foreign culture of the fact that the action is rational, but rather have to convince ourselves. The action is therefore rational according to our own standards. This implies that relativists use a wider concept of rationality than they theoretically admit:

> Notice finally that the interpreter's involvement in this process is such that her evaluations do play a role, albeit a tacit role, in her account of alien beliefs. It is her standards that are at work in her sense of what might reasonably be believed in a given context. (McCarthy, 1989: 329)

The insight that negotiations are possible enables us to return to Alred's therapeutic model of intercultural understanding. I argued that it could be criticised because the mediation between the client's frame of reference and that of the therapist is inappropriate for the intercultural experience because neither of the two parties can claim to be the therapist in this relationship. But from the perspective of negotiation and mediation the therapeutic model of intercultural understanding makes clear that we cannot rest content in our own frame of reference, but instead have to take the others' into account. This is also confirmed by Gupta's model, which stresses that we need the others' frame of reference in order to enhance our self-awareness as cultural beings.

Summary

I have discussed several intercultural situations and have tried to highlight what it means to be intercultural in these situations:

- Being intercultural means to reconstruct the others' frame of reference and see things through their eyes in order to overcome our ethnocentric tendency to impose our categories and values on their behaviour.
- Being intercultural means to enhance our self-awareness as cultural beings. This makes us aware of the relativity of our beliefs and values and protects us from cultivating fundamentalist attitudes.
- Being intercultural means to be able to accept the others' beliefs and values, even if we cannot approve of them. Therefore tolerance plays an important role in the intercultural experience.
- Being intercultural is based on a concept of culture which does not determine the individuals' behaviour but enables them to mediate between contradictory values and to pursue their interests.
- Being intercultural comprises both involvement and the reflection on this involvement. Hence the classroom is not only a kind of substitute

for direct intercultural contact but a necessary place where students can reflect on their intercultural experiences since such reflections are often impossible in direct contact.

- Being intercultural means to be aware of the disquieting tension in the intercultural experience. On the one hand, we must recognise the other culture in its difference. There are no absolute beliefs and values. In Rorty´s terms there is no Archimedean point or skyhook. There are only culture-bound beliefs and values. This is the justification for tolerance, pluralism and identity politics. From this perspective, culture-bound beliefs and values offer the members of each culture a haven of security in which they can rest content. Yet being intercultural also comprises another experience. There are people who suffer under their culture-bound beliefs and values and want to change them. Hence the intercultural experience is in danger of justifying injustices and humiliations if it forbids us to criticise the beliefs and values of another culture because each culture defines for itself what is rational and humane. This implies that we cannot rest content in relativism but must mediate between different frames of reference in order to create a better one. It is ironic that the necessity of intercultural negotiations and mediations is constantly stressed, whereas at the same time philosophers, anthropologists and cultural critics stress emphatically that cultures are incommensurable. These critics make us aware of the dangers inherent in intercultural negotiations, but they do not consider the dangers incurred if we dispense with them and regard the clash of civilisations as inevitable.

References

Asante, Molefi Kete (1995) Afrocentrism. *American Studies Newsletter* 36 (May), 6–8.

Bauman, Zygmunt (1992) *Intimations of Postmodernity*. London: Routledge.

Bloom, Allan (1987) *The Closing of the American Mind*. New York: Simon and Schuster.

Bredella, Lothar (2002) *Literarisches und interkulturelles Verstehen*. Tübingen: Gunter Narr.

Fish, Stanley (1997) Boutique multiculturalism, or why liberals are incapable of thinking about hate speech. *Critical Inquiry* 23 (Winter), 378–95.

Foucault, Michel (1977) Nietzsche, genealogy, history. In M. Foucault, *Language, Counter-Memory, Practice* (pp. 139–63). Ithaca, NY: Cornell University Press.

Gander, Eric (1999) *The Last Conceptual Revolution. A Critique of Richard Rorty's Political Philosophy*. Albany, NY: State University of New York.

Hollinger, David (1995) *Postethnic America: Beyond Multiculturalism*. New York: Basic Books.

Lévi-Strauss, Claude (1985) *The View From Afar*. Oxford: Blackwell.

Lyotard, Jean-Francois (1988) *The Differend. Phases in Dispute*. Manchester: Manchester University Press.

McCarthy, Tom (1989) A Thought-Experiment. *Zeitschrift für philosophische Forschung* 43, 318–330.

Putnam, Hilary (1998) *Renewing Philosophy*. Cambridge, MA.: Harvard University Press.

Rorty, Richard (1991) *Objectivity, Relativism, and Truth*. Cambridge: Cambridge University Press.

Wimmer, Frans M. (1993) Ansätze zu einer interkulturellen Philosophie . In Ram Adhar Mall and Dieter Lohmar (eds) *Philosophische Grundlagen der Interkulturalität* (pp. 29–40). Amsterdam / Atlanta, GA: Editions Rodopi B.V.

Wimmer, Andreas H. (1997) Die Pragmatik der kulturellen Produktion. In Manfred Brocker and Heino H. Nau (eds) *Ethnozentrismus Möglichkeiten und Grenzen des interkulturellen Dialogs* (pp. 120–40). Darmstadt: Wissenschaftliche Buchgesellschaft.

Wittgenstein, Ludwig (1972) *On Certainty*. New York: Harper Torchbooks.

Index